CLICHÉS
of Politics

Edited by Mark Spangler

The Foundation for Economic Education
Irvington-on-Hudson, New York

The Foundation for Economic Education, Inc.
30 South Broadway
Irvington-on-Hudson, NY 10533
(914)-591-7230

Publisher's Cataloging in Publication
(Prepared by Quality Books, Inc.)

Cliches of politics / edited by Mark Spangler
   p. cm.
   Includes index
   ISBN 0-910614-962
   1. Political science—Philosophy I. Spangler, Mark.

HM33.C54 1996   320.01
                             QBI9520782

Library of Congress Catalog Card Number: 95-83127

First edition, March 1994
Second printing, September 1994
Third printing, March 1996

Cover design by Doug Hesseltine
Manufactured in the United States of America

Contents

Introduction   1
Mark Spangler

Publisher's Note   6

I. HUMAN RIGHTS AND THE NATURE OF GOVERNMENT

1. "I have a right!"   9
Charles W. Baird

2. "We have a right to this service."   12
Lawrence W. Reed

3. "Human rights are more important than property rights."   15
Paul L. Poirot

4. "In a just society, food is a right."   18
Cecil E. Bohanon

5. "Don't I have a right to a job?"   22
John Hospers

6. "Civil rights laws increase freedom."   27
Llewellyn H. Rockwell, Jr.

7. "We must abide by the majority. That's democracy."   30
Charles W. Baird

II. GOVERNMENT PLANNING AND REGULATION

8. "Government regulators know best."   35
Matthew B. Kibbe

9. "All we need is the right people to run the government."   38
Melvin D. Barger

(The names of authors responding to clichés are listed in italics.)

10. "No one advocates censorship, but what's wrong
with government control of the economy?"   42
Gary North

11. "An unregulated economy was part of the horse-
and-buggy era."   45
Murray N. Rothbard

12. "Pass a law!"   47
Lawrence W. Reed

13. "There ought to be a law!"   49
W.C. Mullendore

14. "To solve the problem, we need government
regulation."   52
Tibor R. Machan

15. "Federal aid is all right if it doesn't bring federal
red tape."   58
W.M. Curtiss

16. "Big business and big labor require big
government."   61
Edmund A. Opitz

17. "The government must set standards for living
and working conditions."   65
Joan Kennedy Taylor

18. "Rent control protects tenants."   68
Henry Hazlitt

19. "Government should control prices, but not
people."   72
Dean Russell

20. "In a national emergency, government must
control the economy."   75
Robert Higgs

21. "Weak regulation and bankers' greed caused the
savings and loan crisis."   80
Hans F. Sennholz

22. "Government deregulation of the airlines was a disaster." 84
    John Semmens

23. "If free enterprise really works, why the Great Depression?" 87
    Paul L. Poirot

24. "Fact-finding is a proper function of government." 90
    Murray N. Rothbard

III. PRIVATE ENTERPRISE, GOVERNMENT SPENDING, AND HUMAN WELFARE

25. "Politicians are to blame for the fiscal mess in government." 97
    Hans F. Sennholz

26. "There is too much inequality of wealth and income." 100
    Lawrence W. Reed

27. "Americans no longer need to worry about how to produce goods and services." 102
    John Hospers

28. "But we already tried cutting the budget." 107
    Llewellyn H. Rockwell, Jr.

29. "The size of the national debt doesn't matter because we owe it to ourselves." 110
    Paul L. Poirot

30. "The 'Trickle-Down Theory' has caused our economic problems." 112
    K. L. Billingsley

31. "A shortage of tax revenues creates budget deficits." 115
    William R. Allen and William Dickneider

32. "The free market ignores the poor." 118
    Leonard E. Read

33. "Government should guarantee freedom from want." 121
    Paul L. Poirot

34. "Freedom from want requires population control." 126
    Kyle S. Swan

35. "Isn't government investment necessary for economic prosperity?" 130
    Paul A. Cleveland

36. "Military spending brings jobs and prosperity." 133
    Henry Hazlitt

37. "Government spending programs create jobs." 135
    Gregory B. Christainsen

38. "If we had no Social Security many people would go hungry." 138
    Paul L. Poirot

39. "We need government to build the infrastructure." 141
    John Semmens

40. "Americans squander their incomes on themselves while public needs are neglected." 145
    Edmund A. Opitz

IV. THE COMPETITIVE PROCESS

41. "Mankind was born for cooperation, not competition." 149
    Llewellyn H. Rockwell, Jr.

42. "Business is entitled to a fair profit." 152
    Leonard E. Read

43. "We need antitrust laws to prevent monopoly." 155
    D. T. Armentano

44. "Advertising is immoral and wasteful, and debases taste."   158
    Ronald H. Nash

45. "General Motors is too big."   160
    Dean Russell

46. "The laissez faire of Adam Smith is irrelevant to modern society."   163
    Cecil E. Bohanon and James E. McClure

47. "Speculation should be outlawed."   166
    John Fiske

V. LABOR AND EMPLOYMENT

48. "Government should create and protect jobs."   171
    Richard B. McKenzie

49. "The government must guarantee a job for everyone."   174
    Tibor R. Machan

50. "Every employee is entitled to a fair wage."   177
    C. W. Anderson

51. "Women are at a disadvantage in the marketplace."   180
    Jean L. Baker

52. "Employees often lack reserves and are subject to 'exploitation' by capitalist employers."   186
    Paul L. Poirot

53. "Temporary workers are bad for the economy."   189
    Llewellyn H. Rockwell, Jr.

54. "Labor is not a commodity."   191
    Paul L. Poirot

55. "Labor unions are too powerful today, but were useful in the past."   194
    Hans F. Sennholz

56. "Without legislation, we'd still have child labor and sweatshop conditions."   196
    Paul L. Poirot

VI. THE HEALTH-CARE MARKETS

57. "The government should provide free medical care."   201
    Lawrence W. Reed

58. "Health care is 'unique' and should not be left to the market."   203
    Terree P. Wasley

59. "For safety's sake, government must regulate the market for medical products."   206
    Robert Higgs

60. "National health care is working in Canada."   210
    Terree P. Wasley

VII. THE AGRICULTURAL INDUSTRY

61. "Government should support agriculture—the backbone of America."   217
    E. C. Pasour, Jr.

62. "The government should stabilize agricultural markets."   221
    Gary M. Galles

VIII. THE ARTS, MEDIA, AND EDUCATION

63. "We can rely on the media to bring us an unbiased political outlook."   227
    Melvin D. Barger

64. "Public finance of the arts advances a nation's culture."   232
      Paul A. Cleveland and Benjamin L. Crawford

65. "Government grants are required to perpetuate the arts."   236
      Melvin D. Barger

66. "We ought to have sex education in the schools."   240
      Walter Block

IX. FOREIGN TRADE AND THE WORLD ECONOMY

67. "International trade is different and thus requires government management."   245
      William H. Peterson

68. "America consumes too much of the world's resources."   249
      Lawrence W. Reed

69. "In order to develop, Third World countries need foreign aid."   251
      David Osterfeld

70. "Industrialization assures progress in undeveloped countries."   254
      Henry Hazlitt

71. "Foreign imports destroy jobs."   257
      Russell Shannon

72. "A balance of trade deficit hurts the domestic economy."   260
      William R. Allen and William Dickneider

X. RESOURCES AND THE ENVIRONMENT

73. "Government is the key to protecting the environment."   265
      Lawrence W. Reed

74. "Private enterprise leads to pollution."   267
    Walter Block

75. "Only government is farsighted enough to
    protect resources for future generations."   271
    Richard L. Stroup and Jane S. Shaw

XI. PHILOSOPHICAL AND ETHICAL
    PERSPECTIVES

76. "Private enterprise panders to greed and
    selfishness."   277
    Ronald H. Nash

77. "I prefer security to freedom."   280
    Sanford Ikeda

78. "Society is to blame, not I."   283
    Benjamin A. Rogge

79. "All people should perform some type of
    national service."   287
    Tibor R. Machan

80. "If government doesn't relieve distress, who
    will?"   291
    Leonard E. Read

81. "From each according to his abilities, to each
    according to his needs."   294
    Thomas J. Shelly

82. "If we don't get our share of government money,
    someone else will."   296
    John A. Sparks

83. "The more complex the society, the more
    government control we need."   299
    Leonard E. Read

Authors and Editor   301

Index   307

Introduction

The razing of the Berlin Wall in 1989 and the collapse of the government of the Soviet Union just two years later are striking testimony against Communism and state socialism. These events left indelible images in the minds of free people throughout the world. What American didn't feel a sense of triumph and pride as freedom and the American way once again were vindicated?

Those pivotal turns in human history were cause not only for jubilation but also for America to reflect upon the source of its own strength and the course of politics at home. Soul searching, if deep enough, would have revealed that the United States suffers under the influence of a more insidious form of government control—political interventionism. As Eastern Europe retreats from socialism, Americans are inviting government authority, action, and regulation with growing intensity. The commentary of the late Percy L. Greaves, Jr., although written forty years ago, still aptly describes the political course on which America embarked at the turn of the century:

> The mass myopia of our age has been a reactionary reverence for government intervention. When anything goes wrong, from a train wreck to a change in stock market prices, the craven crowds always clamor for just one more law. Throughout the world there is a spirit of . . . trust in government omnipotence that blinds people to the inevitable and undesirable consequences of the very intervention they currently advocate. There can be little question that the great majority of our fellow men believe that governmental action is the answer to every economic problem of poverty or prosperity.

1

The growth of American government in the twentieth century has been so gradual that the populace has slowly adapted and become accustomed to a regulated way of life. Recent generations know of no other way. Yet there has been a dramatic shift of resources to the public sectors. Federal, state, and local governments combined consume 100 times more resources today than at the start of the century; they actually employ more civilian employees than manufacturing companies do.

The federal government alone consumes 25 percent of all goods and services produced in the economy. Ninety years ago federal consumption was only 5 percent. Spending on social programs and entitlements during the same time has increased 1,000 times, to where 40 percent of the federal budget is now devoted to such programs.

While spending trends alone indicate a swelling presence of political control in our lives, they do not tell the whole story. The cost of compliance with government rules is staggering. A recent article in *The Wall Street Journal* reported that U.S. corporations on average pay four dollars in costs of compliance for every dollar paid in taxes. And there is no way to calculate the lost opportunities and suppressed innovation wrought by political regulation and taxation.

The insidious aspect of political intervention is the subtle and alluring way in which it attracts support and advances. Lenin was explicit in his belief that Communism should suppress capitalism. But the politicians of today at least pay lip service to freedom and free enterprise. Government authority is proposed only to "fix" perceived flaws in the market economy, and public spending is used simply to "compensate" for deficiencies in the private sector. Political action is couched in plausible terms and spirited slogans. But political solutions, however well intended, invariably lead to unintended consequences. They are like wolves in sheep's clothing—benign on the outside but treacherous underneath.

Politicians, for instance, justify much of government spending on the grounds that it creates employment. Attending ribbon-cutting ceremonies, these government officials boast about the number of jobs public funds will create. But just the opposite occurs. The visible actions of politicians are only an illusion which hides the destruction of jobs as resources are diverted from private competitive concerns to the coffers of less efficient government bureaus.

Minimum-wage legislation has long received widespread endorsement for assuring that no one is employed at "substandard" pay. In reality, such laws only assure that someone whose productivity does not yet command a market rate exceeding the legal minimum is barred from employment. Labor legislation has restricted opportunities and condemned whole generations of less fortunate workers to lives of unemployment and dependency.

Occupational licensing by governments adds false assurance to the quality of services performed; it, in fact, reduces competition by barring newcomers from challenging the establishment. The Great Depression, popularly believed to be the result of unrestricted free enterprise, was caused by political control of the credit markets and was protracted by labor and tariff legislation.

Foreign aid programs, while noble in purpose, usually miss the root cause of poverty and actually prolong problems by stunting the development of activities which are subsidized. Price controls, designed to alleviate shortages, in reality cause them by encouraging consumption and discouraging production. Politicians are then expected *not* to remove controls but to further intervene and ration available supplies. Antitrust laws prevent rather than promote competition by focussing on numbers and sizes instead of the process and conditions under which competing firms can dominate the marketplace.

Even civil rights laws—sacred cows of the modern political society—have hidden dangers and counterconsequences. Their enactment has erected a system of government favoritism and controls rather than expanding and ensuring full property rights—ownership of one's own life and the fruits of peaceful labor—to groups of persons previously denied equal protection from violent transgressions.

Social Security was introduced more than forty years ago as national retirement insurance. Yet, most younger Americans doubt the program will be sound enough to provide benefits when they retire—despite the government's extracting higher rates of Social Security taxes (from 2 percent in 1940 to more than 15 percent now). Its appearance notwithstanding, Social Security bears little resemblance to insurance; it has become a massive transfer program tragically pitting one politically defined group against another—the young against the old.

And now on the political agenda is the decision to entrust lawmakers and bureaucrats with national health insurance. An examination of existing government medical programs (Medicare and Medicaid), established barely thirty years ago, reveals costs already ten times greater than originally predicted. This spending coupled with government practices of cost-plus pricing has created an enormous demand for medical goods and services while deterring price competition.

To catch a glimpse at a future with politically managed health care, a person need only look to the generally inferior care that the federal government now provides veterans through its own hospital system. National health insurance merely promulgates false assurances that electing the correct politicians provides better health care than exercising choice and responsibilities in the medical marketplace. National health insurance, like Social Security, will become a massive entitlement program; it will one day create political confrontation between the sick and the healthy.

What accounts for the infatuation with political solutions and control? Perhaps citizens too often consider government in ideal or abstract terms without contemplating the harsh realities of bureaucrats wielding the power of legal coercion. Wishful thinking also sustains the notion that government can simply pass a law to correct some perceived problem. Implicit in the willingness of people to transfer control over their lives to politicians is the belief that government is somehow omniscient and benevolent. But what week passes that a public official isn't implicated in a fresh political scandal?

The desire to achieve a secure life—a guaranteed life—motivates and tempts individuals to seek out government favors. A citizen may qualify for certain entitlements, but his pockets tend to be picked by fellow citizens far faster than he can fill them at the public dole as entitlement programs escalate into a system of political plunder. In the meantime, greater power is given to government officials, the economy degenerates, and people are left with diminishing opportunities and choices. Self-responsibility is relinquished for a dependency on the whims of politicians, who can give nothing that is not first wrested from private citizens. Life becomes less certain.

The twentieth-century thirst for government favoritism has generated proclamations of "rights" from every corner of society—rights to food, clothing, shelter, jobs, medical care, child care, public transportation, education, sports participation, club memberships, smoking, nonsmoking—with little regard for the essential right of private property. This view of America differs drastically from the vision held by the framers of the Constitution, who believed the right to life meant the peaceful pursuit of one's desires without obligating others to fulfill those wants—either by law or with personal violence.

Four generations of people were forced to suffer miserably under the tyranny of Soviet dictators, whose "living experiment" with government authoritarianism failed tragically. It was only sheer economic collapse that swept away the Communist stronghold and disengaged the government of the Soviet Union. The turmoil of the aftermath demonstrates the difficulty in restoring meaningful freedom based on private property and free markets, once it is abandoned. Yet today Americans, with reckless abandonment, are turning away from limited government and beckoning political control at a breathless pace.

An informed citizenry must be suspicious of political wolves parading as sheep. We must understand the hidden consequences of political intervention and avoid a reverence for government solutions. Look beyond popular clichés and seek a richer understanding of a free society. A renewed commitment to individual initiative, freedom of choice, and self-responsibility in an institutional setting of private property and limited, peacekeeping government will enable individuals to realize their greatest potentials.

—MARK SPANGLER

Publisher's Note

In the 1960s, Leonard Read, founder and president of The Foundation for Economic Education, added a new dimension to his efforts in making the positive case for limited government and a free economy. He and his staff identified and refuted dozens of socialist clichés—"bromides, plausibilities, catchy phrases"—which often left those just beginning to comprehend the case for freedom "speechless, and often with their faith shaken."

The resulting *Clichés of Socialism* were printed first as single-sheet releases, then as a spiral bound collection, and eventually in a professionally produced paperback book. A revised and expanded paperback edition was last reprinted in 1970 —with a print run of 20,000 copies.

The book was sold through FEE's book catalogue and distributed to hundreds of people who attended seminars here in Irvington-on-Hudson and throughout the country. Within a few years the supply of the 1970 edition was exhausted.

FEE continued to receive numerous requests for *Clichés*— and was urged to reprint the book. But by then many of the original contributors were deceased, and much of the material was dated. Bringing out a new edition was a daunting task, and no one undertook the challenge.

The encouragement and financial commitment of Mr. Harry Langenberg of St. Louis, Missouri, a long-time FEE trustee, kept alive the notion of a new edition of *Clichés*. In 1993, Mark Spangler, a former FEE senior staff member, volunteered to revise and edit such an edition. Over one-third of the original cliché responses were retained for their enduring messages—some with little alteration. These "Classic Clichés" can be appreciated as period pieces, too.

To complete this new edition, the editor enlisted the writing talents of three dozen of FEE's associates, many of whom contribute regularly to the foundation's monthly journal *The Freeman*. The resulting volume of *Clichés of Politics* blends the old with the new and once again provides the reader with a valuable ally in understanding and defending the case for limited government.

I. HUMAN RIGHTS AND THE NATURE OF GOVERNMENT

1

"I have a right!"

Lots of people make this claim without even thinking about the nature and source of rights. What are rights, and where do they come from?

The interventionist view is that so long as legislation is adopted under the rules of procedural due process, government creates and extinguishes rights. For example, Congress, by following the rules of legislative process outlined in the Constitution, can create or extinguish a right to a job, a right to an education, or a right to food.

When interventionists wish to expand the scope of government they often make a distinction between a "privilege" and a "right." In this view, something is a privilege only if a person can acquire it through his own means; and something is a right if government uses tax money or other coercive powers to provide it to individuals irrespective of their means. Really important things, they say, ought to be rights not privileges. Thus in 1993, health care in America was a privilege, but now the Clinton administration is studying ways to convert it into a right.

In the Declaration of Independence Thomas Jefferson wrote about "unalienable" rights that all individuals have irrespective of government. According to him, all humans are "endowed" with these rights by God. Some of Jefferson's colleagues said that "nature" endowed humans with rights—i.e., that rights are inherent in human nature. In either case, rights are logically prior to government. Government has no legitimate authority to add to or subtract from such rights. Its role is to protect them.

If something is a human right in the Jeffersonian sense, it applies to all individuals merely by virtue of their humanity. If one person has such a right, all other humans must logically have the same right. One cannot, without self-contradiction, claim a human right for himself and deny it to others. To do so would be to admit that the right is not a "human" right.

Moreover, it must be possible for all individuals to exercise the claimed right simultaneously without logical contradiction. If when I exercise a right I have claimed, it is thereby impossible for someone else to exercise the identical right at the same time, my action implies that the alleged right does not inhere in human nature. My action implies that it is my right and not the right of the other person.

For example, suppose I claim a right to a job. If that claim means that I will be employed anytime I wish to be (what else could it mean?), there must be some other person who has the duty to provide the job. But then that other person does not have the same right I have. My right is to be employed, his "right" is to provide the job. My right creates a *duty* for him to undertake some positive action that he may not want to undertake. Notwithstanding that we both are human, his freedom of choice is subordinated to my freedom of choice.

Is there any job-related fundamental human right in the Jeffersonian sense? Yes. It is the right of all individuals to *offer* to buy or sell labor services at any terms they choose. I have a right to offer to sell my labor services at terms I like, and so do you. We all can exercise that right without thereby denying it to anyone else. I have a right to offer to buy (employ) the labor services of any other person at terms I like, and so do you. We can do so without thereby denying the right to anyone else. Those to whom you and I extend our offers are free to reject them. In exercising these rights we impose no duty to undertake any positive action on any other person.

Apply the same test to the right to food, the right to an education, and the right to health care. Are any of these fundamental human rights? If they are interpreted to mean that individuals will receive food, education, and health care no matter what other people want, they are not fundamental human rights. We all have a fundamental right to *offer* to buy or sell food, education services, and health care at any terms we like, but if we cannot find others who are willing to accept our offers we have no right to force them to do so.

Apply the same test to the rights guaranteed by the First

Amendment: freedom of religion, freedom of association, freedom of speech, and freedom of the press. These are all fundamental human rights. We each can exercise free choice of religion without denying that right to others. Note, however, we have no right to join a religious organization that doesn't want to accept us. We each can associate with any individuals or groups, but only so long as they are willing to associate with us. Exercising that right does not make it impossible for others to do the same. We each can say what we like without denying that same right to others. Note again, however, we have no right to force people to listen, or to provide us with a forum in which to speak. We each are free to try to assemble the necessary resources, by voluntary agreements with others, to publish a newspaper or a magazine. But we have no right to force people to provide those necessary resources or to purchase or read our publications.

Note that the interventionist and the Jeffersonian views of rights are not only different, they are incompatible. Any time a right claimed by anyone imposes a duty on another to undertake positive action, the alleged right cannot possibly be exercised by both simultaneously without logical contradiction.

The interventionist view of rights is often called the positivist view because such rights necessarily impose duties to undertake positive actions on others. It is part of a larger philosophy called legal positivism which asserts that rights are whatever government says they are.

The Jeffersonian view of rights is often called the negative view because the only duty imposed on others by such rights is a duty to *refrain* from undertaking a particular action. It is a duty to refrain from interfering with others. Moreover, in this view, government itself is bound by the rights justly claimed by all individuals.

The next time you say "I have a right," ask: "Who has the duty?" If there is anyone who has a duty to do anything except refrain from interfering with you, ask: "On what grounds do I claim a right to subordinate that person's will to mine?"

—CHARLES W. BAIRD

2

"We have a right to this service."

When the Reagan administration proposed abolishing subsidies to Amtrak, one of the television networks interviewed a dissenter who phrased her objection this way: "I don't know how those people in Washington expect us to get around out here. We have a right to this service."

When in 1985 the Congress voted to stop funding the printing of *Playboy* magazine in Braille, the American Council of the Blind filed suit in federal court charging that the Congressional action constituted censorship and denial of a basic right.

The issue of "rights" has ignited passions throughout the ages—to the point of bloodshed more often than anyone can count. In 1776, a nation was founded with a declaration that listed but three and its citizens have not stopped talking about their "rights" since.

But something ominous has surfaced in the discussions of late. When so many Americans speak of rights these days, they mean something much removed from the thoughts of Jefferson, Madison, Franklin, and Locke. Taken as a whole, the newly presumed "rights" of recent years constitute an endless litany of claims upon others, a checklist of wants and wishes that escape any generic categorization save that affirmed by the word "plunder."

Sadly, the lofty notion that individuals possess certain rights, definable, unalienable, and sacred, has been cheapened and mongrelized beyond recognition. I wonder how many Americans really know what a "right" is anymore. The sum of all the confusion is this bizarre and destructive fancy: if you claim it, it must be yours.

Does anyone really have a "right" to subsidize rail service? Is there such a thing as a "right" to a copy of *Playboy* in Braille? And what about so many other alleged rights: to a job, to an

12

education, to free day care, to decent housing, to a fair wage, to a chicken in every pot, and on and on *ad infinitum?*

Such questions raise the all-important one: just what is a legitimate "right" anyway? In my belief, the all-time top authorities in this field were the men who crafted this nation at its very start. Though not all of precisely the same mind on every score and not without their faults, none of them treated the concept of rights with the sort of reckless abandon that characterizes our age.

When those gifted individuals asserted the rights to "freedom of speech" or "freedom of the press" or "freedom of assembly," they did not mean to say that one has a right to be given a microphone, a printing press, or a lecture hall.

When the Declaration of Independence spoke of the "right to life," it did not mean the right to live at someone else's expense. Likewise, the "right to liberty" did not translate into a right to do to others whatever one desired. Nor did the "right to the pursuit of happiness" imply Paul's right to rob Peter to pay for Paul's like in art, literature, or music.

The Founding Fathers' concept of rights did not require the initiation of threats or force against others, or the elevation of any "want" to a lawful lien on the life or property of another citizen. It assumed that each individual was a unique and sovereign being and it required only that others either deal with him voluntarily or leave him alone. It is the only concept of rights that does not degenerate into a conflict-ridden free-for-all.

To the founders, a "right" was a moral imperative by which each person exercises the freedom to be what his qualities and potentials make of him, secure in his person and property, and without transgressing that same right of others. His "rights" thus impose no obligation on others except that they abstain from violating them.

In this context, Jefferson's advice as to the proper role of government bears repeating: " ... Still one thing, more, fellow citizens—a wise and frugal government, which shall restrain men from injuring one another, shall leave them otherwise free to regulate their own pursuits of industry and improvement, and shall not take from the mouth of labor the bread it has earned. This is the sum of good government...."

So what does it all mean? Alas, there is no right to Amtrak subsidies, only a right to enjoy the transportation service you freely contract with and pay for.

There is no right to *Playboy* in Braille, only the right to read the copy you might buy, assuming you first find someone who is willing to produce it.

Similarly, you have a right to look for a job, pursue an education, seek the best day care, search for or provide yourself with the housing you desire, shop for the highest wage, or persuade your neighbor to sell you that chicken, but you have no legitimate right to compel (or have the state compel for you) another free person to provide these things to you, unless that other person has breached a contract to do just that.

That knocks into a cocked hat most of what are claimed as rights these days. But the difference between this basic, time-honored, rational view of rights and today's emerging, mindless hodgepodge is the difference between peace, freedom, and mutual respect on the one hand, and the brutality of the lawless jungle on the other.

—Lawrence W. Reed

3

"Human rights are more important than property rights."

It is not the right of property which is protected, but the right to property. Property, per se, has no rights; but the individual—the man—has three great rights, equally sacred from arbitrary interference: the right to his life, the right to his liberty, the right to his property. . . . The three rights are so bound together as to be essentially one right. To give a man his life but deny him his liberty, is to take from him all that makes his life worth living. To give him his liberty but take from him the property which is the fruit and badge of his liberty, is to still leave him a slave.

—U.S. Supreme Court Justice George Sutherland

Tricky phrases with favorable meanings and emotional appeal are being used today to imply a distinction between *property* rights and *human* rights.

By implication, there are two sets of rights—one belonging to human beings and the other to property. Since human beings are more important, it is natural for the unwary to react in favor of *human* rights.

Actually, there is no such distinction between property rights and human rights. The term *property* has no significance except as it applies to something owned by someone. Property itself has neither rights nor value, save only as human interests are involved. There are no rights but human rights, and what are spoken of as property rights are only the human rights of individuals to property.

Expressed more accurately, the issue is not one of property rights versus human rights, but of the human rights of one person in the community versus the human rights of another.

15

What are the property rights thus disparaged by being set apart from human rights? They are among the most ancient and basic of human rights, and among the most essential to freedom and progress. They are the privileges of private ownership which give meaning to the right to the product of one's labor—privileges which men have always regarded instinctively as belonging to them almost as intimately and inseparably as their own bodies. Unless people can feel secure in their ability to retain the fruits of their labor, there is little incentive to save and to expand the capital base—the tools and equipment for production and for better living.

The Bill of Rights in the United States Constitution recognizes no distinction between property rights and other human rights. The ban against unreasonable search and seizure covers "persons, houses, papers, and effects," without discrimination. No person may, without due process of law, be deprived of "life, liberty, or property"; all are equally inviolable. The right of trial by jury is assured in criminal and civil cases alike. Excessive bail, excessive fines, and cruel and unusual punishments are grouped in a single prohibition. The Founding Fathers realized what some present-day politicians seem to have forgotten: A man without property rights—without the right to the product of his own labor—is not a free man.

These Constitutional rights all have two characteristics in common. First, they apply equally to all persons. Second, they are, without exception, guarantees of freedom or immunity from governmental interference. They are not assertions of claims against others, individually or collectively. They merely say, in effect, that there are certain human liberties, including some pertaining to property, which are essential to free men and upon which the state shall not infringe.

Now what about the so-called human rights that are represented as superior to property rights? What about the "right" to a job, the "right" to a standard of living, the "right" to a minimum wage or a maximum work week, the "right" to a "fair" price, the "right" to bargain collectively, the "right" to security against the adversities and hazards of life, such as old age and disability?

The framers of the Constitution would have been astonished

to hear these things spoken of as rights. They are not immunities from governmental compulsion; on the contrary, they are demands for new forms of governmental compulsion. They are not claims to the product of one's own labor; they are, in some if not in most cases, claims to the products of other people's labor.

These "human rights" are indeed different from property rights, for they rest on a denial of the basic concept of property rights. They are not freedoms or immunities assured to all persons alike. They are special privileges conferred upon some persons at the expense of others. The real distinction is not between property rights and human rights, but between equality of protection from governmental compulsion on the one hand and demands for the exercise of such compulsion for the benefit of favored groups on the other.

—PAUL L. POIROT

4

"In a just society, food is a right."

"Every human has a right to food." From the United Nations Declaration of Human Rights to the policy statements of a variety of other organizations, people assert rights to food.[1] Few politicians are willing to challenge this orthodoxy. Indeed, how can one argue against such a "right" without appearing callous and niggardly? Of course, the implication is that it is the government's obligation to provide food to anyone inadequately supplied (whatever inadequate means). A variety of so-called food assistance programs are the logical consequence of this food-as-a-right construct.

Yet food entitlements are not a new political concept. History is replete with examples where governments have granted the right to food and a host of other economic entitlements. Ironically, but predictably, this has often led to a deterioration in the nutritional well-being of the population.

In ancient Rome citizens of the city had rights to food. Political competition led to an expansion of those rights until food became "free." Of course, the food rights of urban dwellers did not come out of thin air. Someone had to produce the food that the Roman citizen consumed. The Roman historian Galen's 148 A.D. description of how city dwellers obtained food is graphic:

> For those living in the cities, in accordance with their habit of procuring sufficient grain at the beginning of the summer to last for the entire coming year, took from the fields all the wheat, barley, beans and lentils. . . . Consequently the peasantry of the districts . . . were literally compelled for the rest of the year to feed on noxious plants, eating the shoots and tendrils of trees and shrubs, and the roots of unwholesome plants.[2]

18

The food rights of city dwellers came at the obvious expense of the rural food producers. Today's expropriations to provide food entitlements may be less obvious than their ancient counterparts, but the effect must be the same: government grants of food must come at a cost. To provide a food entitlement, someone somewhere must lose an economic right.

China's Great Leap Forward (1958–1961) is universally recognized as generating one of the greatest food disasters in history. It is estimated that over 15 million people died in the famine that was a result of the policies of the period. The Great Leap involved collectivizing agriculture, a fact that is well remembered. However, just as relevant, and not as often noted, is the fact that the Great Leap introduced collective dining halls where food was "free." Food was a right of all![3]

It is not surprising that famine was a result. Under the Chinese scheme, peasants had little incentive to produce food, and a great incentive to consume food. The ancient Roman and modern Chinese case were somewhat different in structure, but identical in outcome: incentives to produce food were destroyed. In the Roman case the urban dwellers' confiscation of the peasants' crops destroyed the peasants' incentive to produce. In the Chinese case collectivization destroyed the peasants' incentive to produce while simultaneously and schizophrenically asserted their "right" to consume!

Sydney Webb, an English socialist hailed the 1936 Soviet Constitution for providing " . . . the right to full economic provision, according to need, in all the vicissitudes of life . . ."[4] Of course, just as Western intellectuals like Webb were lauding the Stalin's Russia for granting of economic rights, a tragedy of unheralded proportions had just occurred in the Ukraine. Stalin had ordered the confiscation of all the grain of the Ukraine, and had banned importing food into the region. Even bringing a sackful of potatoes into the Ukraine could lead to execution on the charge of speculation.[5] Many scholars believe the Ukraine was intentionally starved by Stalin for political reasons. Yet the irony is no accident. "Food rights" mean food is politicized. As one commentator aptly stated: "So even as governments have come to see it as one of their responsibilities to supply their people with food, they have also been willing to withhold the food supply from segments of their population who are declared 'enemies.'"[6] What government can give, it can take away! The government provision of today may be the government confiscation of tomorrow!

There are then, at least, three problems with food entitlements. First, the food rights of some must come at the sacrifice of the economic rights of others. Second, the sacrifice of others' economic rights inevitably reduce incentives to engage in productive economic activity. Third, as government interferes with the food market the population becomes vulnerable to the political whims of the state.

The lessons from these three cases are relevant for the modern welfare state. Taxes must finance food transfers. Taxes are a confiscation of producers' economic rights. Moreover, both the taxes and transfers dull incentives to produce. The taxed party produces less to avoid taxation, the recipient avoids productive activity to obtain the transfer. Finally, dependency is created: the poor come to rely on the transfer, and are correspondingly vulnerable to its withdrawal.

Of course, private property provides a bulwark against the horrors outlined in the historical examples above. If the Roman rustic, the Chinese peasant, or the Ukrainian kulak had had individual property rights to the land they worked and the right to exchange freely the product of their labor, no such tragedies could have ensued. What is ironic is that their fellow citizens, who were often identified as having "rights" to the output of the farmers' labor, would also have enjoyed increased food security if property rights had been secure. The reason is remarkably simple: more food would have been produced.

Private property is inconsistent with the assertion of a right to food (or for that matter any other economic good) because its provision *must* come at the expense of a property right. The contemporary welfare state which asserts the right to economic goods of some *must* violate property rights of others. However, if property rights were not violated, if agricultural markets were deregulated, and if producers were taxed less, the subsequent decline in food prices and expansion of economic opportunities would provide real food security to today's poor.

—CECIL E. BOHANON

1. For example, *The Children's Defense Budget* (Washington, D.C.: Children's Defense Fund, 1990), asserts a "fundamental human right to adequate food," p. 131.

2. Quoted from J.E. Evans, "Wheat Production and Its Social Consequences in the Roman World," *Classical Quarterly,* 31: 428–442 (1981), pp. 441–442.

3. See Laszlo Ladany, *The Communist Party of China and Marxism* (Stanford, Calif.: Hoover Institution Press, 1988), Chapter XV for a description of the Great Leap Forward.

4. From *Constitution of the USSR* (London: Committee of the Congress of Peace and Friendship with the U.S.S.R., 1936), p. 7.

5. See James Mace in *The Man-Made Famine in the Ukraine* (Washington, D.C.: American Enterprise Institute, 1984), p. 22.

6. From William Cosgrove, *et al.* "Colonialism, International Trade, and the Nation State" in *Hunger in History,* pp. 215–241, Lucile F. Newman ed. (Cambridge, Mass.: Basil Blackwell, 1990), p. 223.

5

"Don't I have a right to a job?"

We are witnessing today a huge proliferation of rights—or at any rate, of *claims* to rights. "I have the right to a job." "I have the right to a paid vacation at my employer's expense." "I have the right to a decent living." "I have a right to the free use of municipal tennis courts and swimming pools." And so on, with no end in sight. When people become accustomed receiving a certain service, which often began as a privilege extended by someone else, before long they tend to think of it as their right and of the withholding of the service as a violation of their right. Lost in these allegations are such questions as: *Are* these rights? What makes them so? Where do they come from, and who is to provide them?

Our country was founded on the concept of rights. Certain moral rights were conceived to be possessed by all human beings, simply because of their nature as rational beings. "I have a right to X" meant that no one else is to interfere with me with respect to X; a right is like a "no trespassing" sign saying, "You may go so far, but no farther, in dealing with me." Rights give me an autonomy of action within the area of the right, a "moral space" which is not to be transgressed. (By contrast, a legal right is simply what the law permits in the nation or state in which you live. There is still a moral right to life, for example, even if you live in a totalitarian nation which does not respect that right.) Rights preserve the dignity and autonomy of each individual.

A right is not merely a privilege. You may extend me the privilege of walking across your lawn each day as a short-cut to your house, but you may revoke this privilege at any time—it is not mine by right. A driver's license is a privilege (usually extended by the state) which can be revoked if there is clear evidence that you are an unsafe driver.

Having a right is inseparably tied to having certain duties

or responsibilities. If you have a right, there is always something that others must do or refrain from doing because of your right. A right of one person involves a duty of all others to respect that right. Many people, however, have become so insistent of claiming certain things as rights that they do not think of the duties that those rights impose; the "duty" side of the coin is less popular and less emphasized than the "rights" side.

What duties or obligations, then, do rights carry with them? Here it is important to distinguish between *positive* and *negative* rights. A positive right of one person involves a duty of others to *do* something to respect that right, usually an expenditure of money, time, or effort. If you have a right to be supported, then others must do something to support you. A negative right of one person does not involve a duty of others to do something, but only the negative duty of non-interference, or forbearance—of not doing anything to interfere with that to which the person has a right. If you have a right to engage in a certain activity, others have a duty or obligation not to interfere with that activity.

All human beings, according to the Declaration of Independence, have a right to life, liberty, and the pursuit of happiness (sometimes the list is: life, liberty, and property). The crucial terms here, however, are somewhat vague: what exactly is the right to life, and does one have liberty to do anything one chooses? The Bill of Rights helps to spell out the scope of these rights, though jurists are disagreed to this day about how to interpret them in individual cases.

The right to life means at least that you should be protected against those who would take your life, or even threaten it. When a person does not deal with you through voluntary means, but by force or threat of force, you have a right to use force in retaliation in order to defend yourself (this is the right of self-defense), or to use your delegated agent, the police, in your defense. The right to life would be meaningless without the right of self-defense against those who would violate it. As a means to such defense you have the right to bear arms (Second Amendment).

"Congress shall pass no laws abridging freedom of speech or press. . . ." No matter what views you espouse, you will not be forcibly prevented from expressing them. The exact range of application is not specified; can you express your views on another person's property? or loudly at midnight, disturbing the peace, or inciting to riot? At any rate, you will not be stopped because of the content of what you say. (As always in the Constitution, the individual has rights which the government may not violate; the emphasis is on what the federal government may not do.) It is important to be clear about what the right does *not* involve; it does not guarantee you a forum, a lecture hall, or a free ad in a newspaper to disseminate your views, for that would interfere with the rights of others to make their own decisions. The right is not to a thing, but to engage in an activity. It does not place any restriction on others except that of non-interference with your activity; it does not require them to accept what you say or even to listen to you. If the newspaper had to accept your ad, this would interfere with the publisher's right to make his own decision on the matter. There can be no right to interfere with the rights of others.

The right to property (whether personal possessions or land) is not the right to seize it from others, but only to do something to attain it that does not interfere with the equal rights of others. Ordinarily property is transmitted through sale, exchange, gift, or inheritance; one does not have the right to obtain it by theft.

Your right to the pursuit of happiness is not a right to do anything you like to enhance your happiness, for example, by robbing banks or taking pot shots at other people. You may endeavor to enhance your happiness by peaceful means which do not violate rights. As Herbert Spencer said in his *Man versus the State,* each person may do as he chooses as long as he does not forcibly interfere with the equal right of others to act as they choose (Spencer's Law of Equal Freedom).

All of the above are negative rights, requiring of others only the duty of non-interference. It is not so with the so-called positive rights (real or alleged). If you have a positive right, I and others must do something to honor that right; you can have a positive right only at the expense of someone else. Positive rights, or talk of them, is very popular today. One hears, for example, "I have a right to a job." But if I have a right to job, others must supply the job. What if there are no jobs in the field in which I am trained, or because of advancing technology there is no longer a market for my product? Or what if no employer finds it worth his while to pay me wages for my services? What if I am lazy and repeatedly skip work? What if I turn up drunk on the job or am a constant irritant to other workers, or appear for work late every day, or take afternoons off during nice weather? Do I still have a right to the job, or to some other? To say yes would be to take away the employer's freedom of choice in the matter. I do have a right to seek a job, to accept or reject one if offered, or to create one myself (start my own business)—as always, my (negative) right is to engage in an activity, and the only obligation on others is not to interfere.

Similarly, if I have a (positive) right to be supported by you, you must part with some of your income in order to keep me fed and housed. If individuals have a right to support at government expense, then everyone in that state or nation is required to help support me, without being able to exercise their individual judgment as to whether I am worthy of that support. (By contrast, generosity with what is yours does not violate any right.) The right to support seems very humane, but no one can exercise such an alleged right without picking someone else's pocket. The same with the right to a house, the right to a car and a telephone, and so on. These are (alleged) rights to things which must be provided by others.

Moreover, what if the supply runs out? What if so many people claim the right that not everyone can receive it? If a resident of Bangladesh claimed the right to three meals a day, there would not be enough food in the entire country to fulfill this demand. And if in the Middle Ages people had claimed the right to a forty-hour work week, most people would have starved, for in a pre-industrial age they could not have kept body and soul together on so little labor. This problem does not occur with negative rights; my right to life implies only that others not attempt to take it, and it does not matter how many people there are for this right to be honored.

The Founding Fathers of the United States were wise not to list, among the rights of man, any of these alleged positive rights. Doubtless they foresaw where such alleged rights would lead. Better, they thought, to leave industry and agriculture free to produce, and leave the consumer to choose among competing products. Better to leave people free to accumulate capital if they can, thus creating extensive employment and a prosperous economy. Then, though people do not have a right to jobs, there would *be* more jobs, and though they do not have a right to the income of others, they will be much more able to do for themselves what most modern liberals say they should get from government as a positive right.

Letting people free to rise as high as their ability will carry them will create the prosperity that presumably the liberals themselves desire. It is the way they want to achieve it that cannot succeed; theirs is a formula for universal poverty, whereas leaving people free to act in their own best interests, to produce, to expand, to test their ideas in the marketplace, will create an economy in which people will no longer feel tempted to claim rights at the expense of others. To the extent that the (alleged) positive rights are granted, the negative rights must be violated, and with that violation comes the poverty which we all wish to avoid.

—JOHN HOSPERS

6

"Civil rights laws increase freedom."

Even though they are a relatively recent policy development, civil rights laws are considered necessary to insure rights for blacks. But they are, in fact, among the most draconian forms of intervention into the free market. They attack the essence of private property, the ability to exercise control over it. Such laws have resulted in lessened economic freedom, lowered prosperity, heightened social tension, and more trouble for the groups the laws are supposed to help.

Civil rights laws can be broadly grouped into those interfering with free-market labor contracts and those classifying private business as public goods. The labor-related laws forbid discrimination on grounds defined by the government (race, sex, religion, and disability). These are an intervention in the freedom of contract, the legal right to use one's property as one sees fit.

In a market exchange, two parties agree to a contract involving property they own or labor services they can offer. Both expect to benefit from the exchange, or it would not take place. Such market exchanges insure that resources find their most highly valued uses, as determined by their owners. Civil rights laws limit the range of possible legal exchanges, thereby diminishing the use-value of labor and property.

Such legal restrictions generate no social benefit. If the most-preferred choice on a person's rank of preferences is an action the law regards as discriminatory, then maximum benefit is denied to him. To put it another way, civil rights law compel certain results—market exchanges of property—that would not have taken place under a purely voluntary system.

In popular political rhetoric, advocates of antidiscrimination laws say that they guarantee rights but do not themselves discriminate. For example, the 1964 Civil Rights Act forbids dis-

27

crimination against anyone on grounds of race, and ensures that there will be no "reverse" discrimination either. But it is impossible to forbid certain types of exchanges without necessarily compelling others. By limiting the range of options and placing a legal restriction on the most preferred ones, parties must settle on less-preferred outcomes.

All civil rights laws, therefore, necessarily tilt the field so as to advantage one side. If an employer must choose between a white and a black employee, either choice he makes will be in some sense "discriminatory," but by compelling only one possible choice, two of three parties are harmed. The only institutional setting that insures a level playing field is one that allows everyone the freedom to contract, which means not compelling the hiring, firing, or promotion of the members of any group.

If racism is a concern, competitive markets will tend to discourage irrational discrimination in hiring. As a free contractor, any person who thinks himself injured by another's discrimination is free to take his services elsewhere. It is not a socially relevant problem for an employer to pass up a good employee on grounds of race, for by doing so he is effectively paying a premium to discriminate that another competitor does not have to pay. If nearly all employers and firms discriminate irrationally, one employer can break the cartel by hiring passed-over but more productive employees and thereby gain a competitive edge over the other firms.

Civil rights laws, moreover, may actually increase discrimination. Employers forced to pay or promote people out of fear of the civil-rights police will tend to avoid hiring them in the first place. And those who do get hired under such circumstances will be the cream of the labor pool, further marginalizing the least skilled and least experienced.

At the same time, it is wrong to think that the free market will produce "color-blind" results, since a degree (even a high degree) of racial and sexual discrimination will probably persist in any free society. There may be written rules about dress codes and the kinds of music piped into the office, or unwritten rules about how loudly people should speak in the office. As every employer knows, the less divergence in tastes to be found among employees, the easier it is to agree on rules for the common good.

A Korean grocer may want to employ only Korean clerks, a magazine for black professionals only black editors and writers, and a German restaurant only German cooks and waiters. An employer may think that Iraqi-Americans have been unfairly treated and want to favor them. A women's health club may want only women customers and a men's bar may want only men. There is nothing wrong with any of these behaviors, although civil rights laws seek to end them.

In addition to violating the free labor contract, civil rights laws guarantee everyone the right of "access" to "public accommodations" like restaurants, movie theaters, and shops. In fact, what the civil rights laws call public is really private. These businesses are established by private entrepreneurs with private money. The owners should no more be required to serve everyone who comes into their place than they are required to invite everyone to their home for dinner. A large downtown restaurant is as private as a small house in the country. The real difference between private and public is one of ownership, not function or location.

By redefining restaurants, theaters, and shops as public, civil rights laws invade the private property of business owners. Far from establishing a level playing field, they actually give non-owners preference over owners. When trade is compelled, one party must be coerced. Under "public access" it is the owner who must submit to the demands of a trespasser. This is the essence of socialism, which denies that any property is private.

When minorities are allowed to force their way onto private property, the entire character of social and economic life changes. Rather than being based on voluntarism and contract, it is based on intimidation and force. It is therefore predictable that such laws have increased tension between groups rather than abetted it.

Far from increasing freedom, civil rights laws have dramatically reduced it. Conflicts over race, sex, religion, and disability are best left to the free market, which develops natural solutions.

—LLEWELLYN H. ROCKWELL, JR.

7

"We must abide by the majority.
That's democracy."

This cliché is used by the statists to insinuate the coercive authority of government into every aspect of human action. They assert that one who opposes a measure supported by a majority must be antidemocratic and therefore an enemy of freedom. But freedom and democracy are not the same thing. Democracy is a form of government wherein the governed, based upon a majority vote, have some influence over the government. Freedom is a state of affairs in which individuals are able to pursue their own interests without interference from others—including government—so long as they don't trespass against the fundamental rights of others.

For people to be free, government—even democratic government—must be limited. Majorities can be just as tyrannical as dictators. Indeed, the authors of the *Federalist Papers* warned us against the dangers of "despotic majoritarianism." A principal motive of the delegates to the Philadelphia constitutional convention in 1787 was to constrain the "democratic excesses" of the states under the Articles of Confederation.

In an unlimited democracy, anything and everything is subject to a vote. In a limited democracy, the private sphere of human action is not subject to a vote. There, individual choice, not majority voting, is the proper decision rule. In the words of the U.S. Supreme Court:

> The very purpose of the Bill of Rights was to withdraw certain subjects from the vicissitudes of political controversy, to place them beyond the reach of majorities.... One's ... fundamental rights may not be subject to vote; they depend on the outcome of no elections [*West Virginia State Board of Education v. Barnette*, 319 US#624 (1943)].

It is easy to show that there are some things that should not be subject to a vote. For example, suppose a majority of citizens in a country vote to confiscate the wealth of all black citizens and transfer it to all white citizens. Must we abide by the majority in this case? If your answer is "yes," on what grounds do you justify subordinating the rights of blacks to the interests of whites? If your answer is "no," you recognize that there must be some limits on what a majority should be allowed to do.

Suppose a majority of citizens vote to confiscate 50 percent of the income of all people whose annual income is over $150,000 and transfer it to people whose annual income is less than $25,000. Must we abide by the majority in this case? If your answer is "yes" and, assuming your answer to the first question was "no," on what grounds do you differentiate the two cases? Is it because the first is based on race and the second is based on ability to pay? Why should that matter? Isn't theft theft no matter who is the victim and who is the beneficiary?

If we start with the axiom that all people have equal rights and are entitled to equal treatment by the law, logic implies that any taking from some to benefit others is illegitimate. Discrimination on the basis of income is no more defensible than discrimination on the basis of race. Voluntary transfers are permissible, but coerced transfers are not.

The term "economic democracy" is often used to describe a situation in which democratic government extends mandatory majority rule to private production and exchange activities. For example, the National Labor Relations Act (NLRA) forces all employees of a firm to accept the representation services of a labor union chosen by a majority of those workers. The same law compels the employer to recognize the union as the exclusive bargaining agent for the workers. When a union wins a certification election, individual workers, even those who voted against the union, are forbidden to represent and bargain for themselves. Unions justify this monopoly representation privilege by saying that all workers must abide by the majority. They say, "That's democracy."

However, negotiating the sale of one's own labor services is a private, not a governmental, matter. The act of hiring a lawyer is by individual choice from among those lawyers who are willing to take the case. The decision does not involve majority rule voting. A union is an organization that specializes in representing workers in the sale of their labor services. Hiring a union to represent you is logically like hiring a lawyer to represent you. It should be a matter of your individual free choice among those unions who are willing to represent you. But Congress has declared that choosing a union must be like choosing a president, not like choosing a lawyer. Your labor, says Congress, is owned by a majority of your fellow employees.

Suppose Congress declared that choosing a spouse, or choosing a church, or choosing friends must be by majority vote. If we have economic democracy, why not spouse democracy, church democracy, or friends democracy? What is the difference? Is it only because of the Bill of Rights? The First Amendment guarantees individual free choice of religion. It also guarantees individual freedom of association. Choosing a spouse and friends is protected by that freedom of association. Isn't the decision about union representation also a matter of freedom of association?

Where do we draw the line between that which is legitimate to decide by mandatory submission to the will of the majority and that which is not? The authors of the United States Constitution tried to draw such a line, but since then statists have found ways across the line, especially when it comes to economic freedoms. The NLRA, legal minimum wages, rent controls, mandatory family leave, and mandatory racial preference in hiring are only five of the hundreds of acts of Congress that have crossed that line.

In a free society, government itself is limited by fundamental rights of individuals that exist independently of government. Indeed, in a free society the sole purpose of government is the enforcement and defense of those fundamental rights. Democracy cannot expand the legitimate scope of government. There are only two legitimate applications of democracy in a free society: first selecting the people who will wield governmental authority, and then determining the concrete activities of government within its limited scope—and no more.

—CHARLES W. BAIRD

II. GOVERNMENT PLANNING
AND REGULATION

8

"Government regulators know best."

It is fashionable today to ascribe all of life's ills to the inevitable workings of unregulated market processes. This view, originally delineated by Karl Marx, was popularized during the 1960s by Nobel prize-winning Keynesian economist Paul Samuelson. It manifests itself today in the Nanny State. Benevolent government regulators, we are told, are the only things standing between hapless individual consumers and the relentless pursuit of profits under market capitalism. Every problem, from worker safety to airport gridlock, from escalating health care costs to global warming, can be corrected simply because government officials know best. Or at very least, unlike profit-seeking businessmen, they have the public's best interests at heart.

This view—that federal legislators and bureaucrats protect the public from private markets—demonstrates a profound ignorance of the political dynamics that drive the federal regulatory process. This "public interest" perspective wrongly assumes that government officials possess both the relevant knowledge and correct incentives needed to restructure private markets rationally. Unfortunately, politicians and bureaucrats don't, and can't, leave their private interests at the door when they enter public service. Even if they could, government officials have no special access to the boundless body of knowledge conveyed and coordinated by market processes.

As it turns out, both politicians and bureaucrats have something to gain by imposing new, complex regulatory schemes onto private enterprise. Some are simply anti-market zealots. Most, however, are responding to pressures or payoffs from special interests. One concentrated interest group will lobby government officials for a transfer of wealth from the rest of society through the political process. Farmers will seek crop subsidies and price supports; automobile producers will seek tariffs on foreign cars;

labor unions will seek a higher minimum wage and mandated benefits.

Legislators secure the votes needed for re-election by pandering to such special interests. But they also benefit by increasing their control over private markets. Bureaucrats inevitably create new demands for their own regulatory skills by creating a broad, complex web of rules through which all enterprises must pass. In short, politicians and bureaucrats have no economic incentive to pursue the general welfare at the expense of their own.

But even benevolent dictators would often fail to improve upon market outcomes because of what Austrian economists refer to as "the knowledge problem." According to Nobel Laureate Friedrich Hayek, the public interest, mainstream view of regulation begs the key question of economic organization: "If we possess all the relevant information, if we can start out from a given system of preferences, and if we command complete knowledge of the available means, the problem which remains is purely one of logic." Unfortunately, such complete knowledge is never available to any one individual or group. Each individual, argues Hayek, possesses a unique perspective and "the knowledge of the particular circumstances of time and place." Through the process of free exchange, market prices serve as a dynamic telecommunications system, expressing and coordinating these "bits" of knowledge dispersed throughout society.

It was this understanding of market processes that originally led the eminent Austrian economist Ludwig von Mises to question Marx's socialist vision in the 1920s. According to Mises, Marxian central planning was unworkable because the relevant information was not readily available to the government planners: "No single man can ever master all the possibilities of production, innumerable as they are, as to be in a position to make straightaway evident judgments of value . . . ."

This knowledge problem faced by would-be central planners is also faced by regulators who ostensibly seek to fine tune the economy. Unlike the central planner, the bureaucrat does work within a market framework. But he still faces similar problems: At what price, quantity, or quality will the perceived problems of a regulated industry be corrected? Without the feedback of market signals, the regulator has no basis of knowing which actions are "correct" and which are not.

Inevitably, government intervention in private markets produce unintended consequences decidedly more harmful than the "problem" itself. Indeed, most instances of "market failure" can be traced to past instances of government failure. Minimum wage laws and mandated worker benefits artificially raise the cost of labor and produce unemployment among the poor and unskilled; Medicare, Medicaid, and other government spending programs reduce price competition and drive up the costs of health care and health insurance. Tariffs and price supports shift higher costs and inferior quality goods onto individual consumers.

All of this brings us full circle to the question of incentives. For, as Israel Kirzner points out, one of the most likely consequences of any government regulatory scheme is the creation of unintended profit opportunities in the regulatory process itself—opportunities that manifest themselves in "the bribery and corruption of the regulators."

As government intervention grows, so does the incentive to invest less in the pursuit of profits and more into the pursuit of government protection from competition. In such a vicious cycle of political intervention, consumers are never protected, and only government benefits.

—MATTHEW B. KIBBE

9

"All we need is the right people to run the government."

It's been a time-honored practice in America to "throw the rascals out" when things go wrong in government. This supposedly is merely the political version of what happens when the manager of a losing baseball team is replaced, or the chief executive officer of a failing corporation gets the axe.

Nobody should dispute the fact that government operations require capable, experienced people who know how to do their jobs. We've all probably had unpleasant bouts with incompetent public officials and clerks, and we wish they could be replaced.

But when government expands beyond its rightful limits, problems arise that have little to do with the competence and abilities of its officials and employees. The delusion that these problems can be solved by replacing officials only delays the day when people really face the hard questions about what government should and should not do.

Thanks to the relentless expansion of government, however, these questions are being asked the world over, with surprising solutions in some cases. There is growing criticism of government operations and regulations. There is also a rush to "privatize" many services. Though privatization moves are being made for economic reasons rather than to restore liberty, they still appear as hopeful signs.

The most important reason for limiting government to its rightful peacekeeping functions is to preserve and promote liberty. If this is done, people working singly or in groups will eventually find wonderful ways of dealing with the many human problems that government promises to solve, and meeting the human needs that government promises to meet. But as we now know, problems and needs continue to grow while the government colossus has created dangers, such as mountainous public debt and group conflicts, that threaten us all and seem beyond solution. These problems worsen no matter who seems to be running things in government. Even people who used to have almost religious faith in the powers of government are becoming disillusioned as its clay feet become more exposed.

A second dilemma with excessive government is that it must always be run bureaucratically. Bureaucracy can be a maddening thing for people who have been accustomed to the speed and efficiency of market-driven services. When confronted with bureaucratic actions that displease us, we tend to blame the officials in charge and call for their replacement.

But unless the officials we want replaced are completely incompetent, rooting them out is usually a waste of time and effort. As Ludwig von Mises explained many years ago, bureaucracy is neither good nor bad. Bureaucratic management is the method applied in the conduct of administrative affairs the result of which has no cash value on the market, though it may have other values to society. It is management bound to comply with detailed rules and regulations fixed by an authoritative body. "The task of the bureaucrat is to perform what these rules and regulations order him to do," Mises explained. "His discretion to act according to his own best conviction is seriously restricted by them."[1]

Thus bureaucracy is good when it is applied in public operations such as police departments, military forces, and records bureaus. But it becomes oppressive and deadly when it is imposed on business enterprises and other human activities. As Mises shrewdly saw, the evil of bureaucracy was not in the method itself. "What many people nowadays consider an evil is not bureaucracy as such," he pointed out, "but the expansion of the sphere in which bureaucratic management is applied."[2]

Mises then contrasted this bureaucratic system with business management or profit management, which is management directed by the profit motive. Managers, driven by the need to stay profitable, can be given wide discretion with a minimum amount of rules and regulations. And customers will quickly let them know whether the business is providing proper goods and services at prices which customers consider favorable.

This profit-driven system has its opponents, of course, and

this creates problems and frictions for entrepreneurs who want to compete for our business. Some opponents fear the new competition, while others deplore the entrepreneurs' use of resources. And one of the most effective ways of hampering entrepreneurs is to put them under either limited or total government regulation and control—that is, replacing profit-driven management with at least some degree of bureaucratic management.

So what we have in today's world is a great deal of government with additional regulation and control of private business. There is lots of grumbling about the fact that "the system doesn't seem to be working," but nobody is likely to fix it. At election time, glib office-seekers promise to reform the system and "get the country moving again." This doesn't happen, and general dissatisfaction is growing.

And there still seems to be a persistent delusion that "putting the right person" in charge will fix the problem. One favorite government response, when conditions worsen in an area, is to appoint a "czar" with special powers to bring everything together with businesslike efficiency. We have had numerous "czars" to control energy and prices, and one was recently named to deal with the health reform. However highly touted, these czars soon turn out to be no more effective than the Russian rulers who gave rise to the term.

Another common fallacy, a favorite idea with pro-business political administrations, is that government operations will work better if capable business executives are found to head them. But as Mises perceptively noted, "A former entrepreneur who is given charge of a government bureau is in this capacity no longer a businessman but a bureaucrat. His objective can no longer be profit, but compliance with the rules and regulations. As head of a bureau he may have the power to alter some minor rules and some matters of internal procedure. But the setting of the bureau's activities is determined by rules and regulations which are beyond his reach."[3]

Some people thrive in this sort of work and turn out to be excellent bureaucrats. They are the right people to run government operations when it is limited to its rightful peacekeeping functions. But if our purpose is to preserve and promote liberty while seeking the benefits of a market-driven economy, we'll look in vain for reasonable answers and solutions from government—no matter who runs it. We are slowly learning this lesson, though at great cost. We should, of course, continue to follow the time-honored American practice of "throwing the rascals out" when elected officials are performing badly. But in today's world, the officials we're criticizing might not be rascals at all, but just conscientious people trying to do jobs that shouldn't have been created in the first place.

—MELVIN D. BARGER

---

1. Ludwig von Mises, *Bureaucracy* (William Hodge & Company, Limited, Glasgow/Edinburgh/ London, 1945), p. 58.

2. *Ibid.*, p. 57.

3. *Ibid.*, p. 62.

10

"No one advocates censorship, but what's wrong with government control of the economy?"

The call for national economic planning is in principle a call for international economic planning. It is also a call for the international censorship of information, as we shall see.

We live in a world economy. Goods cross borders. Because of electronic communications, so do services. These services come in the form of information. As an economy grows, we have learned, an ever-larger percentage of resources is devoted to the discovery and distribution of information.

The call for national economic planning is a call for government controls over information: censorship. This coercive censorship is aimed not at something deemed by government agents as inherently immoral but at something deemed by them as in some way economically harmful—above all, at *harmful information*. Yet those who call for economic planning are rarely willing to admit in public that they are in principle calling for coercive censorship by a world government.

The lower the price of information, the more demand there is for it. Information comes in bite-sized portions. Buyers want specific information, not information in general. Specific information is what the free market provides. *Ultimately, the call for government economic planning is the call for political restrictions on the voluntary flow of information.* A government agency is established that restricts people's legal right to act on their own behalf in terms of the best information—from their point of view—that they can afford to buy.

Knowledge cannot be controlled at zero price. The more demand there is for individual bits of information, the higher the cost of restricting their flow. Like a juggler who has too many oranges in the air, so is any government that attempts to restrict the flow of information. The juggler's assistant keeps tossing in

42

more oranges. Eventually, he drops most of them. So does the government.

The Soviet Union learned this lesson in August, 1991. It collapsed politically; it had already collapsed economically. Its top leaders could no longer conceal the prosperity of the West from Communist Party members; nor could Soviet businesses, or even its conventional military forces, compete with the productivity of the West, which the free flow of information has made possible. A nation in which typewriters were rationed by the government to politically correct people could not compete in a world of microcomputers. Complexity overwhelmed the government's planners.

The modern international economy is highly complex. Each of several billion people makes numerous economic decisions daily. These decisions all boil down to this: "To buy or not to buy? That is the question." How could any government planning agency make even a tiny fraction of these tens of billions of daily decisions "in the name of the people"? By what moral standard should such representative, coercive decisions be made?

One of the most important decisions a person can make is the decision not to buy. How could a national government planning board decide for a million or a hundred million people that they should not buy specific items? I am not referring here to the purchase of high-tech nuclear weapons. I am referring to consumer goods and tools and, above all, information.

The complexity of the modern economy is in fact one of the strongest arguments against government planning. Members of a government planning agency must act representatively for all of the people under their lawful jurisdiction. The more people represented, the more difficult the task of central planning. Furthermore, the greater the number of choices available to individuals, the more complex the task.

Economists have difficulty in defining precisely what economic growth is, but one of the most useful definitions is this one: "An increase in the number of choices affordable for a large number of individuals." As an economy grows, the number of options grows. As people grow richer—richer in choices—the task of economic planning grows more complicated as it approaches infinite complexity.

As people grow richer, they can afford to buy more information. They want to know what their options are, and the only way to discover this is to gain access to accurate information. Advertising is one source of information, but there are many others. Magazine reviews of products, independent consumer testing organizations, and word of mouth are all important sources of information. The potential buyer makes decisions in terms of both his own desires and the information he can afford.

Is a government planning agency capable of making valid representative decisions regarding the most appropriate information and the appropriate goals (desires) of all or most people under its jurisdiction? How can the members of such an agency get inside the minds of those whom they represent? By what standard will they make their decisions to cut off access to specific bits of information by the general public, or at least by certain groups?

Those who defend the idea of central planning are rarely willing to identify the moral standard by which the government agency will ration specific information. A moral standard is never mentioned in the enabling legislation. So, bureaucrats are left without explicit moral guidelines regarding the legitimacy of the public's access to information.

A defender of government planning might respond: "I am not advocating controls over ideas. I am merely recommending controls over how people spend their money." But prices are extremely important bits of information. To the extent that there are controls over how people spend their money, there are controls over how they live their lives. Such controls are in fact controls over the spread of ideas: *thought control by means of implementation control.* Yet a person who would never deliberately recommend government control over ideas may enthusiastically recommend controls over people's ability to act in terms of their ideas with their own money.

The more complex an economy, the stronger the technical case for the free market: the planning authority of acting individuals. Only the free flow of information, including prices and money, can provide the rational means of decision-making.

—GARY NORTH

11

"An unregulated economy was part of the horse-and-buggy era."

The basic fallacy of this all-too-common cliché is a confusion between technology and such other aspects of human life as morality and political principles. Over the centuries, technology tends to progress: from the first wheel to the horse and buggy to the railroad and the jet plane. Looking back on this dramatic and undeniable progress, it is easy for men to make the mistake of believing that all other aspects of society are somehow bound up with, and determined by, the state of technology in each historical era. Every advance in technology, then, seemingly requires some sort of change in all other values and institutions of man. The Constitution of the United States was, undoubtedly, framed during the "horse-and-buggy" era. Doesn't this mean that the railroad age required some radical change in that Constitution, and that the jet age requires something else? As we look back over our history, we find that since 1776 our technology has been progressing, and that the role of government in the economy, and in all of society, has also grown rapidly. This cliché simply assumes that the growth of government must have been required by the advance of technology.

If we reflect upon this idea, the flaws and errors stand out. *Why* should an increase in technology require a change in the Constitution, or in our morality or values? *What* moral or political change does the entrance of a jet force us to adopt?

There is no necessity whatever for morality or political philosophy to change every time technology improves. The fundamental relations of men—their need to mix their labor with resources in order to produce consumer goods, their desire for sociability, their need for private property, to mention but a few—are always the same, whatever the era of history. Jesus' teachings were not applicable just to the oxcart age of first-century

45

Palestine; neither were the Ten Commandments somehow "outmoded" by the invention of the pulley.

Technology may progress over the centuries, but the morality of man's actions is not thereby assured; in fact, it may easily and rapidly retrogress. It does not take centuries for men to learn to plunder and kill one another, or to reach out for coercive power over their fellows. There are always men willing to do so. Technologically, history is indeed a record of progress; but morally, it is an up-and-down and eternal struggle between morality and immorality, between liberty and coercion.

While no specific technical tool can in any way determine moral principles, the truth is the other way round: in order for technology even to advance, man needs at least a modicum of freedom—freedom to experiment, to seek the truth, to discover and develop the creative ideas of the individual. And remember, every new idea must originate in some one individual. Freedom is needed for technological advance; and when freedom is lost, technology itself decays and society sinks back, as in the Dark Ages, into virtual barbarism.

The glib cliché tries to link liberty and limited government with the horse and buggy; socialism and the welfare state, it slyly implies, are tailored to the requirements of the jet age and computer era. But on the contrary, it is socialism and state planning that are many centuries old, from the savage Oriental despotisms of the ancient empires to the totalitarian regime of the Incas. Liberty and morality had to win their way slowly over many centuries, until finally expanding liberty made possible the great technological advance of the Industrial Revolution and the flowering of modern capitalism. The reversion in this century to ever greater statism threatens to plunge us back to the barbarism of the ancient past.

Statists always refer to themselves as "progressives," and to libertarians as "reactionaries." These labels grow out of the very cliché we have been examining here. This "technological determinist" argument for statism began with Karl Marx and was continued by Thorstein Veblen and their numerous followers—the real reactionaries of our time.

—MURRAY N. ROTHBARD

12

"Pass a law!"

It's no secret that lawyers are not among the most popular people in American society. Opinion polls measuring public esteem for a variety of occupations rather consistently put them near the bottom. That's unfortunate because it tars an entire profession with the same nasty brush. In law, as well as in every other endeavor, there are both honorable people and scoundrels. The special, often outrageous, cases often capture media attention but I know of no study or competent claim that the scoundrels are anything but a small minority of the whole. Most of those who practice law are decent individuals who sometimes get blamed for bad laws that Congress has first written.

Nevertheless, the abundance of lawyers says something fundamentally frightening about the course of our society. To ignore it or to take the easy path of scapegoating the legal profession for it will only compound our problems.

Figures released by the U.S. Department of Education indicate that of the 74,000 professional degrees awarded one year in the mid-1980s, the law field accounted for the greatest percentage—48 percent!

Writing in the *Detroit News,* Professor Ralph Slovenko of Wayne State University Law School pointed out that the number of lawyers in the United States more than doubled during the 1970s and 1980s.

Professor Slovenko says the United States has more than 90 percent of the world's lawyers, five times as many per capita as Western Europe, 36 times as many as Japan. He quotes former Supreme Court Chief Justice Warren Burger, who says that the United States "has the largest law factory the world has ever known."

One reason U.S. productivity has lagged behind Japan's in recent years is apparent from this startling fact: While Japan produces 50 engineers for every one in the United States, the United States produces 100 lawyers for every one in Japan. The explosion of litigation unique to the United States, Slovenko says, "has sent a chill through fields as diverse as medicine, computer science and food processing."

Surely, any society that devotes less of its energies and resources to production and more of those things to lawsuits is destined for the back seat in the world economy.

Ultimately, there is only one comprehensive solution: Stop passing so many laws. More laws mean more lawyers, pure and simple, and new laws have been pouring forth at a breakneck pace for years.

We live in an age in which worship of government is the unofficial state religion. Congress and state legislatures measure their success each year by the number of laws they pass. Our representatives are often called "lawmakers," never "law repealers." Most Americans, even while complaining about government, nonetheless are falling over themselves by the millions to get government to take charge of their problems, their kids' education, their retirement, you name it. "Pass a law" is becoming as much a part of Americana as mom and apple pie.

What Americans must realize is that they can't have their cake and eat it too. Too many are asking for more government and fewer lawyers and lawsuits in the same breath. The fact remains that the bigger government gets and the more laws it passes, the more the legal profession must grow. How can it possibly be otherwise?

—Lawrence W. Reed

13

"There ought to be a law!"

The power of government usually grows in this manner: A specific situation attracts the sympathy or disapproval of one or more sincere citizens. They, in turn, call this situation to the attention of one or more sincere legislators. The situation so impresses the well-intentioned citizens and legislators that they jump to the conclusion: "There ought to be a law."

Seldom does the particular problem or situation apply to each of the 256 million American citizens. But the law that deals with the problem *does* apply equally to all. The results which flow from this fact are not always what the authors and proponents of the particular law had in mind.

In the hands of its interpreters and administrators, a new law—a grant of power to government—becomes an invitation to expand. As soon as the law is passed, the question arises as to whether or not it applies in this or that particular situation. Some of these may be like the original case, and others may not. But decisions must be made. The executive—or, more likely, an administrative clerk or junior legal counsel—generally decides that it does apply. This is understandable; not only is he a "hardworking and patriotic public servant upholding law and order," but also the scope of his bureau, branch, or department of government is thereby increased. It is the accepted political way "to get ahead." Liberal interpretations of new grants of power mean more work and more jobs for more administrators—at the expense of the freedom and the income of the forgotten taxpayers.

If the law happens to be one under which certain citizens can qualify for some "benefit," these citizens are all too willing to help the administrator expand his job and power. And the minds and imaginations of many hundreds of thousands of other citizens are stimulated to invent ways and means of also "qualifying for the benefits"—and then increasing them. Thus the force arising from the creative imaginations of millions of citizens is added to the force that is created by the natural desire of government administrators to increase their power. All join in seeking to enlarge the scope of the law because each sees a way of gaining from it. This hope of gain is the most powerful expansive force on earth. It is this force that can conquer a wilderness and create the greatest industrial society ever known. But if this natural hope of gain is turned by law in another direction, it can—and will—create the largest and most powerfully concentrated government ever devised by man. In fact, it *has*—in our own country as well as abroad.

The maximum flow of creative human energy and the utmost in voluntary cooperation among individual free men are called forth only when government is limited to the equal *protection* of the inherent rights of free and responsible human beings. To the extent that this basic life principle of a free society is implemented and safeguarded within a nation, the people of that nation will achieve balanced development and growth. Most of our reform laws violate this basic principle in that they penalize the producer and reward the "free rider" who consumes more than he produces. Thus the flow of creative human energy is increasingly inhibited as "liberal" laws authorize more and more unearned withdrawals from the stream of goods and services provided by the producers.

The citizens of America are now entrapped in a vicious circle. The administrators must necessarily have more and more tax money if they are to enlarge the scope of their activities under new laws to "help the people." The increase of taxes causes the citizens to try even harder to qualify for the benefits, in order to regain some of the money that was taken from them to finance previous laws.

Hence it is that *additional* problems initiated and intensified by each new law almost always exceed the problem which the law was designed to alleviate in the first place. This could continue until the taxpayer is extinguished and the government is in complete control. It has happened several times before in history.

The only way to avoid this end result is to avoid passing the law that starts it on its way or, if it is already in existence, to get rid of it. We must remember that the principal instrument of government is coercion and that our government officials are no more moral, omnipotent, nor omniscient than are any of the rest of us. Once we understand the basic principles which must be observed if freedom is to be safeguarded against government, we may become more hesitant in turning our personal problems and responsibilities over to that agency of coercion, with its insatiable appetite for power. The hour is late, and we have much to learn.

—W. C. MULLENDORE

14

"To solve the problem, we need government regulation."

Just how widely embraced this cliché is can be gleaned from the fact that nearly every major newscaster takes it for granted. A while ago *NBC Nightly News* reported on some problems with private security services in certain parts of the country. Sure enough, the news anchor concluded, aghast, that government is not regulating this industry, presumably accounting for the trouble. As if meat never poisoned anyone despite elaborate government regulations of the industry, as if no airplanes ever crashed despite the Federal Aviation Administration's presence throughout the last few decades, and as if government regulators somehow had a superior nature to the rest of us. And all the while these broadcasters are reporting on scandal after scandal involving politicians, bureaucrats, judges, and the police, making no connection at all between their blind faith in government and the facts of reality they are hired to tell about.

There are essentially four arguments for government regulation: the creature of the state argument advanced by Ralph Nader and his followers; the two types of market failure argument invoked by, among others, John Stuart Mill and John Kenneth Galbraith; the positive rights to provisions argument advanced by such political philosophers as Alan Gewirth and John Rawls; and the judicial inefficiency argument proposed by the Nobel Laureate economist Kenneth J. Arrow. Let us look at each briefly and see why they do not support the institution of government regulation, despite the belief in its absolute necessity by some many influential people.

The "creature of the state" argument applies to nearly all businesses since most all are incorporated enterprises. It states that corporate commerce is a creature of government itself—it was brought into existence by acts of the British mercantilist government so as to enhance the wealth of the country. And governments still charter corporations. Since government created them, it is authorized and, indeed, ought to regulate them to accord with the public purpose. Clearly, morally, if one has created something, one is responsible for it and may do with it what is reasonable and responsible. So, government ought to regulate corporate commerce to the various good ends government sets out to promote—safety, social equality, affirmative action, environmental purity—especially now that the goal of creating a wealthy country has been largely achieved.

The creature of the state argument fails, however, because the mere fact of history does not establish a moral claim. States used to establish churches and printing presses, yet few defend their authority and responsibility to do so in Western countries, seeing that they should never have done so in the first place. When the state was sovereign, it was taken to be the initiator of nearly everything of importance in society. But when it was learned that the state's sovereignty simply meant the sovereignty of some people over the lives of other people, individuals began to be recognized as sovereign. At that point the state became, by moral right, merely a hired agent of the individuals it was to serve in certain limited capacities.

Now if individuals are sovereign, there is no justification for regulating their lives, be it in commerce, religion, romance, or athletics. Barring their violation of someone's rights to his or her own sovereign authority, they have their own right to liberty to run their lives as they choose. Not that this has always to be wise or good, but it must be their own. The defender of government regulation simply aims to put us back into the age of feudalism wherein the state was seen as a superior entity and its citizens subjects. Only most wish to apply this selectively, primarily to those engaged in commerce. But that is entirely arbitrary and unjustified, and amounts to a perpetration of gross injustice and unfair treatment. When religion and the press are free, so should every other endeavor of human life. Indeed, it is a violation of the rule of law to do as we do now, namely, apply government regulation to business but respect the rights of others, e.g., priests, authors, or poets, to carry on unregulated.

Those who advance the "market failure" theory have argued

that although the free market is a wonderful provider of goods and services, certain public services such as water or electricity would be unnecessarily inefficient in a market setting. Duplication of water or electrical lines, for example, would amount to an inefficient use of resources, so in such cases the free market should be limited, companies should be made into monopolies or taken over by the state, and the industry should be regulated by bureaucrats, not made subject to market forces. And, indeed, throughout the world this view has led to the abolition of free markets in some industries and the institution of extensive government regulation of prices, wages, and labor relations.

Others have taken this idea of market failure even further and have said that government must correct the unwillingness or inability of markets to provide certain values. A clear example is public libraries—the market simply will not furnish us with what we value here, namely, the opportunity to read, so government must take over. But the same basic argument is used to justify regulation of the workplace for health and safety. Affirmative Action, minimum wages, fair trading practices, and the like are all supposed to be values the market fails to produce, so government must rectify matters. All government regulation, then, is but the legitimate effort of a government to remedy what the market ought achieve but fails. The underlying idea here is utilitarianism—the central obligation of the state is to secure the greatest happiness for the greatest number of people, and when the market fails to achieve this, government must step in with its remedial regulatory policies.

Neither argument for government regulation based on market failure is any more successful. The claim that because some inefficiency may occur in the market, thus we ought to take it out of the market, is presumptuous in favor of a kind of raw utilitarianism that ignores individual rights. First of all, what of a bit of inefficiency? Is eliminating it so important as to sacrifice human liberty? But the argument actually depends on showing, also, that government regulation does not introduce its own set of failures—market versus government regulator failures need to be compared. And there is ample reason to conclude, as the scholars of public choice have argued, that when one understands the nature of bureaucracy, one can expect far more damage to society from government meddling than from some market inefficiencies. For example, when an industry is taken out of the market, competition ceases. In case of work stoppages or strikes the entire industry can be shut down, and the only remedy for that is to impose legislative restrictions on the free movement of laborers. That is surely an awesome price to extract to obtain efficiency—it is, indeed, far more *in*efficient than occasional duplication of facilities and resources.

As to the values the market does not always provide, it is once again dubious to suppose that government will supply them in the right proportion, according to a sound set of priorities, effectively, without enormous cost at some other point of the social order. Libraries are now nearly obsolete, except for a few people who could probably be helped much better without building them. Government response to political sentiments expressed in the voting booth is extremely risky since such sentiments are merely voiced, not reconciled with one's budgetary restrictions. Furthermore, the creation of a common pool of valued resources creates a tragedy of the commons, whereby people recklessly overuse resources and create, as is quite evident, huge debts and deficit spending by the state. That, in turn, has its own enormous costs, but at this point identifying who has done the wrong thing is no longer possible. That is part of the tragedy. We all wish to advance our own objectives. When it seems we can do so without having to dip into our resources, we will try ever more vigilantly, taking advantage of the chance to get something free of charge (especially if we are all being told that a good society must be run this way). Government regulation is, once again, a bad idea.

The "positive rights" argument deviates from the American political tradition and classical liberalism's emphasis on the basic human rights not to be killed, assaulted, or robbed (to life, liberty and property, that is), and holds that in fact we have the right to be provided with various goods and services from other persons around us. Thus we have the positive right to health care—currently so high on the government's agenda—or Social Security or public education or unemployment compensation or safety and health protection at the workplace. Because we have these basic rights, and because government was established among us to secure these rights, government regulation must be instituted to adjust private endeavors so that these provisions will be forthcoming. The argument is really dependent for its force on the theory of positive rights.

But we do not have positive rights—because we are not owed involuntary servitude from our fellow citizens. Yes, our parents and some next of kin have some responsibility to help us reach maturity. But thereafter we must secure what we need and want by way of voluntary exchange, not government protection of positive rights. These rights are impossible to protect consistently anyway, and certainly their protection makes protecting negative rights—our rights to life, liberty, and property—impossible. If doctors have the right to liberty but patients the right to be healed, whose right prevails if a doctor wishes to attend the graduation of his or her daughter at the same time someone in the neighborhood needs medical attention? And on what basis is that going to be decided, now that the system of rights has been corrupted?

The government's effort to protect positive rights by way of government regulation is utterly misplaced and puts citizens into a state of subservience to one another. It is clearly immoral.

Finally, some argue that "inefficiencies" prevent even the most vigilant privatization efforts from solving certain problems, that is, pollution, chemical seepage, and similar environmental offenses. When Smith pollutes and Jones suffers, neither can Smith find Jones so as to secure permission, nor can Jones find Smith to launch a lawsuit, so there is neither a market nor a judicial solution available to the parties. Ergo, government must set standards and establish some system of rationing and balance of cost and benefits arising from activities that leave injuries which cannot be litigated.

What of this troublesome case of judicial inefficiency? The problem is not helped at all by government regulation—it merely produces discontentment and injustice. Government cannot rationally decide which firm or individual ought to dump harmful wastes on to others' bodies and properties. It cannot establish collective priorities for individuals who are diverse and may flourish in utterly different ways.

Accordingly, when, for example, air pollution faces us, the best approach is the one offered by classical liberals in their theory of basic human rights to life, liberty, and property. Dumping simply may not be undertaken when no permission can be obtained, unless the result does not increase the prevailing risk of harm to individuals. When manufacturing firms pollute, they utilize other people who did not give their permission for their own purposes. They avoid the full cost of their activities by stealing the resources of others, sometimes even others' lives. It is as if one could simply use another without his or her consent for sexual gratification or some other purpose one may value because, well, it is important. Jobs are important, yes, and getting from one side of town to the other is important, and attending the opera and the PTA meeting—these are all important but not on the backs of other people.

The way to control pollution, then, is to invoke a strict enforcement of personal autonomy and to privatize as much as possible. In areas where this is difficult, a policy similar to what must be done in cases of highly communicable diseases needs to be implemented, namely, quarantine. Those who cannot perform without hurting others must desist, period. And the criminal justice system must develop means by which to determine when homicide, assault, or other forms of rights violation occurs and not hope for government regulation to solve the problem.

Generally, government regulation assumes that some people have superior intellects and moral character, that we can find them, and that it is wise to give them power over the rest of us. This is precisely the bad idea our political tradition nearly succeeded in superseding. Let's regain that initiative instead of squandering it on vain hopes.

—TIBOR R. MACHAN

15

"Federal aid is all right if it doesn't bring federal red tape."

One might think that this tired old cliché would have been laid to rest long ago. But whenever a proposal is made for a new way to hand out federal funds to states or local units of government, some spoilsport is certain to say: "We don't want control along with the money." And advocates of the new legislation will say: "You won't get federal control; we have written the bill in such a way that control of the funds will stay with the local unit."

In the early days of "farm programs," farmers were told that federal subsidies for this and that didn't mean they would have to submit to federal controls. Fortunately, this unsound theory was tested in the United States Supreme Court. In 1942, in the case of *Wickard v. Filburn,* the Court opined: "It is hardly lack of due process for the government to regulate that which it subsidizes."

Who would deny that the regulation of that which is subsidized is sound fiscal policy? It would seem to be the height of irresponsibility for any unit of government, or other organization for that matter, to hand out money without control over its expenditure. This principle applies whether the subsidy is from federal to state, federal to local, or state to local units of government. The question here discussed is *not* whether such subsidies should be made, but rather, whether we can expect control to accompany the grants.

Officials of a given city recently concluded that their welfare costs were getting out of hand. The city's share of these costs was greater than the cost of police protection and almost as much as the cost of fire protection and public works. Some families were receiving welfare payments each month in excess of the take-home pay of some city employees with comparable-sized families.

So, it seemed logical for the city to have a look at the rules and regulations under which welfare payments were being made. The decision was to draw up their own rules and regulations—a new code to cover the handing out of welfare funds. This decision ran straight into the principle we are discussing. It seems that, of the total amount of money distributed under the city's welfare program, more than half came from federal and state grants. With the funds came rules and regulations for their use. And, why not?

Illustrations abound of grants-in-aid from larger units of government to smaller, and of the controls that accompany the grants. Federal aid for education comes with the usual arguments that control need not go with the aid. But we have had long experience with aid for education at the state level, and the evidence is conclusive. There is no reason to think that federal aid should be different. What local school board has not been faced with the rules laid down by the state regarding education and certification of teachers, choice of textbooks, questions of transportation of pupils, tenure of teachers, building programs, curriculums, days of attendance, examination of students, and a host of others? Is there no federal or state regulation of the school lunch program where "surplus" food is involved?

Can you imagine a multi-billion dollar federal highway program with no regulation of engineering specifications, location, signboards, and so forth and so on?

Or federal or state housing? Why shouldn't rules and regulations be established regarding nationality, race, and income of the renters? Or government contracts? When a government contracts with private firms for the manufacture of its many requirements, it would seem proper for it to write any specifications it pleases with regard to wages and hours of the workers.

A classic example of how controls accompany grants is our treatment of the American Indians. Who can imagine what the status of the Indian would be today had he gained the freedom exercised by other Americans—the freedom to be responsible for himself? Instead, he has been a "ward of the government" for decade after decade: controls accompanying handouts.

The solution to what many feel is too much federal or state control of our daily lives is not to be found in trying to write laws that would, in effect, make these units of government irresponsible in their fiscal affairs. Sound fiscal policy requires control by the unit of government that makes the funds available. Whether or not it is a proper function of government to make such funds available is quite another story and cannot be considered here.

The principle involved is not unlike that which governs the finances of a family. So long as the parent supplies a child with spending money, it is proper for the parent to have something to say about the spending, even though the child may be saying or at least thinking: "Boy, will I be glad when I get to earning my own money and can spend it as I wish!"

The solution is so simple and obvious that it hardly needs stating. If we don't want state or federal control of certain of our activities, we must not have state or federal financing of them.

—W. M. CURTISS

16

"Big business and big labor require big government."

It's axiomatic that the shoe must fit the foot; too small and it pinches, too large and walking is painful. Size is a relevant consideration in our judgment of a thing; a power mower is too large for a tract home lawn, but a house set on half an acre couldn't get along without one.

Considerations along these lines might be applied to government. "Do you think our government is too big?" asks the poll-taker. "Yes," is the answer given by nearly everyone. Why has government become so big and such a costly burden on taxpayers? The answer is self-evident: government at national, state, and local levels has assumed many new functions not contemplated by the statesmen of two centuries ago. Why has government grown so big and so expensive? The answer is simple: millions of Americans have discovered that getting money or services from the tax fund is easier than working for a living, and safer than stealing. They join pressure groups and they hire lobbyists—as of this writing there are 77 registered lobbyists per Senator and 25 for every member of the House. We have a big government today because the roughly 100 million Americans who benefit directly from government largesse could not get what they want from a small government.

The men who wrote the Declaration of Independence and the Constitution focused on the proper function and scope of government, knowing that if they resolved that issue properly, the question of the size of the political establishment would virtually take care of itself. It was the proper role of government, they believed, to secure the rights and immunities of the individual person; rights endowed by the Creator to life, liberty, and property. The coercive power vested in government, operating under the Rule of Law, was empowered to punish those who impaired another's life, or his liberty, or his property. This meant a police force, a court system, and a house of detention; with a military force on tap in the event of a foreign threat.

Such a political system presupposed an exemplary citizenry. "The Constitution was written," John Adams has told us, "for a religious and virtuous people; it will serve for no other." Churches and schools were relied upon to develop men and women of sound character and sober thought, such as the people who populated the village of Concord in the days of Emerson and Thoreau. We know that Concord had a jail because Thoreau spent a night there for refusing to pay a tax to the government involved in its war against Mexico. But the citizens of Concord were peaceful and the chances are that the local constabulary never worked full time.

The men who wrote the Constitution, and the citizens who voted to adopt it as their governing rules, had experienced political intrusions into their personal affairs under monarchical auspices and now had a document designed to prevent this. Such was "the original intent," as witness the fact that the words "no" and "not" in restraint of governmental power occur 44 times in the Constitution and Bill of Rights.

When a government is limited to securing individual rights to life, liberty, and property, we have a government whose actions are designed to redress injury and otherwise let people alone. In short, a "big enough" government is one that is able to deter criminal actions and resist foreign aggressors. Beyond this it is "too big."

When the law provides "a free field and no favor," every business enterprise operates according to the rules of the free market, competing for an opportunity to convert the scarce factors of production—people, raw material, and capital (tools and machines)—into goods which will please consumers. Well, how big should a given business be? And who should decide? In a free market economy it is the customers who by buying or not buying, decide the fate of any given business. If they take their trade elsewhere the business faces failure; this is the profit and loss "game" that every business in a free market economy is involved in. When the customers stop buying, for whatever reason or no reason, they are telling the proprietor to stop wasting scarce resources in the manufacture of things people do not want. It seems paradoxical, but it is true, that business failure is a necessary element in economic progress. J.C. Penney failed more than once before finding the right formula; Sam Walton, within the memory of all of us, started small and then became just as big a business as his customers wanted him to be. This is exactly the right size for a business to be.

A business, when it abides by the rules of the free market, has no special privilege legislation designed to give it an advantage over its competitors or charge higher prices to customers. Free market rules occasionally frustrate, however; and if governments traffic in the granting of special privileges (most do), then some businesses lobby for handouts, even while continuing to produce goods and services.

Steel making, coal mining, automobile manufacture, and transportation have each generated big unions which wield enormous political power. Steel was produced, coal mined, automobiles appeared, and people and freight were transported before unions came along. The very existence of unions presupposes manufacture. Things will still be manufactured when unions have vanished from the scene. They came into power because of the widespread belief that capitalistic bosses, however decent they might be, expropriated a portion of each employee's product. Marx's exploitation theory gave this sentiment a certain plausibility for a time, but it was demolished 120 years ago by Böhm-Bawerk and several times since. Nevertheless, it is still part of the folklore, exploiting the grievance, widely felt, that other people fail to give us our due. Lawmakers, looking to gain from the powerful political influence of unions, license unions to use force or threat of force to gain above market wages for their members. Unemployment is one consequence of this maneuver. The reason: when labor costs go up fewer employees will be hired.

To sum up: government should be big enough to keep the peace of the community by securing the right of every person to enjoy individual control over his or her life, liberty, and property ... The size of a business in the free market economy is decided by customers: consumer sovereignty ... A labor union is created by unjust laws favoring one segment of society at the expense of all the rest. The solution? Repeal all special privilege legislation.

—EDMUND A. OPITZ

17

"The government must set standards for living and working conditions."

This cliché is based on the false assumption that one of the functions of government is to forbid people to live and work in unpleasant or dangerous conditions. This in turn is based on another false assumption—that if you pass a law forbidding "substandard" conditions, conditions meeting your standards will miraculously arise.

In fact, this is not the case. Take the example of New York City housing, for instance. Did you ever wonder how the city managed to house the waves of immigrants that poured into its slums in the mid-to-late nineteenth century? It had a "substandard" private housing market that included slum dwellers who took in boarders and so-called cage hotels that rented out 5 × 7 feet spaces with doors that locked, containing a bed with a mattress and quilt, a chair, a locker, and a light bulb—with limited access to a toilet and one shower for several hundred men. There were also some dormitory-style public shelters, but most people preferred the cage hotels or doubling up with another poor family in conditions that would make a modern health department inspector scream.

In the late twentieth century our standards are higher; crowded conditions are illegal and everyone must have a certain number of square feet—except, of course, for luxury situations like half-shares in weekend vacation homes, where young urban professionals are still allowed to sleep three and four to a room. In the late 1970s and early 1980s, New York City targeted a number of cheap hotels known as single-room occupancy (SRO) lodgings as substandard and began demolishing them at a time when a combination of rising real estate taxes and rent control was squeezing many landlords out of business. Not surprisingly, the SRO's place in the housing market was not filled by anything else. To make things worse, this happened at a time when state-run mental hospitals were deinstitutionalizing all former patients who were judged harmless to themselves or others. These deinstitutionalized people were by definition mentally handicapped and had few, if any, job skills, and they increased the demand for cheap housing. By the time the city officials recognized that the SRO's were an important endangered species, it was a bit too late. So the city that had housed waves of poor people in the nineteenth century had homeless on the streets in the late twentieth century. This can be seen as a direct result of too many people in power believing in the fallacy that simply forbidding what is seen as a bad option will result in a better option being created. In fact, the options created were worse than they would have been if no attempt had been made to improve conditions by outlawing the substandard.

Child labor is still the example everyone loves to bring up as a horror of capitalism that cried out for government regulation. In fact, capitalism didn't invent child labor: under primitive conditions *everyone* works, including children. We have a pioneer and agricultural history, and the children in such families worked, just as the women worked—they simply didn't get paid for it. As Charles Murray has pointed out, until a few generations ago, the majority of families in the United States were poor and rural. We must remember that long and harsh as the hours and working conditions in the early factories and mills were, they were still better than the hours and working conditions on the farm, to say nothing of the opportunity they gave to earn a money income. (Historian Robert Smuts reports that whenever a factory opened in a rural area, it was besieged by young girls hoping to find work.) As long as such conditions existed, so did child labor. The laws that were passed have created a situation in which many young people (particularly impoverished ones) now grow up with no knowledge of how to hold a job. As a matter of fact, a case can be made that child labor laws, in conjunction with laws forbidding such other "substandard" methods of making money as cottage industry, industrial home work, and taking in boarders, destroyed the inner-city poor family as an economic unit, leading directly to today's welfare culture.

But the most destructive false assumption here is that the

free market is rigged in favor of the employer, the landlord, the producer—at the expense of the employee, the tenant, and the consumer. Prices do not reflect costs; they are arbitrary, goes this assumption, so if we just force the employer, the landlord, and the producer to lower prices or increase costs, this will not result in a "real" loss; merely in less profit. Experience seems to have no impact on this wishful assumption. Economists have long observed that the result of minimum wage laws is unemployment, and if we didn't have such restrictions everyone looking for work could find *some* employment. Yet politicians continue to pass such laws. Regulations that increase costs have to increase prices unless they are balanced by government handouts, yet we continue to ask for regulation. Only the enormous productivity of a relatively free economic system has allowed these facts to be ignored.

—JOAN KENNEDY TAYLOR

18

"Rent control protects tenants."

Government control of the rents of houses and apartments is a special form of price control. Its consequences are substantially the same as those of government price control in general.

Rent control is initially imposed on the argument that the supply of housing is not "elastic"—i.e., that a housing shortage cannot be immediately made up, no matter how high rents are allowed to rise. Therefore, it is contended, the government, by forbidding increases in rents, protects tenants from extortion and exploitation without doing any real harm to landlords and without discouraging new construction.

This argument is defective even on the assumption that the rent control will not long remain in effect. It overlooks an immediate consequence. If landlords are allowed to raise rents to reflect a monetary inflation and the true conditions of supply and demand, individual tenants will economize by taking less space. This will allow others to share the accommodations that are in short supply. The same amount of housing will shelter more people, until the shortage is relieved.

Rent control, however, encourages wasteful use of space. It discriminates in favor of those who already occupy houses or apartments in a particular city or region at the expense of those who find themselves on the outside. Permitting rents to rise to the free market level allows all tenants or would-be tenants equal opportunity to bid for space.

The effects of rent control become worse the longer the rent control continues. New housing is not built because there is no incentive to build it. With the increase in building costs (commonly as a result of inflation), the old level of rents will not yield a profit. If, as commonly happens, the government finally recognizes this and exempts new housing from rent control, there is still not an incentive to as much new building as if older buildings were also free of rent control. Depending on the extent of money depreciation since old rents were legally frozen, rents for new housing might be ten or twenty times as high as rent in equivalent space in the old. (This happened in France, for example.) Under such conditions existing tenants in old buildings are indisposed to move, no matter how much their family grows or their existing accommodations deteriorate.

Because of low fixed rents in old buildings, the tenants already in them, and legally protected against rent increases, are encouraged to use space wastefully, whether or not the size of their individual family unit has shrunk. This concentrates the immediate pressure of new demand on the relatively few new buildings. It tends to force rents in them, at the beginning, to a higher level than they would have reached in a wholly free market.

Nevertheless, this will not correspondingly encourage the construction of new housing. Builders or owners of pre-existing apartment houses, finding themselves with restricted profits or perhaps even losses on their old apartments, will have little or no capital to put into new construction. In addition, they, or those with capital from other sources, may fear that the government may at any time find an excuse for imposing new rent controls on the new buildings.

The housing situation will deteriorate in other ways. Most importantly, unless the appropriate rent increases are allowed, landlords will not trouble to remodel apartments or make other improvements in them. In fact, where rent control is particularly unrealistic or oppressive, landlords will not even keep rented houses or apartments in tolerable repair. Not only will they have no economic incentive to do so; they may not even have the funds. The rent-control laws, among their other effects, create ill feeling between landlords who are forced to take minimum returns or even losses, and tenants who resent the landlord's failure to make adequate repairs.

A common next step of legislatures, acting under merely political pressures or confused economic ideas, is to take rent controls off "luxury" apartments while keeping them on low-grade or middle-grade apartments. The argument is that the rich tenants can afford to pay higher rents, but the poor cannot.

The long-run effect of this discriminatory device, however, is the exact opposite of what its advocates contend. The builders and owners of luxury apartments are encouraged and rewarded; the builders and owners of low-rent housing are discouraged and penalized. The former are free to make as big a profit as the conditions of supply and demand warrant; the latter are left with no incentive (or even capital) to build more low-rent housing.

The result is an encouragement to the repair and remodeling of luxury apartments, and a boom in new building of such apartments. The effect is not only to provide better accommodations for comparatively wealthy tenants, but eventually to bring down the rents they pay by increasing the supply of luxury apartments available. But there is no incentive to build new low-income housing, or even to keep existing low-income housing in good repair. The accommodations for the low-income groups, therefore, will deteriorate in quality, and there will be no increase in quantity. Where the population is increasing, the deterioration and shortage in low-income housing will grow worse and worse.

When these consequences are so clear that they become glaring, there is of course no acknowledgment on the part of the advocates of rent control and the welfare statists that they have blundered. Instead, they denounce the capitalist system. They contend that private enterprise has "failed" again; that "private enterprise cannot do the job." Therefore, they will argue, the state must step in and itself build low-rent housing.

This has been the almost universal result in every country that was involved in World War II or imposed rent control in an effort to offset monetary inflation.

So the government launches on a gigantic housing program—at the taxpayers' expense. The houses are rented at a rate that does not pay back costs of construction or operation. A typical arrangement is for the government to pay annual subsidies, either directly to the tenants or to the builders or managers of the state housing. Whatever the nominal arrangement, the tenants in these buildings are being subsidized by the rest of the population. They are having part of their rent paid for them. They are being selected for favored treatment. The political possibilities of this favoritism are too clear to need stressing. A pressure group is built up, which believes that the taxpayers owe it these subsidies as a matter of right. Another all but irreversible step is taken toward the total Welfare State.

A final irony of rent control is that the more unrealistic, Draconian, and unjust it is, the more fervid the political arguments for its continuance. If the legally fixed rents are on the average 95 percent as high as free market rents would be, and only minor injustice is being done to landlords, there is no strong political objection to taking off rent controls, because tenants will only have to pay increases averaging about 5 percent. But if the inflation of the currency has been so great, or the rent control laws so harsh and unrealistic, that legally fixed rents are only 10 percent of what free market rents would be, and gross injustice is being done to owners and landlords, a huge outcry will be raised about the dreadful evils of removing rent controls and forcing tenants to pay an economic rent. Even the opponents of rent control are then disposed to concede that the removal of rent controls must be a very cautious, gradual, and prolonged process. Few of the opponents of rent control indeed have the political courage and economic insight under such conditions to ask even for this gradual decontrol. The more unrealistic and unjust the rent control is, the harder it is to get rid of it.

The pressure for rent control, in brief, comes from those who consider only its supposed short-run benefits to one group in the population. When we consider its effects on *all* groups, and especially when we consider its effects *in the long run,* we recognize that rent control is not only increasingly futile, but increasingly harmful the more severe it is, and the longer it remains in effect.

—HENRY HAZLITT

19

"Government should control prices, but not people."

Perhaps you recall the fable of the scorpion who asked the beaver to carry him across a lake. The beaver declined the request with this deduction: "If I let you get on my back, you'll sting me and paralyze me and cause me to drown."

But the scorpion out-deduced him with this rejoinder: "I can't swim. Thus if I sting you while we are in the lake, I'll drown too. Obviously I wouldn't do anything to cause that."

The beaver could find no fault in that logic. So, being a kind-hearted fellow, he invited the scorpion aboard and set out across the lake. Right in the middle of it, the scorpion stung the beaver and paralyzed him.

As they sank together to the bottom of the water, the beaver reproachfully pointed out to the scorpion that *both* of them would now drown. "Why did you sting me?" he asked.

"I couldn't help it," tearfully replied the scorpion. "It's my nature."

Fables, of course, contain morals that can be applied to human affairs. This one pertains to several of our current problems. For example, the *nature* of price controls is people control. A quart of milk or an aspirin obviously is not concerned about the price tag it carries. Prices are of concern only to human beings. And the only thing that can be controlled by government in this process of minimum and maximum prices is people.

The nature of the operation is this: Persons who exercise the police powers of government use those powers to control the people who produce milk, distribute milk, and buy milk. The price of drugs is never controlled by government; the controls apply only to the persons who produce, sell, and use the drugs. When the government enforces a minimum wage, it is persons, not things, that the officials watch and control.

The person who favors rent control wants the police powers used to control individuals who own houses for rent, and families who wish to live in such houses. Purely and simply, he favors controlling people and forcing them to do what *he* wants them to do.

But when such a person is flushed out from behind his euphemistic and comfortable word-shield, he is usually honestly astounded that anyone could possibly believe that he favors people control. Try it sometime. You will invariably get a response somewhat as follows: "I am *opposed* to controlling people. In fact, I support all sorts of organizations and causes to give people more freedom. True enough, I do believe that the government should control certain *prices* for the benefit of all; but control *people*—never! Now stop spouting this nonsense about people control. There is a limit to my patience."

And so it goes. Actually, when you stop and think about it, no government can ever really support a price. Prices don't give a hang about supports; it's not their nature. The nature of all governmental schemes to "support prices" is this: Some people who control the police powers of government use them to take money from other people who have earned it, and to give it to still other people who have not earned it. That's all it is. Calling it by another name cannot change its nature, for better or for worse.

Why do persons object to coming right out with it and saying, "Of course I'm in favor of people control. I don't need you to tell me that it's only people, not inanimate objects or ideas, that can be controlled. But don't forget that I am doing it for their own good. In various of these vital economic areas, I am convinced that I know what is best for them and for us all."

While I would disagree with that candid person, I could still admire him after a fashion. At least he would have the courage of his convictions. For example, Robin Hood was a robber in every sense of the word, but at least he had more personal courage than do the despicable characters who sneak up on their victims and sandbag them from behind.

Perhaps the reason for our preference for the euphemistic "price controls," rather than the realistic "people controls," lies deep in our own natures. All of us seem instinctively to want to help our kindred human beings. But we observe that there are so many of them who want help of various sorts, and that our own personal resources are so limited. But by voting to have the government do it, we can satisfy both our charitable instincts and our sense of fair play. Also, that easy procedure has several other fringe benefits. When we vote to help others, we are thereby fulfilling our patriotic duty as good citizens to participate in the affairs of government. In addition, this procedure doesn't require much personal effort. Also, we are usually promised that somebody else will have to pay the cost.

The next time you hear a politician or a neighbor advocating price supports or rent control or some similar subsidy, ask him why he favors people control, and forcing other peaceful persons to do what he wants them to do, and taking money from people who have earned it and giving it to others who haven't.

At that point, however, you had better duck. For the nature of the ambitious politician and the well-intentioned do-gooder is to consider only the "fine objectives" of their plans and to ignore completely the shoddy means used to enforce them. They won't appreciate your calling this to their attention.

—DEAN RUSSELL

20

"In a national emergency, government must control the economy."

Whenever serious threats arise, modern Americans immediately call on the federal government to "do something," and the government commonly responds by imposing economic controls. In the national emergencies of the world wars and the Great Depression the federal government adopted wide-ranging policies to change people's economic behavior, reallocate resources, and redistribute income. In each case the government subsequently took credit for acting wisely and effectively, but careful analysis of these episodes reveals that the alleged successes either did not occur or occurred in spite of the government's controls rather than because of them.

The habitual resort to government in a crisis reflects a disposition to believe that the government (a) has the capacity to solve the problem, (b) has the moral right to impose its chosen solution, and (c) will not create other—perhaps more serious or intractable—problems while dealing with the one at hand. Each of these suppositions may be challenged.

Governments are not unbiased, dispassionate automatons programmed to promote the public interest. They are collections of human beings endowed with power over their fellows and subject to all the intellectual and moral frailties of their species. Even when their motives are benevolent, their power tends to corrupt them. History shows that citizens take grave risks when they trust the government to solve their pressing problems by means of its coercive powers. Moreover, by demanding that the government respond to every perceived crisis, citizens create an incentive for the government to contrive bogus crises to justify expansions of its power.

In 1917 the government plunged the nation into a war that few Americans were eager to fight. To obtain the resources necessary to prosecute the war successfully the government drastically increased the income tax rates, conscripted nearly three million men into the army, fixed the prices of scores of strategic commodities, intervened in hundreds of labor disputes, and nationalized vital industries including telecommunications, ocean shipping, and interstate railroads. After the war the government abandoned most of its emergency policies, but some of them, including the government's operation of a fleet of merchant ships, its subsidization of agricultural and export credit, and the higher income-tax rates, persisted. More importantly, the wartime controllers, led by the economic czar Bernard Baruch, spread the false message that the United States had triumphed in the war *because of* the economic controls rather than in spite of them.

When the Great Depression began, many prominent political figures, recalling the supposedly successful economic controls exercised during the recent war, supported the imposition of similar controls to cure the depression, which Justice Louis Brandeis characterized as "an emergency more serious than war." Under the leadership of former wartime planners such as Franklin D. Roosevelt, Felix Frankfurter, George Peek, Hugh Johnson, and William G. McAdoo, the federal government brought forth the New Deal, a hodgepodge of new subsidies, taxes, confiscations, regulations, and direct government participation in markets that distorted and hobbled the economy in countless ways. Even though the depression lingered, the textbooks later declared that FDR and his fellow New Dealers had "rescued" the economy and "restored hope."

During World War II the federal government fell back on precedents established during the previous world war and the depression, only this time it pushed most policies much farther than before. The government adopted comprehensive price, wage, and rent controls, conscripted ten million men into the armed forces, allocated strategic commodities through a system of physical allocations and official priorities, and directly financed most of the wartime investment in new mills and factories. In short, the government created a uniquely American command economy. Again, victory encouraged the economic planners to take credit for the triumph. Again, not all the wartime policies were abandoned when peace returned—some of them, like the payroll withholding of income taxes and the trade controls used for conducting "economic warfare," still exist half a century after the end of the war that prompted them.

The federal government emerged from World War II with an unprecedented reputation for effective economic management. An immediate consequence was passage of the Employment Act of 1946, which authorized the government to take permanent and continuous responsibility for "fine-tuning" the economy, making sure that it would always operate at high levels of production and growth and low levels of unemployment and inflation. Thereafter Americans would routinely look to the federal government for a solution whenever any economic problem arose, whether it were slow growth, persistent poverty, declining international competitiveness, or rising costs of medical care. Few people noticed that many of the problems they asked the government to solve were themselves the product of government policies.

Politicians never forgot the leverage to be gained from a perceived crisis. To deal with an "urban crisis," President Lyndon B. Johnson declared a "war on poverty." President Richard M. Nixon twice declared a national emergency, triggering an array of standby economic powers, first because of a strike by postal workers and later because of a perceived balance-of-payments problem. The National Emergencies Act of 1976 and the International Emergency Economic Powers Act of 1977 codified an assortment of statutory powers, including virtually complete control of international trade and finance, available to any president who declares a national emergency. These powers were employed extensively during the 1980s to deny economic liberties to Americans so that the government could conduct economic warfare against such states as Iran, Libya, Nicaragua, and South Africa.

Even more damaging than the legislative and institutional legacies of the great emergencies is their ideological legacy, a propensity to rely on government as the problem solver of first resort. Americans, who once exemplified self-reliance and individuality, now demand that the federal government solve all their problems, real and imagined. In response the government places its heavy regulatory hand upon virtually every part of the economy, from the day-care centers to the stock exchanges. Hardly ever does one hear the opinion expressed that a particular form of government intervention is not only counterproductive or expensive but improper or unconstitutional. In the light of the currently dominant ideology, the public views the scope of permissible government action as unlimited. From the bedroom to the boardroom, no one is surprised to see the federal government intervene, and many are disappointed if it does not.

Unfortunately, the government destroys far more effectively than it creates. By its very nature, government lacks the capacity to solve most economic and social problems. With only coercion to support its actions, it cannot elicit positive, creative human energies; it cannot bring forth the eager cooperation and harmony that exist when people deal with one another through voluntary agreements and associations. Modern Americans vastly overrate what the government can accomplish.

But even if the government were more capable, it would not be morally justified in using its coercive power for any and all purposes. When the government serves the interests of *all* the people—excepting only those who violate the just rights of their fellows—its actions may be morally justified. Lacking the unanimous support of all rights-respecting citizens, it becomes nothing more than a club wielded by some to violate the rights of others. Too often, as in its many redistributive schemes and most of its regulations, government plays the role of a blatant predator.

Moreover, government interventions have tended to proliferate as James Madison warned they would: a new one gives rise to "a long chain of repetitions, every subsequent interference being naturally produced by the effects of the preceding." Rarely does the government do just one thing. Instead, one thing leads to another.

National emergencies have been the outstanding occasions for the expansion federal power in the U.S. history. Collectivists know well—and exploit the knowledge—that war or any emergency likened to war in its seriousness is "the health of the state." The so-called medical care crisis, along with the sweeping government interventions it has spawned, is only the latest example. If Americans are to retain even a small part of the economic freedom they once enjoyed, they must learn to resist the crisis-mongering of politicians and the news media and to remember that what is done today in reckless haste may be regretted for many years to come. Calling on the federal government for a remedy usually results only in compounding and perpetuating the problem while further throttling our freedoms.

—ROBERT HIGGS

21

"Weak regulation and bankers' greed caused the savings and loan crisis."

Federal Reserve Chairman Alan Greenspan shocked the financial world in 1990 when he estimated the eventual cost of the savings and loan bailout at half a trillion dollars. And Treasury Secretary Nicholas Brady added a jolt by admitting that taxpayers must bear most of the burden.

It is a scandal, all agree, the greatest ever in U.S. financial history. It is greater by far than the bailouts of Chrysler, Lockheed, and New York City, even greater than the costs of the default of Third World debtor countries. In ages past, it would have been ignored as a malicious story that was absurd and impossible. Yet, it is as real as the S&L losses and bankruptcies.

It is even more scandalous that most of the perpetrators are escaping unscathed. The legislators and regulators who created the system during the 1930s have left the stage of life and can no longer be held accountable. But there are many who helped to fashion the S&L structure, who drafted and enacted the Depository Institutions Deregulation and Monetary Control Act of 1980 that stoked the fires of inflation, and the Garn-St. Germain Act of 1982 that invited crooked appraisals and dubious accounting. They are making their escape.

A few politicians actually paid a nominal price for the damage they inflicted. Representative Fernand St. Germain of Rhode Island, co-author of the law that made matters worse, was defeated for re-election. Speaker Jim Wright, who badgered federal regulators for his favorite S&L bankers, resigned in disgrace. Five Senators are at risk because they intervened with regulators on behalf of big campaign donors. Yet, no representative or senator is expected to lose a penny from the debacle. In fact, they voted themselves several boosts in salaries and pensions.

The politicians who created and nurtured the system are

quick to point at the bankers who saw an opportunity to splurge and steal. Some 50 thrift officials and accountants already have been convicted, and more are likely to face indictments as inquiries proceed. But even if a few hundred incompetent and corrupt owners and managers should be found out, their numbers are puny when compared with some 50,000 employees laboring in the industry. It is unlikely that the number of industry perpetrators will ever reach 1 percent of employees, but it is obvious that more than one half of the legislators created and fashioned the system and that regulators guided it every step of the way.

The greatest outrage, however, is the lack of Congressional interest in the causes of the disaster. There are no hearings, no investigations, no special prosecutors, not even committee debates on the real causes of the scandal. Congress is visibly skirting the real issue.

The reasons for such conspicuous silence may be as numerous as the voices against the hearings and investigations. Some legislators undoubtedly are convinced that they have the answer: the irresponsibility and greediness of bankers. Many newspapers and broadcast media share this opinion, which implicitly exculpates the legislators.

The conspicuous silence may also hide an awareness of guilt. Many legislators not only cast their votes for the system but also have used it, and continue to use it, for their own ends. Savings and loan associations and other government-sponsored and regulated institutions are among the most generous contributors to the re-election campaign funds of the politicians who legislate and regulate the conditions of S&L existence. The contributions amount to many millions of dollars, bolstering the political and financial fortunes of incumbents. Surely, any Congressional investigation would soon discover the connection, which would be rather embarrassing to the legislators.

Public opinion, which offers a ready answer to all things, usually points at a lax Reagan Administration and a reckless industry. It neither theorizes nor analyzes, nor argues on grounds of inexorable principle. In vague and eclectic fashion, public opinion clings to simple notions of good and evil, command and obedience. It places the blame on evil bankers and lazy regulators who neglected their police function.

Actually, the bankers' greed and the regulators' negligence merely are visible symptoms of much greater evil. The real cause of the disaster is the very financial structure that was fashioned by legislators and guided by regulators; they together created a cartel that, like all other monopolistic concoctions, is playing mischief with its victims.

The structure was erected on the foundation of government force rather than voluntary cooperation. Held together by numerous laws and regulations, it weakened from the inflation fever of the 1970s and growing institutional competition during the 1980s. It suffered severely during the Nixon, Ford, and Carter Administrations which lifted interest rates high above the rates S&Ls were permitted to pay and charge. As depositors withdrew their deposits and turned to higher yielding money market funds, S&Ls were caught in the vise of inflation and regulation. Moreover, rising interest rates caused S&L instruments consisting primarily of long-term mortgages to plummet in price. All S&Ls suffered staggering losses. It is surprising that some actually managed to survive.

In desperation about their sinking ship, the legislators finally consented to "deregulate," that is, they relaxed some rules while they tightened others. They passed the Depository Institutions Deregulation and Monetary Control Act which reduced aggregate reserve requirements for Federal Reserve member institutions by about 43 percent and tightened Federal Reserve control over financial institutions.

To lower reserve requirements is to pour more fuel on the fires of inflation. The 43 percent reduction that member banks experienced was unprecedented in scope and magnitude; it flooded the markets with new credits, caused interest rates to skyrocket to a 20 percent prime rate, and precipitated an inflation rate that reached a staggering level of 18 percent. To control the price inflation, the Carter Administration then invoked the Credit Control Act of 1969 and placed controls not only on banks and thrift institutions but also on all consumer lenders, such as retailers and auto dealers.

The Depository Institutions Deregulation and Monetary Control Act extended Federal Reserve credit controls by imposing reserve requirements on all transaction accounts. At the same time credit unions, savings banks, savings and loan institutions, and nonmember banks were required to keep their reserves with the Fed. In short, the extension of Federal Reserve controls and the expansion of Federal Reserve funds greatly tightened the vise that was to crush more than 3,000 thrift institutions.

The S&L industry is a component part of the American financial cartel that builds on legislation and regulation. Federal deposit insurance was added in 1933 to prevent a repeat of the sad banking picture of the Great Depression. Unfortunately, government insurance is self-defeating. The greater the protection government provides, the greater the risks the insured are willing to take. Depositors who are fully insured have no incentive to select a solid bank over a poorly managed bank. Federal deposit insurance contributed to the debacle of the S&L industry.

As with so many government programs gone awry, the S&L system was born of good intentions and economic ignorance. Unfortunately, the economic ignorance of politicians and officials is always visited on the people. It is visited anew on the American people who are facing a bailout bill of some $500 billion.

—HANS F. SENNHOLZ

22

"Government deregulation of the airlines was a disaster."

For the last 15 years, commercial air service in the United States has been largely free of economic regulation. Critics of this freedom have made strident assertions that the results of deregulation have been detrimental to the traveling public. Every time there is an airline crash or an airline experiences financial losses, these critics blame deregulation.

These crashes and losses, though, are hardly conclusive evidence against deregulation. After all, deregulation never promised to eliminate accidents or guarantee perpetual profits for all airlines. A look at more comprehensive measures of the post-deregulation aviation environment reveals results diametrically opposed to the charges leveled by deregulation's critics.

One of the problems with regulation of an industry is the suppression of competition. The suppression of competition in the airline industry during its 40-year regulatory period (1938-1978) was legendary. In this whole period, the Civil Aeronautics Board (government's airline regulatory agency) refused to allow any new nationwide airlines to be formed. Establishing service to new markets was extremely difficult. No matter how much potential customers might want or need new air service, none could be implemented without government approval. Obtaining this approval required time-consuming and expensive regulatory hearings. If new service was permitted by the government, it would frequently be *via* the award of a monopoly franchise for a specified route. Price competition was virtually forbidden.

The regulatory regime increased the inconveniences and costs of flying for most passengers. In contrast, deregulation has seen both a dramatic improvement in flying convenience and a reduction in fares for the majority of air travelers. The big losers from deregulation have been the lawyers who earned fees from the cumbersome regulatory processes, the bureaucrats who have had to move on to more productive work, and the minority of customers who gained when regulations forced other passengers to subsidize their fares.

The post-deregulation bankruptcy of unsuccessful airlines is what one would normally expect from a competitive environment. In the free market, a majority of business firms eventually fail. The more efficient firms with the better products succeed. Firms less efficient or with less desirable products lose the competitive battle. This turnover is a necessary part of a vital economy. Regulation that prevents this turnover ensures that less desirable products and less efficient methods continue to waste scarce resources.

Some critics of deregulation find it too difficult to argue against the gains in service and reductions in fares achieved by deregulation. Instead, they argue that these benefits have been obtained at the cost of reduced safety. They argue that competitive pressures for efficiency have induced airlines to skimp on safety. Any air crash is immediately cited as proof of this allegation.

The argument that deregulation has undermined air travel safety is short on both logic and evidence. First of all, despite the deregulation enacted in 1978, the government retained all of its authority to regulate safety. The Federal Aviation Administration's (FAA) control over air safety was not diminished one iota by the airline deregulation act. If there are any safety problems, it is not because the government lacks authority to impose regulations.

It is the FAA that has blocked the implementation of a privately developed air-collision avoidance system for over a decade. While the FAA has been slow to implement air traffic safety innovations, the taxes imposed on commercial air travelers that could be used to finance safety improvements have been appropriated by Congress to be spent on something else.

Second, there is no reason to presume that a regulatory regime designed to limit competition would tend to enhance safety. In fact, since regulation made routing more circuitous and flying more expensive, it seems likely that regulation would tend to decrease safety. The more circuitous routing under the previous regulatory regime resulted in more passengers spending more time on planes making more take-offs and landings. Obviously, this exposed more people to more risk.

The lower fares under deregulation have shifted more travel to airlines from other modes. The biggest shift has been from automobiles. On a per-passenger-mile basis, intercity auto travel is about 100 times more likely to result in a fatality than commercial air travel. Consequently, deregulation has probably been responsible for saving over a thousand lives per year since 1978.

Third, there simply is no evidence that deregulation has resulted in less safety. There have been fewer accidents and fewer fatalities in the 15 years since deregulation than in the 15 years prior to deregulation. This is despite the fact that air travel has doubled since 1978. There is no evidence that airlines are "skimping" on safety expenditures. Statistics show that safety expenditures have maintained a constant ratio of airline outlays in the pre- and post-deregulation periods.

Perhaps the best proof that air travel is safer under deregulation is the fact that insurance premiums for commercial airlines have declined. Insurance companies can only make money if the amount they collect in premiums exceeds the amount they pay in damages. If premiums are going down it means that damages are also going down. This is further evidence that flying is safer since deregulation.

Far from being a disaster, deregulation of the airlines has been a roaring success. And why shouldn't it be? Since Adam Smith wrote of "the invisible hand" in 1776, we have known that the free market is a powerful force for channeling human endeavor into productive and beneficial ends. That flying in the post-deregulation era is cheaper, more convenient, and safer should not be surprising. What is surprising is that anyone could seriously propose that the clumsy "visible hand" of the government be called back to undo the benefits we have gained from deregulation.

—JOHN SEMMENS

23

"If free enterprise really works, why the Great Depression?"

To enumerate the blessings and advantages of competitive private enterprise before most any audience in this day and age is to evoke the protest: "Well, if the free enterprise system is so wonderful how do you account for the unemployment, bank failures, and prolonged business depression of the early 1930s? Are periodic depressions an inevitable cost of freedom?"

Free enterprise, of course, does not prohibit or preclude human or business failure. Freedom to choose, to exercise one's own judgment in the conduct of his life and his business, permits mistakes as well as growth, progress, and success. Among fallible human beings, it is to be expected that some of us will fail in some of our ventures. Human failure cannot be eliminated entirely, but the harm can be localized. It is one of the advantages of competitive private enterprise that the penalties for failure are levied against those who fail—the damage is not assessed against the whole society—and that the greatest rewards go to those whom their fellows deem most worthy of success. This is self-responsibility, the other side of the coin of personal freedom to choose. To be held accountable for one's errors is to assure the optimum of responsible human action in society. This is the primary reason that the free enterprise system is so preferable over the only possible alternative: a system of central planning, authoritarian control, dictatorship, where one man makes all the mistakes, usually on a grand scale, and always at the expense of everyone else. The great weakness of socialism is that no one, neither the leader nor any of the followers, assumes any sense of accountability or responsibility; someone else is always to blame.

This is why the advocates of central planning and government control are prone to cast the blame for the Great Depression onto someone else—to make free enterprise the scapegoat. But there is nothing in either the theory or the practice of responsible individualism, with individuals held accountable for their inevitable errors, that will explain a major depression such as the one following the boom and crash of 1929. Such massive social upheavals require some other explanation.

Examining the events and causes of World War I shows that our own government had long been inhibiting free enterprise in numerous major ways. Since 1913, we have had a politically controlled fractional-reserve central banking system capable of irresponsible and uncontrollable expansion of the supply of money and credit—the engine of inflation. And this engine has been used with monotonous regularity in an attempt to finance, implement, camouflage, nullify, or offset the many other costly programs of government intervention.

We have had a steeply graduated income tax to penalize the thrifty and successful. We have had government regulation and control of transportation, public utilities, and many other business enterprises. Much of the legislation giving special coercive powers to the leaders of organized labor had its origin during World War I. Especially in the 1920s, we began experimenting on a major scale with farm support programs. We have had wage and hour legislation, tariffs, and many other forms of protectionism and government control. But, most and worst of all was the inflation growing out of the deficit spending of World War I and the Federal Reserve Board's artificially depressed interest rates of the 1920s.

This government promotion of cheap money during and after World War I led at that time to private speculation and investment of resources in unsound business ventures, just as similar policies are doing now. During such a boom period there always is a great deal of malinvestment of economic resources under the illusion that the government can and will keep on promoting easy money—inflation. The continuing inflation temporarily hides many of the mistaken judgments of business owners, tempting others to make similar mistakes instead of taking sound corrective actions. With government pumping forth the money, all businesses are inclined to be borrowers, until bankers eventually find themselves over-loaned on bad risks.

The crash of 1929 was strictly a crash of confidence in the soundness of the government's monetary policy—the government's dollar—the shocking discovery, accompanied by great despair, that government interventionism or socialism doesn't work as promised.

Free enterprise can accomplish miracles of productivity, but it is wholly incapable of causing a major boom of speculative malinvestment which inevitably ends in crisis of readjustment called depression.

The opening question should be restated: "If government control (socialism) is so wonderful, why the Great Depression?" What happened in 1929, what happens whenever political intervention prices the various factors of production out of the market and leaves idle plants and idle men, must be attributed to socialism—not to free enterprise.

—PAUL L. POIROT

24

"Fact-finding is a proper function of government."

Ours is truly an Age of Statistics. In a country and an era that worships statistical data as super "scientific," as offering us the keys to all knowledge, a vast supply of data of all shapes and sizes pours forth upon us. Mostly, it pours forth from government. While private agencies and trade associations do gather and issue some statistics, they are limited to specific wants of specific industries. The vast bulk of statistics is gathered and disseminated by government. The overall statistics of the economy, the popular "gross national product" data that permit every economist to be a soothsayer of business conditions, come from government. Furthermore, many statistics are by-products of other governmental activities: from the Internal Revenue Service come tax data, from unemployment insurance departments come estimates of the unemployed, from customs offices come data on foreign trade, from the Federal Reserve flow statistics on banking, and so on. And as new statistical techniques are developed, new divisions of government departments are created to refine and use them.

The burgeoning of government statistics offers several obvious evils to the libertarian. In the first place, it is clear that too many resources are being channeled into statistics-gathering and statistics-production. Given a wholly free market, the amount of labor, land, and capital resources devoted to statistics would dwindle to a small fraction of the present total. The amount that the federal government alone spends on statistics can be estimated to be into the hundreds of millions of dollars.

Secondly, the great bulk of statistics is gathered by government coercion. This not only means that they are products of unwelcome activities; it also means that the true cost of these statistics to the American public is much greater than the mere amount of tax money spent by the government agencies. Private industry, and the private consumer, must bear the burdensome cost of record-keeping, filing, and the like, that these statistics demand. Not only that; these fixed costs impose a relatively great burden on *small* business firms, which are ill-equipped to handle the mountains of red tape. Hence, these seemingly innocent statistics cripple small business enterprise and help to rigidify the American business system.

But there are other important, and not so obvious, reasons for the libertarian to regard government statistics with dismay. Not only do statistics-gathering and producing go beyond the governmental function of defense of persons and property; not only are economic resources wasted and misallocated, and the taxpayers, industry, small business, and the consumer burdened. But, furthermore, statistics are, in a crucial sense, critical to *all* interventionist and socialistic activities of government. The individual consumer, in his daily rounds, has little need of statistics; through advertising, through the information of friends, and through his own experience, he finds out what is going on in the markets around him. The same is true of the business firm. The businessman must also size up his particular market, determine the prices he has to pay for what he buys and charge for what he sells, engage in cost accounting to estimate his costs, and so on. But none of this activity is really dependent upon the *omnium gatherum* of statistical facts about the economy ingested by the federal government. The businessman, like the consumer, knows and learns about his particular market through his daily experience.

Bureaucrats as well as statist reformers, however, are in a completely different state of affairs. They are decidedly *outside* the market. Therefore, in order to get "into" the situation that they are trying to plan and reform, they must obtain knowledge that is *not* personal, day-to-day experience; the only form that such knowledge can take is statistics.[1] Statistics are the eyes and ears of the bureaucrat, the politician, the socialistic reformer. Only by statistics can *they* know, or at least have any idea about, what is going on in the economy.[2] Only by statistics can they find out how many old people have rickets, or how many young people have cavities, or how many Eskimos have defective sealskins—

and therefore only by statistics can these interventionists discover who "needs" what throughout the economy, and how much
federal money should be channeled in what directions. And certainly, only by statistics, can the federal government make even
a fitful *attempt* to plan, regulate, control, or reform various industries—or impose central planning and socialization on the
entire economic system. If the government received no railroad
statistics, for example, how in the world could it even start to
regulate railroad rates, finances, and other affairs? How could
the government impose price controls if it didn't even know *what*
goods have been sold on the market, and what prices were prevailing? Statistics, to repeat, are the eyes and ears of the interventionists: of the intellectual reformer, the politician, and the
government bureaucrat. Cut off those eyes and ears, destroy
those crucial guidelines to knowledge, and the whole threat of
government intervention is almost completely eliminated.

It is true, of course, that even deprived of all statistical
knowledge of the nation's affairs, the government could still *try*
to intervene, to tax and subsidize, to regulate and control. It
could try to subsidize the aged even without having the slightest
idea of how many aged there are and where they are located; it
could try to regulate an industry without even knowing how
many firms there are or any other basic facts of the industry; it
could try to regulate the business cycle without even knowing
whether prices or business activity are going up or down. It could
try, but it would not get very far. The utter chaos would be too
patent and too evident even for the bureaucracy, and certainly
for the citizens. And this is especially true since one of the major
reasons put forth for government intervention is that it "cor-
rects" the market, and makes the market and the economy more
rational. Obviously, if the government were deprived of all
knowledge whatever of economic affairs, there could not even
be a *pretense* of rationality in government intervention. Surely,
the absence of statistics would absolutely and immediately
wreck any attempt at socialistic planning. It is difficult to see
what, for example, the central planners at the Kremlin could *do*
to plan the lives of Soviet citizens if the planners were deprived
of all information, of all statistical data, about these citizens. The

government would not even know to *whom* to give orders, much less how to try to plan an intricate economy.

Thus, in all the host of measure that have been proposed over the years to check and limit government or to repeal its interventions, the simple and unspectacular abolition of government statistics would probably be the most thorough and the most effective. Statistics, so vital to statism, its namesake, is also the State's Achilles' heel.

—MURRAY N. ROTHBARD

---

1. On the deficiencies of statistics as compared to the personal knowledge of all participants utilized on the free market, see the illuminating discussion in F. A. Hayek, *Individualism and the Economic Order* (Chicago: University of Chicago Press, 1948), Chapter 4. Also see Geoffrey Dobbs, *On Planning the Earth* (Liverpool: K.R.P. Publications, 1951), pp. 77–86.

2. As early as 1863, Samuel B. Ruggles, American delegate to the International Statistical Congress in Berlin, declared: "Statistics are the very eyes of the statesman, enabling him to survey and scan with clear and comprehensive vision the whole structure and economy of the body politic." For more on the interrelation of statistics—and statisticians—and the government, see Murray N. Rothbard, "The Politics of Political Economists: Comment," *The Quarterly Journal of Economics* (November 1960), pp. 659–65. Also see Dobbs, *op. cit.*

III. PRIVATE ENTERPRISE, GOVERNMENT SPENDING, AND HUMAN WELFARE

25

"Politicians are to blame for the fiscal mess in government."

Most Americans sense that something is wrong. They have an eerie feeling about the federal government spending hundreds of billions of dollars it does not have and owing a debt of trillions of dollars. After all, in their personal lives they learned very early that what they don't owe won't hurt them. He is rich who owes nothing. And they may have learned in their history classes what Thomas Jefferson said about government debt: "I place economy among the first and most important of republican virtues, and public debt as the greatest of the dangers to be feared." And in a letter to a friend he wrote: "The principle of spending money to be paid by posterity, under the name of funding, is but swindling futurity on a large scale."

The federal government obviously lives by fiscal principles which differ diametrically from those of our personal lives and from those postulated by Thomas Jefferson. We are quick to find fault with those principles and place the responsibility on the shoulders of politicians and officials whom we hold in low regard anyway. Unfortunately, we fail to search our own conscience which, if searched in earnest, would reveal our own responsibility and culpability. In fact, the majority of the American people is solely responsible for the federal spending predilection and the pyramid of trillion-dollar debt.

Although most people readily support reduction in federal spending, they balk at virtually every proposal of specific cuts. A nationwide poll conducted by *The Wall Street Journal* and NBC News, for instance, found that 86 percent oppose reductions in Medicare spending, 69 percent oppose reductions on social spending for the poor. There are more than 90 million Americans who benefit directly from one or several transfer programs. They are unlikely to oppose the largess.

Many more Americans benefit indirectly. The retirement benefits of some 35 million beneficiaries lend aid and comfort to millions of young people who otherwise would have to assist their parents. The Medicare and Medicaid programs which finance the medical care of more than 50 million aged, disabled, and needy Americans benefit not only the recipients but also the families which otherwise would provide the medical care. The subsidies to some 7 million students benefit not only the students but also many more parents, relatives, and spouses who otherwise would provide the assistance. The federal government subsidizes more than 100 million meals per day, or 15 percent of all meals served, through food stamp programs, child nutrition programs, nutrition programs for the elderly, and commodity distribution programs. All the recipients are likely to object strenuously to any reduction in benefits although they all are moaning about the budget deficits.

The benefits received are concrete and visible; the harmful psychological, economic, and political consequences of the programs are hidden in the haze of popular notions and prejudices. It takes knowledge and reasoning to perceive that forcible transfer of income and wealth erodes individual character and morale, that it consumes economic wealth and lowers labor productivity and income, and weakens democratic institutions. It is a potent prescription for stagnation and poverty, and an open invitation for social and political conflict.

It is difficult to confront the entitlement system with economic arguments. They are utterly ineffective against passionate descriptions of human need and want. "We cannot afford it" is an invitation to instant rejection and ridicule. At its best, it initiates a search for funds which leads to ugly denunciations of people with funds.

To perceive the evil consequences of political largess requires a sense of morality and justice which must guide all our actions. The established rules of morality must be applicable to individual as well as political conduct. We must keep our promises, fulfill our contractual obligations, and respect the rights of property acquired under contract.

Above all, we must reject the notion that political action is not bound by the decencies of that code of law and morals which governs private conduct.

The present system of political entitlements and largess rests on a universal rejection of that code of law and morals. Our representatives in the Congress deal and wheel and engage in feverish logrolling in order to distribute and redistribute the entitlements. In a democratic society the only principle guiding their action is the majority vote. In all cases the will of the majority prevails; the minority which lacks the vote is likely to become its victim.

More than 200 years ago James Madison clearly foresaw the social and political conditions of our age. In a speech in the Virginia Convention in 1788 he declaimed: "On a candid examination of history, we shall find that turbulence, violence and abuse of power, by the majority trampling on the rights of the minority, have produced factions and commotions which, in republics, have, more frequently than any other cause, produced despotism."

The destiny of a republic in which the majority thrives on entitlements forcibly extracted from minorities is despotism— unless the majority forgoes its numerical power and returns to the code of morals. The road ahead is clear. We may proceed in the old direction toward despotism or veer around and return to the proven ways of the republic. The choice depends on the moral attitude we adopt toward other people, especially the political minority. Morality itself is eternal and immutable.

—HANS F. SENNHOLZ

26

"There is too much inequality of wealth and income."

"Free people are not equal, and equal people are not free."

I wish I could remember who said that. It ought to rank as one of the great truths of all time.

Equality before the law—that is, being judged innocent or guilty based on whether or not you committed the crime, not on what color, sex, or creed you represent—is a noble goal and is not at issue here. The "equalness" I refer to pertains to economic wealth.

Put another way, then, the quotation above might read, "Free people will have different incomes, and where people all have the same income, they cannot be free."

With that in mind, let me share with you what I used to tell my freshman economics students about incomes and how to make theirs grow.

At least three reasons account for differences in personal wealth in a free society. They all stem from the fact that people themselves are different, one from another, in countless ways. The reasons are: talent, industry, and thrift.

Talents are as varied as the day is long. Some people have more than others. The trick is finding which talent or talents you have that other people value, and develop them to their fullest. Maybe you're the best dandelion picker in the valley, but if no one wants dandelions, you'll probably starve.

Industry—the willingness to work—differs from one person to another and even from one day to the next. After you've discovered a talent you have and others will pay for, your income may largely depend on how hard you apply yourself.

Thrift is an attribute that takes an extra measure of discipline these days. Saving and investing, rather than consuming everything now, can even make it possible for you to retire and enjoy a living standard higher than most of those who work. So potent a factor is thrift in accounting for differences in income that if we equalized everybody's earnings tonight, we'd have inequality again by morning. Some would save, and some would not, or would save less.

In a free society, the person seeking higher income must develop his best talents in an effort to supply the needs and desires of others, work hard and faithfully at it, and yet still put something aside for later in the form of prudent investment. Not everybody does these things, or does them as well as others, so differences in income naturally result.

Building on what I've said so far, my best advice to both young and old in the job market is to become indispensable to your employer. I mean, become so uniquely valuable to him (or her) that pay raises are practically automatic.

As a former professor at a small college, I often observed that some faculty members complained about low pay and small raises. The ones who grumbled the loudest were the ones who did the least to distinguish themselves from the rest. They did the bare minimum—punched in and punched out at the appointed times, made no lasting mark on students, other faculty, the college, or their profession.

Becoming indispensable means doing things that others can't or won't do. It means standing out from the crowd, unafraid to put forth a little extra, learning how to get along with employer and fellow employees. At contract time, it causes the employer to think twice about what it would mean to lose you. In short, being different in a positive way accounts for different pay, higher pay. In terms of income, the only way to make people the same is to use force to keep them from being different.

That's the way it works in a free society. It's one of those great features of freedom we too often abuse or take for granted. As the French say, but in a slightly different context, *"Vive la différence!"*

—LAWRENCE W. REED

27

"Americans no longer need to worry about how to produce goods and services."

A vast array of consumer goods is available to most Americans; almost any material thing that people want is available for purchase—a source of envy to millions of people throughout the world.

Yet most Americans take it all for granted. City dwellers have become so detached from the earth that gives them sustenance that they seldom think where all these products come from, or of the kind of economic system that makes them available. Many young people do not trace the origin of their foods further back than the supermarket.

Most teachers, social workers, and members of government bureaucracies appear to have no idea of it either. They are much concerned with how the results of the productive process should be *distributed,* but seldom consider how they have been *produced.* They compete with one another for a share of federal and state handouts, and press incessantly for increased appropriations, as if indifferent to the possibility that the sources of this bounty may cease to exist. One distinguished professor writes that thanks to technology the problem of production has now been solved, and the only remaining problem for society is that of distribution.[1] But we would do well to note what Rose Wilder Lane wrote in 1943:

> ... for countless centuries, multitudes of men have lived on this earth. Their situation has been the everlasting human situation. Their desire to live has been as strong as ours. Their energy has always been enough to make this earth at least habitable for human beings. Their intelligence has been no less than ours.
>
> Yet for all these years, most men have been hungry.

Famines have always killed multitudes, and still do over most of this earth. A century ago the Irish were starving to death; no one was surprised. Europeans had never expected to get from this earth enough food to keep them all alive.

Why did they walk, and carry goods on their backs, for thousands of years, and suddenly, in one century, only on a sixth of this earth's surface, they make steamships, railroads, cars, airplanes? Why did families live in floorless hovels, without windows or chimneys, and then, in a hundred years and only in these United States, they take these all for granted, and regard electricity, porcelain toilets, and window screen as minimum necessities? ... What explains this?

The physical earth has not changed in historical time. Raw materials do not explain what has been done with them here; the raw materials were here when the Mound Builders were. Vast quantities of iron, coal, oil, rubber, have always been available to human beings. Two thousand years ago when Caesar went into Gaul, Europe was a rich and virgin wilderness inhabited by a few wandering savages, as this continent was a century ago. Not raw materials, but *the uses that human energy makes of raw material, create this rich new world ...*

Forty years ago nobody imagined this America. There was a $40-a-month mechanic, working ten hours a day six days a week, tinkering nights and Sundays in the woodshed behind his little rented house—no bathtub, no running water, no light but a kerosene lamp—in a far, cheap suburb of Detroit; even Henry Ford did not imagine this America.

There were no cars, no highways, no radios or planes, no movies, no tall buildings, no electric lights, no toothpaste, not many toothbrushes, no soda fountains, no bottled soft drinks, no hot dog stands, no high schools, no low shoes, no safety razors or shaving cream, no green vegetables in the winter, and none in cans, no bakers' bread or cakes or doughnuts, no dime stores, no supermarkets. An orange was a Christmas treat, in prosperous families.

There was no central heating, and only the very prosperous had bathtubs; they were tin or zinc, encased in mahogany in the homes of the very rich. The rich, too, had gaslights. Spring came to American children when mama let them go barefoot. No moderately prosperous parents thought of letting children wear out good shoe-leather in the summertime. Stockings were cotton. Sheets were made at home, of muslin seamed down the center, for looms had never made muslin as wide as a bed. Mother made all the family's clothes. Forty years ago, a journey of ten miles to the next town (by buggy or mail-hack or train) was planned and prepared for, at least some weeks in advance.

When America began the Revolution, no one expected this. Thomas Paine and the other revolutionists of his time were not thinking of changing living conditions. They were thinking of moral values.

What actually occurred, when men could act freely, was a tremendous outburst of human energy, changing all life-values, and utterly transforming the material world. . . .[2]

The problem of production is never really solved. Only when human energy has been applied to create technology, and then only when people are left free to produce, can a high standard of living be sustained. But when government interposes itself between production and consumption, the production of goods is inhibited and less consumption is possible. When government controls almost all of the productive process, as it did in the late Soviet Union, production falters because goods cannot be produced efficiently—when workers are not rewarded for doing a good job, shoddy goods are made; and consumers then face bare shelves or shelves with unwanted goods. Foods lie rotting in the fields because the state-owned tractors are in disrepair or are a thousand miles away at harvest time. Production is stifled when the conditions for its existence are no longer present.

Some government is necessary in order to prevent crime, arbitrate disputes, and, in general, uphold human rights. But the same government that rightly makes it illegal for a person to dump poisonous wastes into the soil, also has today the power to stop a farmer from using a part of his own land, saying "that mud puddle over there we hereby declare a wetland, and you are not allowed to use it." Regulations tend to multiply without regard to need, but only to give more power to the regulators. Taxes, too, increase until many businesses are forced into bankruptcy and potential entrepreneurs decide not to take the risk of starting. This in turn throws many people out of work who would otherwise be gainfully employed. Government avoids blame by condemning all businesspersons as selfish, greedy, and exploitative, in order to conceal its own inefficiency, corruption, and lust for power. As a rule the public goes along with this, enthusiastically approving still more taxes and regulation, and cheering when another wealthy business owner has bit the dust. They fail to see the connection between the government measures they applaud and the unemployment and economic depression that result.

An economy cannot long remain prosperous by government's taxing and spending more, now absorbing national output at a rate equal to the entire income of every American living west of the Mississippi. If this trend continues, America will gradually sink to the status of a Third World nation—more unemployment, more violence in the streets, more shackles on production, more poverty. That is after all how Rome ended—not through barbarian invasions but because the public sector absorbed so much of the empire's wealth that those who created the wealth on which everyone depended could not continue to produce.[3]

Many Americans apparently believe, and many schools teach, that wealth is an evil and that people must be penalized for trying to accumulate it. We are all supposed to "share the wealth" and equalize incomes. But no productive enterprise can long endure on such a premise; wealth dries up at its source. The very thing that every business requires, capital, is what the "do-gooders" do not want it to have. "What a dilemma!" wrote Dr. Manuel Ayau of Guatemala. "Poverty is bad, and everyone wants to see it abolished. Wealth is the absence of poverty. But wealth is evil. Yet only through the accumulation of wealth can investment occur, and without investment there is only poverty."[4] Indeed, the problem of poverty is solved only so long as the situation of those who produce the wealth is stable and secure.

—JOHN HOSPERS

1. For example, Professor Nicholas Rescher's books *Distributive Justice* (Bobbs-Merrill, 1966) and *Welfare* (University of Pittsburgh Press, 1969).

2. Rose Wilder Lane, *The Discovery of Freedom* (Arno Press, 1943), pp. vii–x, 229.

3. See Ludwig von Mises, *Human Action* (Regnery, 1945), pp. 767–69.

4. Manuel Ayau, in "Yes, We Have No Bananas," a pamphlet published by the Universidad Francisco Marroquín, Guatemala City.

28

"But we already tried cutting the budget."

People who advocate high government spending often claim we have already cut, or tried to cut, the federal budget, but that it did not work. They especially claim this happened in the 1980s, when the president expressed the desire for lower levels of government spending.

In 1980, the federal government spent about $600 billion, but 10 years later, that amount had more than doubled. The growth occurred not only in military-oriented spending, but in domestic welfare as well. Spending on "human resources," which is good proxy for welfare, began at $315 billion in 1980 and then zoomed to $619 billion by 1990. And approximately the same levels of growth occurred in the previous three decades, regardless of the rhetoric of the politicians in charge.

The primary policy change that allowed high spending was the elimination of the gold standard. Every step away from this restraint on government growth allowed more discretion for politicians and bureaucrats.

It was not always thus. In the nineteenth century, the nation's currency was based on gold, and without the ability to print money at will, the government could not dramatically expand except—when Lincoln instituted the inflationary greenback—it went off gold. The dollar was sound, and the Constitution was enforced. But in the age of fiat money, spending has become astronomical. Today, the federal government spends every six hours what it spent in the sixty years between 1789 and 1849.

If we want to have government limited by the rule of law and fiscal responsibility, spending will have to be drastically curtailed. Sometimes, however, it is difficult to know if and when spending is being cut. Politicians often say they have cut the budget, when really they have only cut the rate of increase in a particular program. For example, if spending on welfare has been rising at 10 percent, dropping the increase to 8 percent will be called a spending cut. Even more confusingly, politicians will increase the projected rate of future increases in a particular program just so they can later lower it and claim to be cutting the budget. In reality, the only cut that qualifies as a cut is when the government spends less this year than it spent last year. That has rarely happened in any program, despite claims to the contrary.

Politicians also use a variety of tactics to make sure that the public does not demand spending cuts. First, they will make sure the "benefits" from spending are spread to influential people who can advocate more increases. Second, they will spread them to a diverse group of people so that no one has an interest in cutbacks. Third, they will make conspicuous cuts that will generate public outcries (called the Washington Monument Ploy, because the National Park Service once closed the monument when its budget was cut under Nixon).

In a private business, the price system and its signal of profit and loss make it easy to know where to cut. The business owner cuts costs in ways that do not distract from the goal of serving the consumer. If a business is paying too much in salaries, for example, it will cut pay before it cuts store hours. That way, the business can economize without hurting the consumer. With a little experimentation, business managers achieve a highly productive workplace.

The nature of bureaucracy is different, however. It precludes a rational approach to budget cutting. There are no customers, as with private business. Even if people get services from a bureaucracy, the customer neither provides all the revenue nor drives the decisions of the producers. There is no profit and loss system. The bureaucracy exists outside the market.

The bureaucracy might like to cut its budget in a rational way, but there is literally no way for it to know what is its most valuable and least valuable service.

It is because of the nature of bureaucracy that the effort to eliminate "waste, fraud, and abuse" in government has been such a failure. In most cases, there is no way to distinguish waste from useful spending, fraud from the honest outlays, and abuse from business as usual. Rather than strive for these kinds of reforms, the most successful attempts at cutting government spending have come by the elimination of whole agencies. No agency can be trusted to cut its budget.

The Reagan Administration originally talked about abolishing entire agencies, but in the end did not. Moreover, it actually expanded the budgets of the agencies he said he would abolish (Departments of Education and Energy) and then added a new agency. The truth is we have not tried to cut the government's budget. But we'd better take a chainsaw to it if we want to restore economic sanity.

—LLEWELLYN H. ROCKWELL, JR.

29

"The size of the national debt doesn't matter because we owe it to ourselves."

Some things a person does owe to him or herself—intangibles like respect, integrity, responsibility. "This above all: to thine own self be true." But such duties to self are not a debt in the usual sense of a repayable loan or obligation.

If an individual transfers his own money or his own promise to pay from his right pocket to his left, the transaction clearly leaves him neither richer nor poorer. There would be no point in a person's borrowing from himself; but if for some reason he did, the size of the debt he owed himself wouldn't matter at all. However, if A gives his property to B, we do not say that each is as rich or as poor as before. Or, if C buys extensively on credit, his creditors surely do not believe that C "owes it to himself." They are keenly aware that the size of his debt makes a big difference when the bills fall due.

In a society where the government owns or controls all property and persons and issues money or bonds as a bookkeeping device to keep track of its spending, it wouldn't matter how many promises or bonds had been issued or remained outstanding. Since individuals would have neither property nor rights, the socialized government—as sole owner—would only be dealing with itself. But in a non-socialized society, individuals do have rights and may own property. If the government borrows property from citizen A, then it is obligated to repay that debt to A—not to B or C or D. The individual who owns a government bond may be a taxpayer as well, and thus liable in part for the taxes the government must collect in order to redeem his bond; but B and C and D are also liable as taxpayers even if they own none of the bonds themselves. And the size of the debt makes a real difference to everyone involved.

One of the vital characteristics of the institution of private property is that ownership and control rest with individuals, and whether a person *owns* or *owes* makes a whale of a difference in how rich or how poor he is.

The concept of private ownership and control of property further presupposes a government of limited powers instead of a socialized society in which everything and everyone is government owned and controlled. Private property owners presumably have something to say about the extent to which government may tax or seize their property; otherwise, it wouldn't be a limited government, and there wouldn't be private property.

Now, government debt signifies that government has made certain claims upon private property above and beyond the "due processes" of authorized taxation. The semblance of private property must be maintained, else the government could find no "owner" from whom to "borrow" and no taxpayers upon whom to draw when the debt falls due. But, in essence, the government debt is an existing claim against property—like an unpaid tax bill—and the larger that debt, the less is the real equity of individuals in what is thought to be private property. In that sense, the socialization already has occurred, and the government does "owe to itself" because it owns the property. The size of the debt is important, however, because it measures the amount that taxpayers and property owners owe—not to themselves, but to the government over which they have lost control insofar as it now owns and controls them.

It would be most surprising to find a completely socialized government heavily in debt, simply because no sensible property owner would lend to such an institution if he could possibly avoid it. Though deficit financing seems inconsistent with the original American design of limited government, it is possible in an emergency for a limited government to find voluntary creditors, especially among its own citizens who expect the government to abide by its constitutional limitations and thus leave a large base of taxable private property through which debts may be redeemed. But the growing size of the government debt should be of real concern to every creditor and especially to every taxpayer with any interest whatsoever in private property and personal freedom.

—PAUL L. POIROT

30

"The 'Trickle-Down Theory' has caused our economic problems."

The point of a slogan or cliché is to prevent the listener from thinking and invert reality through altering the meaning of terms and phrases. The "trickle-down economics" cliché has enjoyed tremendous success.

The cliché started during the first administration of Ronald Reagan and quickly became a mainstay of the interventionist vocabulary. The trickle-down tag remains popular with President Clinton and his followers, and television "journalists" attribute it to venal conservatives. It was even mentioned on a popular situation comedy show comparing it to theories about Santa Claus and the tooth fairy.

Self-described socialist John Kenneth Galbraith once explained the concept on a *Firing Line* television program with William F. Buckley Jr. The administration of the time, lamented Galbraith the wealthy economist, was "giving" out all sorts of favors to the wealthy and powerful, in the fond hope that some would eventually "trickle down" to the poor and middle class.

Galbraith further compared the concept to stuffing a horse's trough full of straw, in the hope that some would eventually get tossed around for the chickens, ducks, and other little critters. But sound economics can show that this explanation more properly belongs to what emerges from the other end of the horse.

In the first place, the federal government produces nothing that people would freely buy in an open marketplace. The state is a net *consumer* of wealth, not a producer. Returning to the barnyard anology to find an image of the state, we notice a pig—portly, listless, and, of course, always squealing for more.

Every time the state tries to produce something on any scale, the result is a disaster. The collapsed economies of the Eastern Bloc stand as evidence of that fact. As the late F.A. Hayek explained, no government, however enlightened, possesses the knowledge and moral detachment to "plan" a modern society, with its myriads of daily decisions. Only individuals acting in a free marketplace can do so. But if the government's visible hand has its way, individuals can't have theirs. It's as simple as that.

Only someone with a statist vision could see the government as the flywheel of wealth in America or anywhere else. The typical response is that the government is handing out regulatory and tax concessions, but this too has fatal problems.

In the United States money does not trickle down from the government. It flows upward from the private sector. In a market economy, individuals and corporations earn money by producing goods which uncoerced consumers will purchase. More important, in democratic societies that respect human rights, the government has no *prior claim* to what people earn by their honest labors. There was, however, a system which maintained such a claim. It went by such names as feudalism, slavery, and totalitarianism.

Hence, for the government to allow individuals to keep what they have earned by their own labor is not a favor, subsidy, or "trickle-down" arrangement of any kind. But for popular academicians to profess otherwise only shows the pervasiveness of the statist mindset and its capacity for self-deception.

This is not to say that there is not a true trickle-down theory. Here is how it works.

The government currently ignores its legitimate task of protecting life, liberty, and property, and performing those tasks which it is not practical for individuals to do, such as building interstate highways and maintaining an army. Instead the government sets out to achieve "social justice," largely by the "redistribution" of wealth, which it assumes is the product of exploitation.

In reality, as Frederic Bastiat explained in his masterful treatise *The Law,* the modern state acts like burglars, who are also in the business of redistributing wealth. In like manner, the state plunders the property of its citizens. And with the proceeds, the state is always careful to take care of its own benefits first.

Federal employees, for example, boast their own retirement program, much more generous than Social Security. And postal employees get their choice of—count 'em—five medical plans. Every day brings new revelations of bulging salaries for little effort, outrageous perks, bounced checks, and general corruption.

This same government that plunders wealth proposes spending "programs" that will supposedly benefit the populace, increase prosperity, and eliminate the deficit. Who says there is no Santa Claus or tooth fairy? Here, then, is the true trickle-down theory as an honest partisan would explain it:

You the producer will, on your own initiative and with your own capital, work hard to turn a profit. We, the government, will impede you with regulations and confiscate ever-increasing amounts of your income. With what we confiscate, we will first take care of the needs of the state, but hopefully some of that money will trickle down to those we determine to be needy victims.

Ironically, if you follow this model the cliché is true. The trickle-down theory is the source of our economic problems.

—K. L. BILLINGSLEY

31

"A shortage of tax revenues creates budget deficits."

The latest, if not last, surplus in the federal budget was in 1969. Since then, government has spent vastly more than its taxation receipts. Politicians and journalists love to talk about deficits. They are against them. And most want to reduce the deficit mainly by increasing taxes. But their concern is misconceived and their agitation misdirected. Indeed, in a real sense, there is no deficit.

Consider some common sense. Government acquires resources and products; it cannot have more than it gets from the people. The things government buys, as well as the funds to make the payments, come from you and me in some way. Raising the means to make the payments *is* taxation, even if accountants and statisticians label as "taxation" only the compelled payments to government and not the receipts from borrowing through selling bonds.

Government spending is government spending, whether government directly gets the funds it spends by handing the public a tax receipt or a bond. In either case—conventional taxation or borrowing—its expenditures divert wealth from the public to government. That reduction in wealth left in private hands *is* taxation. So with government absorption simultaneously matched by private cost, the real government budget is always balanced.

We do better to consider the *size* of the budget rather than its purported *imbalance*. And we see that size, not in the amount of traditional *taxes,* but in the amount of government *spending*— the amount of people's wealth that government sequesters and redistributes.

While the real government budget is always balanced, explicit tax payments by the public are still smaller than federal expenditures. How did this bookkeeping deficit get so large, and what might be done about it? Much experience informs us that raising tax *rates* does not invariably increase tax *receipts* (nor does lowering rates always reduce receipts). It tells us also that increasing tax *receipts* does not necessarily reduce the *deficit*.

Indeed, in the forty-eight years since World War II, federal tax receipts and the deficit have moved in the *same* direction—generally both increasing—over half the time. The story is even more sobering if a lag is noted: in more than two-thirds of the time, a change in receipts was followed a year later by a deficit change in the *same* direction. The wretched record is clear: government typically increases its spending by more than the public increases the taxes provided to government.

The growth of the deficit after 1969—slowly for a time and exploding after 1975—has not reflected tax-starvation of government. Over the entire period, receipts rose robustly at 8.2 percent annually, and were nearly six times as great in 1992 as in 1969; but government outlays rose still faster, at 9.2 percent, approaching an eight-fold increase. While the ratio of federal receipts to gross domestic product remained at the 1969 level of 19 percent, expenditures ballooned to over 23 percent by 1992.

The great deficit has stemmed, not from taxing ourselves too little, but from spending on ourselves too much. With tax receipts remaining nearly a constant proportion of national income, changes in federal spending have determined changes in the deficit. And over the past thirty years more spending has persistently been associated with lower growth of business investment and national output.

That excessive spending has not resulted from allegedly massive increases in defense expenditures. Defense comprised half the federal budget and some 9 percent of national output during the early 1960s, when the deficit was tiny. It steadily fell proportionately until 1979, when President Carter began the military recovery. At the peak of the buildup, in 1986, defense still was only a little more than one-quarter of the budget and 6.4 percent of total production. In the last two years, the defense proportion has fallen precipitously—almost back to the level of 1979—while the deficit has soared to new heights.

Spending has indeed raced ahead. But the galloping spending has been overwhelmingly on "social" programs rather than defense. And the bulk of that social spending has not been welfare directed to the poorest; it has been mainly "entitlements" for the middle and upper-middle classes, largely for retirement convenience—Social Security, Medicare, and government pensions, along with such subsidies as price and income supports for the more affluent agriculturalists.

So-called deficits are not "nice" mainly because deficit financing redistributes wealth. This occurs as government takes money from the many taxpayers and pays it to the relatively few holders of government bonds as interest and principal.

Our fiscal fiasco reveals a fundamental flow of focusing simply on the bookkeeping deficit rather than on the magnitude of the whole federal budget. The ratio of federal spending to national output has risen in every administration since World War II. Even if spending were financed fully by conventional taxation without deficits, a budget of overwhelming size and misguided purposes still generates dire economic consequences.

—WILLIAM R. ALLEN AND WILLIAM DICKNEIDER

32

"The free market ignores the poor."

Once an activity has been taken over by the government for a spell, nearly everyone will concede that that's the way it should be.

Without socialized education, how would the poor get their schooling? Without the socialized post office, how would farmers receive their mail except at great expense? Without Social Security, the aged would end their years in poverty! If power and light were not socialized, consider the plight of the poor families in the Tennessee Valley!

Agreement with the idea of state absolutism follows socialization, appallingly. Why? One does not have to dig very deep for the answer.

Once an activity has been socialized, it is impossible to point out, by concrete example, how people in a free market could better conduct it. How, for instance, can one compare a socialized post office with private postal delivery when the latter has been outlawed? It's something like trying to explain to a people accustomed only to darkness how things would appear were there light. One can only resort to imaginative construction.

To illustrate the dilemma: By the middle of the twentieth century, people in free and willing exchange (the free market) discovered how to deliver the human voice around the earth in one twenty-seventh of a second; how to deliver an event, like a ball game, into everyone's living room, in color and in motion, at the time it is going on; how to deliver hundreds of people from Los Angeles to Baltimore in less than 3 hours and 19 minutes; how to deliver gas from a hole in Texas to a range in New York at low cost and without subsidy; how to deliver 64 ounces of oil from the Persian Gulf to our Eastern Seaboard—more than halfway around the earth—for less money than government would deliver a one-ounce letter across the street in one's home town.

Yet, such commonplace free market phenomena as these, in the field of delivery, fail to convince most people that "the post" could be left to free market delivery without causing many people to suffer.

Now, then, resort to imagination: Imagine that our federal government, at its very inception, had issued an edict to the effect that all boys and girls, from birth to adulthood, were to receive shoes and stockings from the federal government "for free." Next, imagine that this practice of "for free" shoes and stockings had been going on for some 200 years! Lastly, imagine one of our contemporaries—one with a faith in the wonders that can be wrought by men when free—saying, "I do not believe that shoes and stockings for kids should be a government responsibility. Properly, that is a responsibility of the family. This activity should never have been socialized. It is appropriately a free market activity."

What, under these circumstances, would be the response to such a stated belief? Based on what we hear on every hand, once an activity has been socialized for a short time, the common chant would go like this, "Ah, but you would let the poor children go unshod!"

However, in this instance, where the activity has not yet been socialized, we are able to point out that the poor children are better shod in countries where shoes and stockings are a family responsibility than in countries where they are a government responsibility. We are able to demonstrate that the poor children are better shod in countries that are more free than in countries that are less free.

True, the free market ignores the poor precisely as it does not recognize the wealthy—it is "no respecter of persons." It is an organizational way of doing things, *featuring openness,* which enables millions of people to cooperate and compete without demanding a preliminary clearance of pedigree, nationality, color, race, religion, or wealth. It demands only that each person abide by voluntary principles, that is, by fair play. The free market means willing exchange; it is impersonal justice in the economic sphere and excludes coercion, plunder, theft, protectionism, and other anti-free market ways by which goods and services change hands.

Admittedly, human nature is defective, and its imperfections will be reflected in the market. But the free market opens the way for men and women to operate at their moral best, and all observation confirms that the poor do fare better under these circumstances than when the way is closed, as it is under socialism.

—LEONARD E. READ

33

"Government should guarantee freedom from want."

Once upon a time the people of the United States waged a war on poverty, the success of which has seen no equal.

They didn't call it war on poverty. They said they were trying "to promote the general welfare," and the device they used was a new Constitution for a government of strictly limited powers. The government was to protect life and private property, thus providing the political framework within which all individuals would be free to produce and trade to their hearts' content. If anyone wanted to be richer or poorer than others, that was his choice and his problem; and how well he succeeded depended on how well he pleased his customers. The laws were designed, as best those men knew how, to render justice impartially, neither harassing nor granting special privilege to the rich or the poor, or any class, or any individual. Of course, there were violations of principle, human nature being what it is, but the principles themselves were sound.

Unlike their modern counterparts in the United States, and unlike their eighteenth-century contemporaries in France, the early political leaders of the United States did not try to promote the general welfare through deficit financing and continuous inflation. They had suffered through the wild paper-money inflation of the Revolutionary War period and concluded that the whole scheme was "not worth a Continental." They took the position that the best way to help a debtor was to let him pay what he owed, thus establishing his credit rating against which he might want to borrow again some other time. They even went so far as to let bankers and borrowers and lenders compete in the money markets, and suffer the consequences of their own folly if financial panic ensued.

If a man acted so as to become a failure, he was permitted to fail. If he couldn't make good at farming, there was no federal farm support program to discourage his trying to be useful in some other way. If he lost one job, he was free to seek another, with no powerful labor unions to bid him nay, and no unemployment compensation or state or federal relief programs to encourage him to remain idle. There wasn't even a minimum-wage law to tell him at what point he must stop working entirely rather than take a lower wage; no programs inviting or compelling him to retire at age 65. And if he chose to enter business at his own risk and responsibility, there was no federal Small Business Administration to help him remain a small businessman.

Perhaps most important of all was a reluctance on the part of many of the early statesmen of America to seek political office and political power. They knew of other ways to find happiness and achieve success. George Washington wanted to return to farming at Mount Vernon; Jefferson longed to be back at Monticello. Neither the governors nor the governed looked to the government as the source and provider of all good things. The government was a police force of limited power for a limited purpose; and most of life was to be found and lived in peaceful and creative ways outside the scope of governmental control.

It would be a gross distortion of the fact to presume that poverty was eliminated from the United States in an absolute sense under the comparatively free-market and limited-government practices of the nineteenth century, or to assert that there were not governmental interferences in the private sphere. Throughout the period, there were many individuals and families in the nation with earnings and savings well below a level they themselves might have considered necessary for a decent standard of living. All that one may conclude, without fear of reasonable contradiction, is that Americans prospered under those conditions to a greater extent than had the people of any other society at any time. If they knew that among them lived "a lower third," it was not cause for panic. Competitive private enterprise kept open the market paths through which anyone could, and most everyone did, find ways to help himself by serving others. And the basic economic theory behind this miracle of progress was: *those who produce more will have more.*

One of the characteristics of human nature is an insatiable desire for more—materially, intellectually, spiritually. The more a person understands, the more inquisitive he tends to be. The more he sees, the more he wants. The more he has, the more acquisitive he becomes. Now, the fact that individuals are forever wanting more and tend to act so as to fulfill their most urgent wants largely accounts for the miracle of the free market, the fabulous outpouring of goods and services through competitive private enterprise and voluntary exchange.

A superficial view of this human tendency to be dissatisfied led Karl Marx and many others to reject the market economy with its emphasis on production. A more satisfactory formula, they have presumed, is that "those who want more should have more." The problem of production has been solved, the modern Marxists contend, and their "multiplier" formula stresses the speed of spending; if each spends his income and savings fast enough, everyone will have more to spend.

This consumer doctrine or purchasing power theory of prosperity has tremendous appeal to human beings who always want more. But it presumes too much. The problem of production has not been solved. There is no endless free supply of the goods and services consumers want. Unless there is some incentive to save and invest in creative business enterprises, all the spending in the world will not promote further productive effort. In short order, all available goods and services will have been consumed if nothing is done to replenish their supply. It is not spending or consuming, but productive effort only, that begets production!

An individual surely must realize that he cannot spend himself rich, if all he does is spend. Nor can two individuals spend each other rich, if all they do is trade back and forth what they already have on hand. Nor can any number of individuals long subsist if all they do is trade among themselves what remains of a non-replenished, initial supply of goods and services.

Monetary transactions tend to obscure some of these most elementary facts of life. In an industrialized market economy money enters into most trades, serving as a medium of exchange, a convenient measure of exchange rates or prices which guide buyers and sellers in their further activities as consumers and as producers. Among these market prices are wage rates for services rendered, and interest rates for savings loaned and invested.

In a freely functioning market economy, prices, wages, and interest rates guide and encourage production for the purpose of satisfying consumer wants; and this occurs so automatically that many consumers spend their dollars without even thinking of the creative efforts that had to be called forth in some manner before those dollars would be worth anything. Failing to understand the market, political planners assume that the whole process of production and exchange might be stimulated to function even better if only the government will create additional money and put it into the hands of consumers. These planners fail to see that money's only purpose, as a medium of exchange, tends to be defeated by such arbitrary tampering with the supply. This inflationary tampering distorts prices and wages and interest rates on which economic calculations are based. It encourages consumption and spending but it discourages saving and lending, weakening the incentive and capacity to produce.

This is why the current political war on poverty is doomed to fail. If the government continues to subsidize the poor at the expense of all taxpayers, the result will be an increase in the number of those being subsidized—more poor taxpayers. If the power of the government is invoked to favor debtors at the expense of creditors, more persons will try to borrow but fewer will be willing to lend. If savings are to be systematically plundered through inflation, the thrifty will learn to be spendthrifts, too.

The poor always will be able to obtain in the open competition of the market more of the life-sustaining and life-enriching goods and services they want than can be had through political warfare against successful private enterprise. The market leaves the planning and managing to those who continuously prove their ability, whereas political class warfare tends to redistribute resources among those most likely to waste them.

When government becomes the guarantor of "freedom from want," this means that the poorest managers within the society have been put in charge of human affairs; for they always do and always will outnumber those of superior talent. What is now advertised as a war on poverty is really a confiscation of the fruits of production; and the consequence has to be disastrous for everyone, especially for the poor.

—Paul L. Poirot

34

"Freedom from want requires population control."

This popular cliché has persisted for centuries, and on this issue many liberals and conservatives are quick to agree. Conservatives may concede that more economic freedom would eventually be beneficial to struggling Third World countries; but they echo their liberal counterparts when they propose that *right now* these countries need to introduce some kind of population control by political means to solve immediate problems.

Both liberals and conservatives conclude that overpopulation causes shortages in food, living space, and resources and is at the root of human misery and the world poverty problem. Their clever lifeboat economic models use a multitude of statistical and demographic data to prove simply that more people always result in poor people. When the number of people vying for a piece of the pie increases, each of their pieces get smaller. However, the lifeboat arguments are full of holes and are easily blown out of the water with sound economic understanding and clear logic. Indeed we shudder when we consider the implications of the vast body politic using coercive measures to arrest the growth of population.

Yet this is exactly what today's influential thinkers and the vast majority of average citizens are advocating. Some may be supportive of the free economy and concede that it could possibly help these poor countries. However they say so grudgingly, and are quick to qualify their statement with assertions that the benefits could only be realized far down the road through a long and tedious process, a transition that would take too long to make the necessary impact on living standards.

Indeed, they urge the governments of poor countries to take drastic measures in the hopes of making noticeable improvements in conditions *right now*. Their constant cry is, "Do *something* to control population!"

Politicians are ever watchful for this "do-something" mentality. They will make lofty pronouncements that assert their commitment to controlling the growth of population. The "population bomb" will be given "high priority." They may create committees and giant bureaucracies to decide the official population stabilization policy. And they will no doubt devise expensive incentive programs and schemes to build motivation for smaller families. Millions of dollars will be dumped into *publicly funded* population deterrents—from sex education and free contraceptives, to voluntary sterilization and free abortion on demand. Inevitably, when all the spending schemes fail to alleviate the situation, government will put away its wallet and pull out its gun. Government will tell you what to do.

What can result is a violent, coercive, and horrifying display of force where government-subsidized sterilization and abortion will turn into *government-mandated* sterilization and abortion— even infanticide. Such are the accounts of the People's Republic of China's vicious one-family, one-child program, the details of which are too grisly to dwell upon.

There is one thing you can say for this brand of statist. Even in today's socialist-engineered semantic revolution of an Orwellian newspeak dialect that converts the meaning of political terminology into its opposite—a tax is now a "contribution" and "equality" means special benefits at the expense of others— population control advocates don't mince words. Their use of terms quite accurately explains their goals. When they say population control, they literally intend to *control the entire population.* One insightful critic of their agenda makes this observation: "Population control is the last desperate act and ultimate weapon of a Welfare State whose lust for power and instinct for survival knows no political or moral limits."[1] This is the essence of the politicization of family planning.

What leads people to call on governments to implement such policies? Are we to suppose that people are innately designed to control and be controlled? These cries for controls are actually rooted in false notions and misinformation. People might not choose control rather than freedom in family planning if they understood one basic economic principle: human effort can multiply the amount of wealth; *people are producers as well as consumers.*

Therefore, human misery and world poverty are not so much problems of population. Population is only an important concern in countries that produce only babies and no goods or services. It is low production that causes poverty. If, on the other hand, the amount of capital investment is high relative to a population, production is facilitated, and there simply is no such thing as overpopulation—quite the opposite. Countries in which there is sufficient capital can always accommodate population increases. New faces are beneficial and always welcome. Free and productive societies therefore not only adjust well to population increases, but thrive on them. Throughout history, rapidly advancing capitalistic societies always had continually growing populations. Economic production always outpaced both the rates of birth and immigration combined. These examples merely confirm the first principle of rational action. Association and cooperation with others always benefit everyone involved more than had each remained in isolation. Surely lifeboat economics holds no water.

The secret of prosperity, then, lies in simply creating an environment that will encourage the greatest accumulation of capital and productivity. Western civilizations led the way in prosperity not because of superior intelligence, strength, or skills. It was solely the result of the ideas that were embraced there; the result of an economic and social order that fostered higher standards of living—the free market and division of labor.

Therefore, only in unfree countries are poverty and overpopulation primary concerns. It is a direct result of their ideology translated into the policies their governments adopt. Radical intervention weakens the incentive to work, save, and be productive. Such policies do not promote capital accumulation, but pave the road to poverty and despair. As one writer put it, "like a horse and carriage, socialism and hunger inevitably go together."[2]

But since the wealth of a nation is exclusively a product of thought and ideas, there is just cause for hope. It means that higher standards of living are open to all countries. People simply must choose them. This calls for no less than a complete disavowal of the social planning philosophy—its premises and corollaries. Yes, any poverty-stricken, overpopulated country with the courage to embrace a radical change in ideology can liberate their society from the dogmas of the past that halted their development.

In this light it is simply absurd to attribute poverty on a national level to overpopulation. Such an analysis does not even break the surface of the real problem. Actually, to correct the statist cliché, freedom from want is impossible. Scarcity is a fact of nature that no government law or program can change, certainly not by attacking the proliferation of its citizens. Only one avenue of thought has consistently promoted incentive, creativity, and an unparalleled productive capacity—freedom, which one day may be rediscovered when all else fails.

—KYLE S. SWAN

---

1. James A. Weber, *Grow or Die!* (New Rochelle, New York: Arlington House Publishers, 1977), p. 183, quoted in David C. Huff, "Freedom, Coercion, and Family Size," *The Freeman,* January 1989, p. 27.

2. "The Third Horseman: Thanks to Socialism, Famine Stalks the Earth," *Barron's National Business and Financial Weekly,* December 20, 1965, p. 1, quoted in Rousas J. Rushdoony, *The Myth of Over-Population* (Nutley, New Jersey: The Craig Press, 1969), p. 6.

35

"Isn't government investment necessary for economic prosperity?"

Politicians and government bureaucrats constantly tell us that we need to make "investments" in our future. What they are really advocating by their admonition are various new government programs which are needed to remedy the lack of such projects produced by the private sector of the economy. The investment in these projects is to be accomplished by raising tax dollars or by obligating all citizens to some future burden through debt financing. The proponents for these government projects tell us that we need to invest in education, technology, and infrastructure if we are to have a vibrant, growing economy because the marketplace alone will not provide enough of these things to ensure economic prosperity.

What is the basis of their argument? Typically, advocates for governmental expansion argue that the new programs are needed because there are external benefits to society associated with the proposal being considered. Therefore we hear statements such as "Education benefits everyone," or "The United States must develop new technologies if it is going to compete in the global economy." The one thing that all such statements have in common is a commitment to the notion that an economic problem exists for which government provides the only solution. In reality though, is this notion true?

In most cases the answer is "no." To clarify my position, consider the following example that recently made news in Alabama. The item of interest was the Renaissance Tower built in Florence. This project was financed by a general revenue state bond issue which carried with it an obligation for tax dollars to be used to guarantee bond payments if the project failed to generate sufficient revenues. The project is a completed tower which houses a restaurant at the top. The restaurant overlooks the

130

Tennessee River. The purpose of the project was to increase tourism in the area; but the tower has been a complete failure, and the taxpaying residents of Alabama are holding the bill for ten million dollars. The locals sarcastically refer to the tower as "the restaurant on a stick," and the restaurant—even though it does have a nice view—remains rather empty save a school outing or two.

How did this circumstance arise? Undoubtedly numerous politicians made many eloquent speeches in favor of the proposal. I'm sure they must have argued that the project would generate benefits for all Alabamians. During the political debate over the project, proponents undoubtedly employed such arguments as, "The state must invest in this kind of project if it is going to compete with neighboring states for tourism dollars." Thus, in the proposal stage, the project was to draw people from all over to visit the new landmark. These tourists would then proceed to spend their dollars dining high above the Tennessee River. Furthermore, the proponents of the project also likely argued that once the tourists had arrived in our state to see this monument, they would no doubt stay and visit other locations as well, thereby bringing new revenues to many other businesses around our state.

It is highly unlikely that private investors would have put their money into such a venture voluntarily. They would have viewed such a proposal as a loser only to be attempted by the foolhardy eager to squander their resources. Why then was such a project undertaken? It was political. Once we can force the financial responsibility for our mistakes upon others, it is no longer necessary to be careful about the projects we undertake. We no longer need to ask the serious questions regarding whether or not any particular project will truly pay for itself by generating revenues in excess of the cost of the resources expended to produce it. Rather, egos and selfish special interests take over so that those with the political power squander other people's money for their own thrills. In the end we are left with restaurants on sticks and large tax bills that we must pay. Such expenditures serve to reduce the living standards of those forced to pay for them while raising the living standards of those few politicians which have special interest in the projects or those few individuals who are fortunate enough to be selected to construct the projects.

Examples of government expenditures like this make me nervous every time I hear politicians and bureaucrats share their plans for new projects. I am convinced that these plans can never outperform the marketplace because the individuals making the decision about how to spend and "invest" my money do not value the same things that I value, nor do they value the same things you value. As a result the projects that they will force us to pay for are not likely to be the ones we want. Personally, I do not want some government official making decisions for me. Unfortunately, in the United States today, it appears that we no longer care about the personal freedom to make our own choices. We are, therefore, likely to see many more foolish government projects constructed which squander our resources in the name of investment. Lunch with a view, anyone?

—PAUL A. CLEVELAND

36

"Military spending brings jobs and prosperity."

A young hoodlum, say, heaves a brick through the window of a baker's shop. The shopkeeper runs out furious, but the boy is gone. A crowd gathers, and begins to stare with quiet satisfaction at the gaping hole in the window and the shattered glass over the bread and pies. After a while the crowd feels the need for philosophic reflection. And several of its members are almost certain to remind each other or the baker that, after all, the misfortune has its bright side. It will make business for some glazier. As they begin to think of this, they elaborate upon it. How much does a new plate glass window cost? Three hundred dollars? That will be quite a sum. After all, if windows were never broken, what would happen to the glass business? Then, of course, the thing is endless. The glazier will have $300 more to spend with other merchants, and these in turn will have $300 more to spend with still other merchants, and so *ad infinitum*. The smashed window will go on providing money and employment in ever-widening circles. The logical conclusion from all this would be, if the crowd drew it, that the little hoodlum who threw the brick, far from being a public menace, was a public benefactor.

Now let us take another look. The crowd is at least right in its first conclusion. This little act of vandalism will in the first instance mean more business for some glazier. The glazier will be no more unhappy to learn of the incident than an undertaker to learn of a death. But the shopkeeper will be out $300 that he was planning to spend for a new suit. Because he has had to replace a window, he will have to go without the suit (or some equivalent need or luxury). Instead of having a window and $300 he now has merely a window. Or, as he was planning to buy the suit that very afternoon, instead of having both a window and a suit he must be content with the window and no suit. If we think of him as a part of the community, the community has lost a new suit that might otherwise have come into being, and is just that much poorer.

The glazier's gain of business, in short, is merely the tailor's loss of business. No new "employment" has been added. The people in the crowd were thinking only of two parties to the transaction, the baker and the glazier. They had forgotten the potential third party involved, the tailor. They forgot him precisely because he will not now enter the scene. They will see the new window in the next day or two. They will never see the extra suit, precisely because it will never be made. They see only what is immediately visible to the eye.

So we have finished with the broken window. An elementary fallacy. Anybody, one would think, would be able to avoid it after a few moments' thought. Yet the broken-window fallacy, under a hundred disguises, is the most persistent in the history of economics. It is more rampant now than at any time in the past. It is solemnly reaffirmed every day by great captains of industry, by chambers of commerce, by labor union leaders, by editorial writers and newspaper columnists and radio commentators, by learned statisticians using the most refined techniques, by professors of economics in our best universities. In their various ways they all dilate upon the advantages of destruction.

Though some of them would disdain to say that there are net benefits in small acts of destruction, they see almost endless benefits in enormous acts of destruction. They see "miracles of production" which require a war to achieve. And they see a world made prosperous by an enormous "accumulated" or "backed-up" demand. After World War II in Europe, they joyously counted the houses—the whole cities—that had been leveled to the ground and that "had to be replaced." In America they counted the houses that could not be built during the war, the nylon stockings that could not be supplied, the worn-out automobiles and tires, the obsolescent radios and refrigerators. They brought together formidable totals.

It was merely our old friend, the broken-window fallacy, in new clothing, and grown fat beyond recognition.

—HENRY HAZLITT

37

"Government spending programs create jobs."

One of the most enduring—and pernicious—myths of inter-ventionism is the view that government programs can be counted on to create employment. Who among us has not seen pictures of the smiling politician at a ribbon-cutting ceremony, telling us how proud he is to have sponsored a project involving "thousands of jobs"?

In fact, many of the people out of work are unemployed *because* of government programs, and such programs impoverish the society as a whole. The main point is simply that government programs have to be paid for, and the method of finance is likely to destroy private sector jobs at the same time that the public payroll expands. Since private sector jobs tend to be more produc-tive than the government jobs that replace them, the general wealth of the society is decreased rather than increased.

Consider the ways by which government programs can be financed. The most common method of obtaining funds is taxa-tion. If taxes are levied, the government obtains funds which can be used to employ workers at a project site. But taxpayers will now have less disposable income. They are then likely to buy fewer consumer goods, and employment in the industries produc-ing consumer goods is likely to decline. Taxation of businesses similarly eliminates employment in related private sector indus-tries.

If taxpayers maintain their consumption levels and instead make tax payments out of funds that they otherwise would have saved, the general effect is the same. For if taxpayers reduce their saving, banks and other financial institutions will now have fewer funds to lend out in support of various capital invest-ments—purchases of new equipment, plants, office buildings, etc.—and employment in the industries producing capital goods will decline.

Consider next the possibility that the government could obtain its funds, not by taxation, but by borrowing—running a deficit. In this case, those who lend funds to the government will now have that much less to lend to the private sector. Once again, government employment will go up, but private employment is likely to go down.

Consider finally the possibility that the government could obtain funds by creating new money.Over time spending of the newly created money will cause the prices of goods and services to be bid up. If wages were unaffected by this process, it would be profitable to increase employment permanently because employers would be receiving higher prices for their products, while labor costs would remain the same. Once workers realize that inflation is occurring, however, the situation will change.

Workers will eventually catch on to the fact that inflation is eroding their purchasing power. What seemed like an acceptable wage will no longer buy as much as it did before. It will then take higher wages to attract workers into positions. The stimulus provided to employment by creating money will be gone. Prices and wages will have increased roughly in proportion to the increase in the supply of money, and employment will be little changed from what it otherwise would have been.

In summary, increased government spending cannot be counted on to increase total spending. Instead, government spending and government employment replace private spending and private employment. Socialism replaces capitalism. Productivity declines. And promoting full employment through expansion of the money supply is only an illusion which fades when labor and other costs adjust to the inflation.

If government programs cannot be counted on to increase total employment, why do we continue to hear politicians making the same old claims? Because even if the arguments are fallacious, they have an enduring appeal. The employment at the site of a public works project is visible. Everyone can see that it was the result of deliberate action taken by government officials. Those officials can take credit for the well-being of the workers involved.

By contrast, the reasons for the loss in private employment are less obvious. The people who are out of work may have no idea that they are unemployed because of the actions of politicians who are many miles away. In addition, the full decline in private employment may not occur except after a relatively long period of time.

What can be done? There can be no solution to this problem as long as the political system rewards representatives for showering benefits on their constituents while shifting the costs of programs onto everybody else. A more constructive system would dismantle the many barriers to productive employment that are currently on the books.

Taxes and regulations, for example, mean that it costs an employer far more to hire someone than the amount a worker actually receives in his paycheck; it may cost $20 per hour to employ someone who will take home only $7 per hour. Minimum-wage laws, to cite another example, continue to price lesser-skilled workers out of many jobs. Finally, it is still illegal to be paid for doing certain kinds of work at home—the making of clothes, for example.

Generally speaking, government employment is not a good substitute for private employment, and a ribbon-cutting ceremony is not necessarily a proper occasion for smiles and celebration. How refreshing it would be to see someone crash the party and declare that the emperor has no clothes. No emperor—or public official—can create jobs without at the same time limiting jobs created by private, tax-paying concerns.

—GREGORY B. CHRISTAINSEN

38

"If we had no Social Security many people would go hungry."

Compulsory Social Security has been the law of the land for almost three generations, and many citizens of the United States are now convinced that they couldn't get along without it. To express doubts about the propriety of the program is to invite the question: "Would you let them starve?"

Many Americans are old enough to remember things that happened prior to passage of the Social Security Act in 1935, but where is one of them who ever watched a human being starve? No, we wouldn't "let them starve." So why is it so widely believed that, without Social Security benefit payments, many people would go hungry?

The social security idea is based on the questionable premise that a person's usefulness ends at age 65. He is supposed to be without savings and without capacity to continue to earn his living. If that premise were correct, it would be easy to see how hunger might develop among the aged. If they're really good for nothing, who wants to be bothered to look after the old folks!

Lumping people into groups and jumping to conclusions about each group (that is, people over 65 would go hungry without Social Security) is standard procedure of government planning. A corollary conclusion is that breadwinners under 65 must be compelled by force of law to respect and care for their elders. These conclusions rest on false assumptions made by those having no faith in anyone else as an individual. Their faith is in coercion, and they thus conclude that government holds the only answer to every problem.

To those of little faith, it is necessary to explain again and again and again that government is noncreative and can distribute only what it first taxes away from the productive efforts of individuals. "The people" are—first, last, and always—individuals, some more economically creative than others, but each worthy of respect as a human being. To tax a man's earnings and savings, for other than defensive purposes, is to reduce his capacity and his incentive to care for himself and for others, rendering him part slave to others and thus less than human. On the flip side, he who either volunteers or is forced to look to the taxing power of government for his livelihood is also enslaved and debased.

Slavery has been tried in the United States, unfortunately, and a major reason for its failure is that it was, and is, an unproductive way of life; it lets people go hungry. It also is morally degrading to slave and master alike. Yet, we are being told that without compulsory Social Security taxes upon the young and strong, the oldsters among us would go hungry—perhaps starve; we are invited to try once again a semi-slave system—under benevolent masters, of course. Well, those socialists are dead wrong. Their premises are faulty. Free human beings may be counted upon to care well for themselves and for their fellow men, voluntarily.

What should concern us all is that, *if we persist* under the false premises of the Social Security idea (socialism), many Americans *will* go hungry—not only physically hungry, but morally and spiritually starved as well.

The prime argument against Social Security is in the moral realm. Giving to one individual or group the fruits of the labor of others taken from them by coercion is an immoral procedure, with destructive effect upon the sense of personal responsibility of everyone involved. But there are sufficient reasons for rejecting the program, even from a strictly materialistic point of view:

1. Social Security is not old-age insurance; it is a regressive income tax, the greatest burden of which falls on those earning lower incomes.

2. The so-called Social Security fund of about $1 trillion amounts to nothing more than a bookkeeping entry, showing how much money the federal government has borrowed from itself in the name of Social Security and spent for other purposes.

3. The fact that an individual has paid Social Security taxes all his life does not mean that any of that money has been set aside or invested for his account; if he ever receives Social Secu-

rity benefits, they must come from taxes collected from others (perhaps even from him) at the time.

4. The matching amounts, presumably paid by employers on behalf of individual employees, are in effect paid by the employees either through reduced wages or through higher prices for goods and services.

5. Offering a subsidy to those who retire at age 65 does not provide additional savings for plant and tools and thus create jobs for younger workers; it increases their tax load.

6. A person now entering the Social Security program and earning in excess of $18,250 annually would do better simply by accumulating his contributions over his lifetime—even if the amounts remained uninvested—rather than depending upon the amount of benefits paid by Social Security (as estimated by the American College of Life Underwriters).

—PAUL L. POIROT

39

"We need government to build the infrastructure."

It almost goes without saying that any analysis of government provided infrastructure will find needs outstripping revenues. Whether it be roads, transit systems, airports, dams, canals, ports, or whatever, the government seems to be consistently falling short of demand, running over budget, or misallocating resources.

These failings supply the rationale for repeated tax increases. People who would have enough sense to stop buying defective products or to stop pouring money into an unprofitable business investment, seem resigned to paying higher taxes for public infrastructure. The presumption seems to be that there is no alternative to paying higher taxes.

Well, as long as we are determined to rely upon the government to provide infrastructure, there may well be no alternative to higher taxes. The problem is that the government, unlike the private sector, has little incentive to be efficient in meeting the needs of consumers. Consider the contrasting methods by which government and private sector businesses obtain money.

Government has the power to tax. The legislature can pass a law requiring anyone to pay over to the government a sum of money. The payment is not voluntary. It need not be in exchange for any benefit or service. In fact, one of the guiding principles of taxation is the "ability to pay." The simple fact that a person has some money is sufficient legal grounds for the government to lay claim to it.

Private sector businesses do not have the power to tax. These businesses can offer a product or service in exchange for money. Any payments they receive are voluntary. If consumers are not persuaded that the prospective product or service is worth the asking price, they will not buy it. This means that private sector businesses must earn their money.

These contrasting methods for obtaining money lead to contrasting standards of performance in the delivery of goods and services. Since government need not provide anything in exchange for the money it compels taxpayers to pay, it should not be surprising to find that many taxpayers do not, in fact, receive anything in exchange for their payments.

It is often argued that so-called highway "user taxes" overcome the difficulties associated with tax-financing. Almost everyone has seen the "Your Highway User Taxes at Work" signs that accompany many road construction projects. However, the fact that the targeted taxpayers are drivers rather than everyone doesn't do much to improve the incentives down at the highway department.

Highway user taxes, like other taxes, are thrown into a common pool. Granted, these funds are usually earmarked expressly for highway purposes. However, there is no assurance that the taxes will be used to provide services for those who paid them. Taxes may be "earned" on one road, but the funds used to build another road. The determination of how funds are to be spent is not guided by any need to satisfy customers. The government monopoly running the highway system may choose to ignore consumer demand. Political favoritism may be the key factor in allocating investments from the common pool of tax funds. Drivers cannot take their business (and their tax payments) to competing suppliers.

Involuntary payment and a captive clientele are not conducive to good performance. Imagine the mess we would be in if we attempted to provide food in the same way we have tried to provide the highway system. Instead of everyone buying their own food, everyone would be taxed and politicians and bureaucrats would decide who gets to eat. Would we be surprised to find that favored insiders would be allowed to overeat? Would we be surprised to find that lengthy bureaucratic procedures raised costs and made many wait in long lines? Would we be surprised to find that a lot of food would be improperly prepared or half-baked? The results would be highly unsatisfying. Yet, this is precisely where we find ourselves now with public highways. Poorly conceived "pork-barrel" projects consume an ever growing share of highway tax dollars. Bureaucratic inertia and resistance to innovation leave many urban regions clogged with rush-hour traffic congestion. Maintenance is neglected. Projects typically go over budget. Promised roads cannot be completed before tax funding is exhausted.

There is an alternative. The frustrations with publicly provided roads have stimulated interest in privately provided roads. The major objection to privately provided roads has always been the considerable inconvenience of toll collection processes. Admittedly, having to stop to pay a toll to an attendant or toss a coin into a box would be a nightmare if it had to be applied to every street and highway.

Fortunately, modern technology has come to the rescue. Inexpensive electronic transponders are available for automated toll collection. These credit card-sized devices would make paying for highway use as easy as paying for long distance telephone calls. Vehicles would not have to stop or even slow down to pay tolls. Everything would be handled electronically. Payment would be made monthly via a credit or debit card.

Private provision of infrastructure would greatly improve the incentives for performance. Unlike the tax-funded government system, private sector firms would have to provide a valued service in order to get paid. The existence of multiple private sector infrastructure providers would obtain the advantages of competition for the driving public's patronage. Users of roads would be more apt to receive what they pay for.

We have observed the collapse of socialism in Eastern Europe. We rightfully conclude that attempting to have the government run all the key businesses in the economy is a formula for failure. Why should we expect government control of the business of providing infrastructure in this country to fare any better? Compulsory tax-funded, non-competitive, bureaucratically controlled—are these features that we would expect for efficient production of quality products capable of satisfying customers?

We don't need government to build the infrastructure. In

fact, government involvement is more an impediment than an aid to achieving an efficient infrastructure.

—JOHN SEMMENS

40

"Americans squander their incomes on themselves while public needs are neglected."

The society is affluent, we are told—but affluent only in the private sector, alas! The public sector—meaning the political structure which our society spends half its energy to maintain—starves. Mr. and Mrs. America bounce along in their tail-finned chariot over a bumpy highway—the best road their government can build with the niggardly resources permitted it. They queue up to pay scalper's prices for tickets to the World Series with nary a thought that this indulgence contributes to the non-building of a political housing project in an already overcrowded city. That evening they dine at an expensive restaurant, and government, as a result, lacks the means to supply water for a dam it has just constructed in a drought area. Americans, in short, go in big for private indulgence at the very time when the Crisis, long anticipated by the Certified Thinkers, demands the Opulent State.

Those who advance this line of criticism are perfectly correct on one point: if there is to be an increase in political spending, there must be a consequent decrease in private spending; some people must do without. The well-being of individual persons in any society varies inversely with the money at the disposal of the political class. All money spent by the governing group is taken from private citizens—who otherwise would spend it quite differently on goods of their choice. The state lives on taxes, and taxes are a charge against the economically productive part of society.

The Opulent State, fancied by levelers who criticize the Affluent Society, cannot exist except as a result of massive interference with free choice. To establish it, a society of freely choosing individuals must yield to a society in which the lives of the many are collectively planned and controlled by the few.

The state, in our Affluent Society, already deprives us of fifty percent or more of our substance. Not enough say the critics. How much then? Seventy percent? A hundred? Enough, at any rate, so that no life shall go unplanned if they can help it. This is the ancient error of authoritarianism. The intellectual, from time immemorial, has dreamed up ethical and esthetic standards for the rest of mankind—only to have them ignored. His ideas may be ever so sound, but his efforts to persuade people to embrace them meet with scant success. The masses are too ignorant to know what is good for them, so why not impose the right ideas on them by direct political action? The state is too weak and poor? Well, make it strong and rich, he urges; and it is done. But when the state is strong and rich, it devours the intellectual together with his defenseless ethical and esthetic standards. The state acts from political and power motives, as by its nature it must. It cannot possibly be the means of realizing the dreams of spiritual advance.

Every society devises some public means of protecting its peaceful citizens against the violent action of others, but this is too limiting a role for government to satisfy the censors of the Affluent Society. Such a government cannot legislate morality or enforce egalitarianism. The massive state interference they advocate is designed, they say, to protect the people from the consequences of their own folly, and the way to do this is to pass anti-folly laws to prevent wrong choices.

There are degrees of wisdom, true, and some people are downright foolish. This being the case, a lot of people will live by the rule of "easy come, easy go." They spend their money at the races when the roof needs repair, or they install color TV even though they are still paying on the motor boat. In a free society this is their right! This is part of what it means to be free! The exercise of freedom invariably results in some choices that are unwise or wrong. But, by living with the consequences of his foolish choices a man learns to choose more wisely next time. Trial and error first; then, if he is free, trial and success. But because no man is competent to manage another, persistent error and failure are built-in features of the Opulent State.

—EDMUND A. OPITZ

IV. THE COMPETITIVE PROCESS

41

"Mankind was born for cooperation, not competition."

Opponents of the market economy have long argued against competition because it supposedly pits man against man, when people ought to be working together for the common good. This cliché is riddled with fallacies. The basis of the market economy is trade and exchange, and nothing could be more cooperative. The competitive part of the market is people striving to serve their fellow man better than others. That also promotes the common good.

No society can survive without the institution of exchange. One's personal resources are rarely sufficient for survival, and never enough for what people call the good life. We must rely on others to give us access to their resources as well. This can be done only in two ways: first, by forcing ourselves on others and taking their property (or arranging for a third party, such as the government, to do it for us), and two, by negotiating a voluntary trade. The first option leads to a war of all against all. The second promotes social peace and cooperation. A society based on the second option is capitalistic because people produce and acquire property through contract instead of force.

When trade occurs, one person trades his goods or services for someone else's goods or services. For this to take place, both parties must come to an agreement. Cooperation must occur because if only one party desires a trade, no goods or services change hands. Moreover, each party to the exchange must feel that he will come out ahead. He must place more subjective value on what he has gained than what he has given up. Through a market transaction, then, both parties are made better off. That is how the wealth in society increases.

The introduction of money into this cooperative process only enhances the efficiency of trade. With money, people who want to trade have a common unit that can be traded for other goods at a later date. Everyone desires money because it enhances the ability to cooperate with other people who also want to improve their lot. That is why money is the most valuable commodity in the economy.

When a society allows for peaceful trade, and has an institutional mechanism that enforces contracts, the composite of exchanges in society create the market. The market is a highly complex network that channels resources to the users who most desire them. And the consuming public is in charge of how this process works itself out, because it is the public that all producers must please. Producers must cooperate with their customers so that both sectors can be made better off.

Another form of trade that requires cooperation is the labor contract. When a person offers his skills in service of consumers on the market, a capitalist pays him in anticipation that these skills will bring in more money than they cost to buy through wages and salaries. This kind of trade is essentially no different from the trade between producers and consumers, for it too is based on voluntary agreement and cooperation. The much vaunted "worker-management conflict," then, does not exist in a free market. It is only through laws that create the cartels of workers called unions that conflicts arise, which interrupt the cooperative nature of the labor contract.

Competition is no less important a characteristic of the market. It is this kind of interaction that allows consumers to get better products at lower prices, which is what consumers desire. Producers do not compete with consumers; they compete with other producers in their ability to serve their customers better. No producer can rest on his laurels, because in doing so others will come along to take his place in providing the public what it needs and wants.

Interventionists often complain that producers make excess profits, but it is precisely the existence of competition that makes this impossible over the long run. When profits rise, it signals other producers that they too should be involved in making the profitable good. The introduction of new producers means more bidding for resources, lower prices, and diminished profits for the initial entrepreneur.

Business owners are often thought of as champions of competition, but that is not always a correct assumption. Too often, people in business seek to use the government to lessen competition. Getting politicians to impose import quotas, for example, means that favored businessmen don't have to worry about foreign businessmen making better products and selling them here. Business also tolerates regulations that hinder themselves so long as competitors are hurt more.

When producers, consumers, and laborers are given the freedom to trade, the result is a balance of the forces of cooperation and competition that makes everyone in society better off in the long run. A system of interventionism—or the mixed economy—injures the ability to both cooperate and compete. This leads to waste and inefficiencies and to a lower standard of living. Man was made to both cooperate and compete, and only the free enterprise system makes both possible.

—LLEWELLYN H. ROCKWELL, JR.

42

"Business is entitled to a fair profit."

This is actually a cliché of socialism, but it often goes unchallenged because the business leaders who repeat it are rarely suspected of endorsing ideas with socialistic overtones.

The notion that a business is entitled to a fair profit has no more to commend it than does the claim that workers are entitled to a fair wage, capitalists to a fair rate of interest, stockholders to a fair dividend, landlords to a fair rent, farmers to a fair price for their produce. Profit (or loss), regardless of how big, cannot properly be described as fair or unfair.

To demonstrate why *fair* should not be used to modify *profit* as a right to which someone is entitled, merely imagine a businessman, heedless of the market, persisting in making buggy whips. If no one were willing to exchange dollars for whips, the manufacturer would fail; not only would he have no profit but he would lose his capital to boot. Would you have any feeling of guilt or unfairness for having refused to buy his whips? Most certainly not!

We do not think of ourselves as unfair when we search for bargains. We have no sense of unfairness when employing a competent rather than an incompetent helper, or borrowing money at the lowest rate offered, or paying a low instead of a high rental. The idea of guaranteeing a fair dividend to one who invests in wildcat schemes never enters our heads. When we shop around, our choices cause profits to accrue to some businesses, losses to others. We do not relate these exercises of free choice to fairness or unfairness or consider that anyone's rights have been infringed.

In marketplace parlance, there is no such thing as a right to a "fair" profit. All that any person is entitled to in the market place, whether a business proprietor or wage earner, is what others will offer in willing exchange. This is the way believers in the free market think it should be.

However, when it is claimed that business is entitled to a fair or reasonable profit, the claimers must have something else in mind than what they can obtain in willing exchange. Otherwise, they wouldn't mention the matter.

While the "something else" these businesspeople have in mind is rarely understood in its full implications, it must necessarily mean something other than individual freedom of choice. In short, it must mean the only alternative to freedom of choice: authoritarianism. When the market—freedom in exchange—is cast aside, there remains but one other determinant as to who will get how much of what, namely, government! And when government determines or controls profits, prices, wages, rents, and other aspects of production and exchange, we have socialism, pure and simple.

When "fairness" is demanded as a substitute for what can be obtained in willing exchange, the asker, consciously or not, is insisting on what naturally and logically follows: a planned economy. This means all forms of protectionism, subsidies, maximum hours, minimum wages, acreage allocations, production schedules imposed by the state, rent control, below market interest rates, free lunches, distressed areas designated and financed by governmental confiscation of people's capital, federal urban renewal, state unemployment insurance, Social Security, tax discrimination, inflation, and so on. These measures—socialism—are government's only means of "fairness," and they institutionalize *un*fairness!

The declaration that business is entitled to a fair profit connotes equalitarianism; that is, a coerced evenness in reward to the competent and incompetent alike. From what does this type of thinking stem?

It may very well be a carry-over from the static society which, as in a poker game, can award no gain to anyone without a corresponding loss to someone else. It is to overlook the economics of the free market and its willing exchange where each party to the exchange gains. If each party did not believe he gained, there would be no willing exchange. There couldn't be!

Or, this type of thinking may stem from the labor theory of

value which holds that the worth of a good or service is determined not by individual evaluations but by the amount of effort exerted: if as much effort is used to make a mud pie as to make a mince pie, they are of equal worth! Marx, acting on this theory, evolved his system: in essence, to have the state take from the mince pie makers and give to the mud pie makers. After all, goes the cliché, aren't the mud-pie makers entitled to "a fair profit"?

Assuming the market is free from fraud, violence, misrepresentation, and predation, the economic failure or success of any individual is measured by what he can obtain in willing exchange—fairness being a state of affairs that is presupposed in the assumption. Everyone, according to any moral code I would respect, is entitled to fairness in the sense of no special privilege to anyone and open opportunity for all; no one is entitled to what is implied by a fair price, a fair wage, a fair salary, a fair rent, or a fair profit. In market terms, one is entitled to what others will offer in willing exchange. That is all!

—LEONARD E. READ

43

"We need antitrust laws to prevent monopoly."

All doctrinaire critics of the free-market system accept the idea that the government must enact and enforce antitrust (anti-monopoly) laws. Indeed, even many "conservatives" who claim to support free enterprise are convinced that "competition" must be preserved by vigorous enforcement of the Sherman and Clayton Acts.

Both modern liberals and conservatives are wrong on this issue. Most "monopoly" has nothing to do with the free market; instead, it is directly derived from government power itself. The historical meaning of the term "monopoly" is "a grant of privilege from the state" that prevents competition by law. Most of the business organizations that held "monopoly" positions in eighteenth-century England or twentieth-century America held "franchises" or "certificates of public convenience" that *legally* restricted anyone else from entering their protected market. When Adam Smith spoke critically of "monopoly" in *The Wealth of Nations*, it was precisely *that* sort of monopoly that he condemned.

Business interests often argue that their particular industry requires "protection" from so-called "destructive competition." Historically, the source of most state monopoly privilege has been particular business interests seeking protection from new firms, new products, and new technologies. Clearly the most efficient way to eliminate this sort of "monopoly" and restore a free market is simply to prohibit (or legally abolish) all government restrictions on market entry.

Even if it is conceded that some "monopoly" is created by government, isn't there also a "free market" monopoly problem and, thus, still a need for antitrust policy?

There are several reasons to believe that antitrust law is

unnecessary in a free market. Some business organizations are more successful than others and, as a consequence, tend to earn a high market share. They earn this high share by being more efficient than their rivals, by rapid and risky innovation, and by maximizing the overall subjective welfare of their customers. Yet it makes no sense (from a consumer perspective) to employ antitrust law and attack the very firms that currently maximize consumer welfare!

Some firms might obtain high market share by vigorously cutting prices and some critics would restrict such "predatory" behavior. Yet clearly to restrict such price changes is to restrict the very price "competition" that the critics claim to support. Why must we restrict "competition" in the name of preserving "competition"? Further, it is ultimately the consumers who will decide whether any price reduction is "predatory" or not. If consumers reward the firm that lowers prices (by purchasing more), then *they* decide that "monopoly" (at the moment) is more efficient then some alternative market structure. Again, it would be strange to have antitrust law interfere with an arrangement that the consumers themselves deem most appropriate.

Supporters of antitrust law hold that competitive firms might "collude" in the absence of antitrust law and that such collusion would harm consumers. Certainly firms would be free to share cost information and jointly determine market prices. But whether this behavior "harms" consumers is a serious matter of dispute.

Most cartel agreements, both before and since antitrust law, have been notoriously unsuccessful at achieving any "restraint of trade." New firms can always enter markets and supply the "restricted" output. Moreover, existing cartel members have strong incentives to cheat on the agreement and produce additional output. Most cartel arrangements quickly dissolve well before the antitrust authorities enter upon the scene.

Even cooperative agreements that don't dissolve are not necessarily bad. Firms may be able to achieve substantial efficiencies in production and marketing through information sharing and other joint activities. Some of these efficiencies can be achieved through formal business mergers. But some can be achieved by less formal agreements (of various length and scope) between firms in the same industry. The antitrust laws currently discriminate against such efficiencies by allowing (some) mergers but condemning nearly all cooperative agreements.

The best argument against antitrust law is to examine its actual history. Most of the government cases are against firms that were expanding output and lowering prices. Standard Oil, U.S. Steel, Alcoa, United Shoe Machinery, and IBM, were all indicted in classic antitrust cases. Yet in each and every instance, the firms were expanding production, innovating, and expanding consumer welfare. The private antitrust cases (where one firms sues another) are even worse. Here, at least, there is no pretense that it is the "public interest" that is being protected. In short, antitrust in practice has been a blatant attack on industrial efficiency and consumer choice.

Economics aside, there is even a more important reason for opposing antitrust law. Antitrust laws always interfere with basic individual rights to property. They legally prevent owners of property from using it in some peaceful manner. As Adam Smith noted more than 200 years ago, any law that the state might enact to restrict businessmen from making price agreements must, by its very nature, interfere with "liberty and justice." Smith's insight into the true nature of monopoly and his wisdom concerning the inherent injustice of antitrust legislation is still perfectly valid today.

—D. T. ARMENTANO

44

"Advertising is immoral and wasteful, and debases taste."

It is true of course that a great deal of advertising *is* less than honorable or uplifting. It is also ironic that many of the worst examples of advertising produced each year come from the campaigns of American politicians, the very people that the ideological enemies of the free market seek to make the overlords of the institution of advertising. If the point to this cliché were simply to condemn specific instances of bad advertising, there would be no quarrel. The intent, however, is to plant the seed that the very institution of advertising is wrong or immoral enough to warrant abolishment or control by the morally superior liberals in our society who want to control what we see and read.

The fact is that advertising is an essential part of a free society and a free market system. Claims that it is a morally questionable or taste-abusing practice are guilty of blaming a legitimate practice because of its misuse by some. The same reasoning would abolish the practice of medicine because some use it corruptly or ineptly.

It is important to recognize the essential function advertising serves in a free society. It is a vital source of information for buyers, alerting them to new products or new opportunities. The charge that advertising unfairly passes along unnecessary costs to the consumer results from a failure to grasp an important fact about production costs.

An entrepreneur's job is hardly finished at the moment he has a completed product ready to offer to consumers. It doesn't do much good to produce something and then make it available if consumers are unaware of the nature of the product, what it offers, and the fact that it is now available. If consumers don't recognize their opportunity to acquire the product, it is as if the product does not even exist. Nor is it enough simply to toss out certain pieces of information. People are often busy, inattentive, and distracted. The information should be presented in a way that gets both the attention and the interest of the consumer.

Advertising also insures accessibility to markets by new and thus relatively unknown sellers. Thanks to advertising, it is easier for new sellers to gain entry to the market. It is untrue that advertising increases the cost of the product, a cost that must be absorbed by the supposedly victimized consumer. Advertising usually reduces price.

Advertising should be viewed as a sign of every entrepreneur's justifiable insecurity. Everyday, when he opens for business, he lacks sufficient information to tell him what will happen that day. He is at the mercy of an innumerable number of unpredictable factors. If he's lucky and guesses right, he can make a profit and thus pay his own bills. If he's unlucky or guesses wrong, he will lose. He can never be sure what the market will do to him and his product or service today. Consequently, the advertiser attempts to allay his fears and draw the consumer's attention to his product or service. While we may sometimes not like the form his advertising takes, the institution itself is an indispensable part of a free market. The questionable values frequently observed in some types of advertising reflect as much on the standards of the potential customer as on the character of the advertiser. The blame for questionable advertising falls on the advertising agency, the seller, *and* the consumer.

There is no need to look to government to remedy the alleged problem of advertising. As we know so well, the people who run government are often the worst practitioners of the advertising art. To the extent that large numbers of people are offended or harmed by tasteless advertising, the market system itself contains the resources to bring about change. To the extent that advertising is deceptive and distorts the truth, it is helpful to remember that a genuine market system can only function within a framework of rules that prohibit acts of force, fraud, and theft. But, once again, the most egregious examples of fraud in advertising are the speeches and ads of people running for public office.

—Ronald H. Nash

45

"General Motors is too big."

A competitor of General Motors once gained national attention by claiming we would all be better off if that giant company were broken up by our government. His plan had been endorsed by several important people, including an influential senator who spent much of his time devising ways and means to accomplish the objective.

Apparently, many millions of sincere Americans were and are quite willing to accept the "unselfish" efforts of political activists to save us from the clutches of the world's largest industrial corporation. But before you and I join them, perhaps we should think a bit more deeply into this issue of bigness and the resulting power that General Motors has over us.

As far as I know, there is not even one person in the entire United States who has to buy anything from General Motors. If GM were closed down tomorrow, there would be only a temporary shortage of cars because even an "unselfish" competitor who wants the government to break up General Motors would be happy indeed to double his own production. And so would any of the other domestic producers of automotive vehicles. And, of course, all foreign producers would like nothing better than to triple their shipments of cars to the United States. Similar sources of both domestic and foreign supply also exist for diesel locomotives and the various other products now sold by General Motors.

There is only one reason you now buy any product. You think you are getting the most for your money. Otherwise, obviously, you wouldn't buy it. Thus the only thing which that senator and the GM competitor wished to save you from is your freedom to patronize whomever you choose.

When we consumers voluntarily choose to buy most of our cars from one company, that company necessarily becomes the largest in the industry. We consumers make that decision when we buy the cars. And the more we buy, the bigger that company will grow. The only way the government can stop that is to tell you and me we can't buy from whom we choose. That's what breaking up General Motors means—depriving you and me of freedom to buy what we please from whom we choose and in whatever amounts we can afford.

I do not know nor care why you think a Chevrolet (or whatever) is a good bargain; that's your business, not mine. Personally, I prefer my little non-GM car. My sole concern here is that both of us shall continue to have absolute freedom of choice in the matter.

There can be no freedom of choice, however, except in a free market. For if producers can't produce what they please—and if you and I can't patronize whom we choose—obviously we have all been deprived of freedom of choice. I am astounded at the number of intelligent people who can't understand that simple truism. When you get right down to it, there are only two ways we can ever be deprived of freedom. And both of them involve government in one way or another—either positively by laws against freedom of choice, or negatively by the government's refusal to stop gangsters who interfere with our freedom to choose.

If we consumers think General Motors is too big, too inefficient, or too anything else, we can easily change the situation. All we need do is stop buying GM products. Then the world's largest industrial company will go out of business within 90 days—and we will still have all the cars, trucks, finance companies, and locomotives we want.

That giant corporation has no control over you and me in any way. It can't force us to buy anything. The secret of General Motors' "power" is its remarkable ability to produce what we fickle consumers most want to buy. A decision to stop that would be the perfect example of cutting off one's nose to spite one's face.

In 1911, and again in 1920, powerful General Motors ceased to be the people's choice. In both instances, it almost went bankrupt. Only by reorganizing, bringing in new management, and borrowing large amounts of capital did it manage to stay in business.

Meanwhile, Ford Motor Company had more than 60 percent of the entire automobile market. And "Old Henry" was doing everything he could to get it all. Since the American people happily bought his "rough and ready" Model-T's by the millions, naturally his company became the largest in the industry. Then something happened—we ungrateful consumers began buying Chevrolets and Overlands. And we willingly paid double the price of a Model-T to get those enclosed cars with a new type of gear shift and a self-starter. In due course, Ford Motor Company closed down—and stayed closed until its engineers could produce a car we consumers wanted.

That's the free market and progress. That's also freedom. And if you and I permit senators and GM competitors to "save" us from it, we will no longer be free to choose. We will lose the most effective and beneficial control ever devised—our right to determine with our purchases which company shall grow large and which shall fail. The government will then decide for us. And that, of course, is the opposite of freedom.

—DEAN RUSSELL

46

"The laissez faire of Adam Smith is irrelevant to modern society."

Detractors of free-market economics often claim that competition, while possibly relevant in Adam Smith's day, is not workable now. Because the world is more complicated, society is increasingly urbanized, and corporations are so large and powerful, the "invisible hand" Adam Smith outlined is a quaint and inoperative notion. Competition, they say, cannot be expected to protect consumers from the excesses of the market; government regulation of the marketplace is imperative. To these critics, free-market economics is a capricious and perhaps dangerous anachronism, a framework not to be taken seriously by modern intellectuals. Of course, that some academic economists teach free-market economics is absolutely baffling and infuriating to these elites.

To assess whether Adam Smith is relevant for the modern age, let's first review the model of a free market. This model grew out of Adam Smith's *Wealth of Nations* (1776), and is often used in the contemporary college economics classroom. It is rooted in four basic assumptions: (1) the number of buyers and sellers in the market is "large"; (2) sellers produce a homogenous product; (3) consumers are well informed; and (4) entry and exit of producers in the market are unrestricted.

Among other things, this model implies that when consumers want more of a particular product, sellers comply by bringing more to market. If consumers want products to have certain qualities, producers will provide those attributes in their product. These results are not dependent on producer beneficence, but are an outcome of producers' search for profits in an arena of competition. Critics rarely deny the implications that follow from the above assumptions. Most critics simply assert that the

163

assumptions of a competitive model are less relevant today than they were in 1776. Let's examine each assumption in turn.

Contrary to popular wisdom, there is good reason to believe that the first assumption, a large number of buyers and sellers, is more prevalent today than it was in Smith's era. The reason for this is so obvious it is illusive. The great advances that have been made in communications and transportation have lowered the costs of exchanges between people in distant locations, thereby increasing the scope of the market. Consumers choose from among a larger number of producers today than in Adam Smith's time.

For example, many small-town householders of Smith's time had to rely on the occasional visit of the transient peddler for most of their household wares. Almost all of modern American consumers are within easy driving distance to a shopping mall offering a profusion of choices for household goods beyond the wildest imagination of those in Smith's time. Reductions in transportation costs along with catalogues and television shopping networks bring the world's supply of household goods to the modern consumer. Seen in this light, Adam Smith's competitive market, far from being anachronistic, is prophetic!

The second assumption, that sellers' products are identical, is certainly less true than it was in Smith's day. This, however, in no way reduces the validity of the competitive model but, indeed, enhances it, as a simple example will illustrate.

The roving troubadour of the 1700s was welcome relief to the boredom of small-town life. Although the modern amusement seeker can still find on-stage entertainment, the emergence of television, radio, motion pictures, compact disc players, and VCR's has expanded choices in the entertainment market and has made it more competitive than ever. That these new entertainment forms are not replicas of the troupes of old is hardly relevant.

Consumers today are able to choose not only from among more producers, but from more types of goods in almost every aspect of their life than could consumers in Adam Smith's day. The availability of ready substitutes, not the uniformity of producer's output, drives the competitive marketplace.

The third assumption requires that consumers be well informed. Increased competition in both number and type of sellers tends to enhance consumer information. Having twenty different automobile dealers to choose from allows consumers to make more discerning decisions than when the village wagonmaker was the only seller within a day's journey. But in addition, information is simply more accessible today than it was 200 years ago. The intervening years have seen many innovations: low-cost mailing, mass production of books, telephone, electronic mail, a proliferation of consumer-interest magazines, fax machines, and so on, all of which lower the cost and increase the reliability of information. Because consumers are more informed than ever before, the competitive model of Adam Smith is more *apropos* than ever.

The fourth assumption (that entry and exit are unrestricted) is an area where conditions are possibly confounded. Smith argued that legal restriction to competition should be eliminated. He recognized allowing new firms to enter the market was crucial for the benefits of competition to accrue to society. Two hundred years later governments still actively inhibit competition by licensing arrangements, antitrust laws, excessive regulation, international trade restrictions, and a host of other measures that prevent potential competitors from entering the market. Interestingly, these restrictions on market entry and exit are frequently advocated by the same people who argue that the market model is irrelevant. Such restrictions, however, kept society from reaping the full benefits of a free market in Smith's time just as they do today. The fault, however, is neither in market forces nor in the modern age as such. Market restrictions result from a flawed philosophy of government intervention that was as pervasive in fashionable intellectual circles 200 years ago as it is today.

—CECIL E. BOHANON AND JAMES E. McCLURE

47

"Speculation should be outlawed."

In 1869 John Fiske, noted American philosopher, scholar and literary critic, wrote an essay on "The Famine of 1770 in Bengal" *(The Unseen World and Other Essays,* Boston: Houghton Mifflin, 1876), pointing out that a major reason for the severity of the famine was the prevailing law prohibiting all speculation in rice. The following is excerpted from that essay.

This disastrous piece of legislation was due to the universal prevalence of a prejudice from which so-called enlightened communities are not yet wholly free. It is even now customary to heap abuse upon those persons who in a season of scarcity, when prices are rapidly rising, buy up the "necessaries of life," thereby still increasing for a time the cost of living. Such persons are commonly assailed with specious generalities to the effect that they are enemies of society. People whose only ideas are "moral ideas" regard them as heartless sharpers who fatten upon the misery of their fellow creatures. And it is sometimes hinted that such "practices" ought to be stopped by legislation.

Now, so far is this prejudice, which is a very old one, from being justified by facts, that, instead of being an evil, speculation in breadstuffs and other necessaries is one of the chief agencies by which in modern times and civilized countries a real famine is rendered almost impossible. This natural monopoly operates in two ways. In the first place, by raising prices, it checks consumption, putting every one on shorter allowance until the season of scarcity is over, and thus prevents the scarcity from growing into famine. In the second place, by raising prices, it stimulates importation from those localities where abundance reigns and prices are low. It thus in the long run does much to equalize the pressure of a time of dearth and diminish those extreme oscillations of prices which interfere with the even, healthy

166

course of trade. A government which, in a season of high prices, does anything to check such speculation, acts about as sagely as the skipper of a wrecked vessel who should refuse to put his crew upon half rations. The turning point of the great Dutch Revolution, so far as it concerned the provinces which now constitute Belgium, was the famous siege and capture of Antwerp by Alexander Farnese, Duke of Parma. The siege was a long one, and the resistance obstinate, and the city would probably not have been captured if famine had not come to the assistance of the besiegers. It is interesting, therefore, to inquire what steps the civic authorities had taken to prevent such a calamity. They knew that the struggle before them was likely to be the life-and-death struggle of the Southern Netherlands; they knew that there was risk of their being surrounded so that relief from without would be impossible; they knew that their assailant was one of the most astute and unconquerable of men, by far the greatest general of the sixteenth century.

Therefore they proceeded to do just what our Republican Congress, under such circumstances, would probably have done, and just what the *New York Tribune*, if it had existed in those days, would have advised them to do. Finding that sundry speculators were accumulating and hoarding up provisions in anticipation of a season of high prices, they hastily decided, first of all to put a stop to such "selfish iniquity." In their eyes the great thing to be done was to make things cheap. They therefore affixed a very low maximum price to everything which could be eaten, and prescribed severe penalties for all who should attempt to take more than the sum by law decreed. If a baker refused to sell his bread for a price which would have been adequate only in a time of great plenty, his shop was to be broken open, and his loaves distributed among the populace. The consequences of this idiotic policy were twofold.

In the first place, the enforced lowness of prices prevented any breadstuffs or other provisions from being brought into the city. It was a long time before Farnese succeeded in so blockading the Scheldt [River] as to prevent ships laden with eatables from coming in below. Corn and preserved meats might have been hurried by thousands of tons into the beleaguered city. Friendly Dutch vessels, freighted with abundance, were waiting at the mouth of the river. But all to no purpose. No merchant would expose his valuable ship, with its cargo, to the risk of being sunk by Farnese's batteries, merely for the sake of finding a market no better than a hundred others which could be entered without incurring danger. No doubt if the merchants of Holland had followed out the maxim *Vivre pour autrui* [Live for others], they would have braved ruin and destruction rather than behold their neighbors of Antwerp enslaved.

No doubt if they could have risen to a broad philosophic view of the future interests of the Netherlands, they would have seen that Antwerp must be saved, no matter if some of them were to lose money by it. But men do not yet sacrifice themselves for their fellows, nor do they as a rule look far beyond the present moment and its emergencies. And the business of government is to legislate for men as they are, not as it is supposed they ought to be. If provisions had brought a high price in Antwerp, they would have been carried thither. As it was, the city, by its own stupidity, blockaded itself far more effectually than Farnese could have done it.

In the second place, the enforced lowness of prices prevented any general retrenchment on the part of the citizens. Nobody felt it necessary to economize. Every one bought as much bread, and ate it as freely, as if the government by insuring its cheapness had insured its abundance. So the city lived in high spirits and in gleeful defiance of its besiegers, until all at once provisions gave out, and the government had to step in again to palliate the distress which it had wrought. It constituted itself quartermaster-general to the community, and doled out stinted rations alike to rich and poor, with that stern democratic impartiality peculiar to times of mortal peril. But this served only, like most artificial palliatives, to lengthen out the misery. At the time of the surrender, not a loaf of bread could be obtained for love or money.

—JOHN FISKE

V. LABOR AND EMPLOYMENT

48

"Government should create and protect jobs."

"Jobilism" is back. Jobilism is the modern-day public-policy philosophy that mistakenly makes the count of jobs the key measure of a country's economic success or failure.

This policy philosophy gained political stature in the early 1980s as the Democrats repeatedly sought to spur economic recovery with massive federal jobs programs, all designed to increase government largess under the guise of jobs. Jobilism's political position was fortified when the Reagan Administration began measuring the success of its domestic policies by the growth in jobs. Jobilism faded from public policy discussions as the recovery continued into 1990.

The return of jobilism was heralded by former President George Bush when he characterized his domestic economic program as having three pillars: "Jobs, jobs, jobs," although he was always vague on how he was going to do it. Now, President Bill Clinton has a "plan" to protect and create "high-paying" middle-class jobs, curiously, by increasing federal taxes on just about everyone (but especially the "rich," who are responsible for much of the country's investment), expanding workplace federal mandates, and enhancing union powers to drive up American labor costs. The jobs at stake are almost always those that represent political clout.

The ongoing policy debate under the banner of jobilism is as misguided as was its intellectual precursor, mercantilism, popular three centuries ago. Under mercantilism, the key measure of national wealth was gold. The bigger the national gold hoard, the greater the national power and pride, or so the public was taught. Mercantilism was found to be intellectually bankrupt when it was discovered that gold was an artificial national icon, representing valuable, productive resources that could have been used to expand national production had they not been traded away for glitter that had to be buried in a vault to be protected.

Jobs are not a form of national gold that should be saved and protected. Indeed, they should be destroyed as rapidly as possible because they represent constraints on what else the economy can do to expand income and wealth.

Economic progress and job destruction necessarily go hand in hand. Jobs are destroyed when a better mousetrap or computer program is developed or when work is made obsolete with the advent of a new, more efficient, or cheaper means of production. No country can afford an idle population. By the same token, no country can afford to treat jobs as so many ounces of gold that must be counted, stored, and protected from obsolescence.

Job creation (and protection) is a favored goal of our political leaders because it appeals to existing political interests and is seductively misleading and counter-productive. It is also one of the easiest goals to achieve. To create or protect jobs, all Congress has to do is obstruct progress, by killing off or retarding opportunities for renewal of American competitiveness and entrepreneurial spirit.

Job destruction is shunned as a national policy goal not only because it appears openly hard-hearted (which, paradoxically, it is not), but also because job destruction is so very difficult to achieve. Job destruction requires ingenuity, creativity, and the guts to take a few risks that others will not take. It requires intensive study, hard work, and detailed knowledge of the multitude of economic circumstances that can only be known by real people in the workaday hinterlands, not Washington, D.C. It requires, in short, the types of skills and understandings that are generally absent in political circles.

Over the past several years, our political leaders and policy pundits have called for renewal of "American competitiveness." They don't seem to get the underlying message in the country's observed failures in domestic and international markets: *America had been destroying too few jobs*. Moreover, they have not yet realized that renewed competitiveness must be built on a commitment to progress, which, in general terms, means relying on people outside of the political capitals to use to their best advantage the knowledge of circumstances that is only known to them.

Revitalized competitiveness mandates a willingness to replace much that is old with much that is new. It requires widespread (not wanton) job destruction, nothing more nor less. And it necessitates that we begin to view, for example, the loss of hundreds of thousands of jobs in the textile industry over the past two decades as a measure of the success of the industry in dramatically improving productivity and maintaining its status as world class. Similarly, the current wave of job destruction in the service industry must be seen as mirroring the long-awaited productivity gains from the computerization of many services.

When renowned Harvard economist Joseph Schumpeter lauded the market as a system of "creative destruction" fifty-some years ago, he meant *every* word. Destruction—specifically, job destruction—is endemic to any economic system that is creative. What we need in this country is more job destruction, not less—because we need more, not less, creativity.

The Communist states of Eastern Europe and the former Soviet Union were good at job creation. Not surprisingly, they ended up with more jobs to do than they had people to fill them. In the process of creating so many jobs, they destroyed not only economic progress, but also the morale of the people to work for a living and to get on with the arduous task of making obsolete the jobs they have.

There is a valuable lesson to be learned from the fate of those countries and the jobs policies their leaders followed for too long. We can only hope that the politicians will soon level with the American electorate on what meaningful progress requires.

—RICHARD B. McKENZIE

This essay was adapted, with permission, from an article which appeared in The Wall Street Journal.

49

"The government must guarantee a job for everyone."

The funny and quite popular motion picture *Dave* featured a political fantasy that fully subscribed to this cliché. The look-alike who took over after the real president, who was a philandering fraud, took ill endears himself to everyone (including, we may presume, the viewing audience) by announcing that the government will henceforth have as its central task to guarantee a job for everyone. How? Nobody knows—because it is impossible to do as well as vicious to try.

As the writers of *Dave* and purveyors of this cliché would have it, no one who is against government spending and for vetoing handouts or public works programs can be compassionate. But the first thing to remember is that, on the contrary, compassion is the trait of those who hand out *their own* wealth to the needy, not those who hand out *other people's*. Even if it were possible by way of government to guarantee everyone a job, it would not amount to something compassionate. It would be a case of stealing from Peter to provide for Paul.

Secondly, in fact government hasn't the faintest idea as to how to make a job for anyone—administrators of the government invent nothing, start no enterprise, discover no new laws of nature to put to use—zilch. Government cannot make jobs—all it can do is take money from some (which kills off jobs), extract funds to support itself (which keeps politicians and bureaucrats well fed), and give a little back in some public works program or subsidy (which restores some of the lost jobs, but only for as long as public funding continues since there was likely no market demand for such work in the first place).

No one who introduces, helps pass, or signs a bill for government to hand out money creates any jobs. Yet this kind of fantasy politics is being supported by nearly all the dizzy dreamers

174

in the world, including many writers, actors, and producers in Hollywood. It is no wonder that the damage is nearly impossible to control. The plain, axiomatic fact is that from nothing, nothing can be produced.

But perhaps the most important point overlooked by those who embark on trying to get people jobs by means of government programs is that even the attempt to guarantee a job to people violates a most precious principle of human interaction. Jobs are, after all, work one can do because others go into the market to obtain the results of the work. The job of the writer exists so long as there are those who want to read; the job of the engineer exists by virtue of some people's willingness to pay for new designs of equipment or computers. Waiters are employed because people patronize restaurants. Company executives have jobs because people want to invest in a firm's business and want someone to run the business.

In short, jobs only exist because people want to and can obtain the results of those jobs. But imagine what it would take to guarantee jobs. The waiter who works in the French restaurant which is no longer patronized by potential customers will lose his or her job unless, of course, the customers are coerced to eat in the French eatery, never mind their wants, choices, capacity to pay, and so on. The makers of typewriters will have a job only if customers are not permitted to purchase computers but are forced to keep using the old-fashioned instrument. There would be no auto workers today had consumers been forced to save the jobs of the buggy industry. Even attempting to guarantee jobs for these people involves establishing universal involuntary servitude—unwilling customers purchasing goods and services they would not purchase if they were not forced to by the guarantor.

So not only is it impossible for the government to guarantee jobs because governments do not make anything and because governments haven't learned to turn nothing into something, but also it is morally vicious for governments to try to make jobs—it entails conscription of customers for the jobs that it would attempt to guarantee. Taxing them really amounts to the same thing, of course, namely, forced labor or involuntary servitude.

No doubt, those who lose jobs are often in dire straits, sometimes because they failed to prepare for hard times, sometimes because they misjudged what people will want to purchase, and at other times simply because people have embraced some fad that has crowded out their possibly superior product or service. The loss of a job need by no means be an leveling experience, although sometimes that's what it takes to motivate some persons to upgrade their careers, to get out of a rut.

But in any case, whether the choice of the potential buyer was sound or unsound, what is crucial is that trying to force him or her to purchase is exactly the same as forcing the person to work at some job he or she does not want. It involves involuntary servitude, the unwilling performance of tasks to keep others employed.

Finally, even the futile effort to guarantee jobs for all can have the devastating side effect of acclimating people to the notion that government can solve their problems—i.e., that those individuals in their society who have the authority to wield lawful force can best solve our various problems, so we need do nothing much in order to make progress in our lives.

Some years back I looked up an old friend from Budapest who had settled in Montreal. During the visit he asked me to lend some help to his daughter who was 13 years old and doing badly in school. I knew nothing of the child so all I could do is ask, "Why are you doing so badly in school?" She answered, "I am not interested in what they teach me." So, trying to get a handle on the situation, I pressed on: "How will you succeed at living reasonably well without an education?" The child's reply stunned me: "The government will take care of me." The Canadian, British, Swedish, and, not to forget, Soviet welfare states, which have been in far worse shape than the United States, have not only foisted a weak system on their citizens but prepared them for a lifetime of dependence.

Government cannot guarantee jobs. Its attempts to do so threaten us with involuntary servitude and the demoralizing impact of becoming dependent on a myth of getting something out of nothing.

—TIBOR R. MACHAN

50

"Every employee is entitled to a fair wage."

Being "fair" in the determination of wages is an axiom of good management, a "demand" of union leaders. But at the risk of appearing to be "unfair," let us examine the notion that "every employee is *entitled* to a fair wage."

Suppose, for instance, that a man is employed to produce ordinary aluminum measuring cups. Working with only such hand tools as a hammer and cutting shears, he is able to cut and form two cups an hour—16 in an 8 hour day; and these are hardly the streamlined models which grace a modern kitchen.

A block away, a man using a press, dies, and other mass production equipment turns out high quality aluminum measuring cups at a rate of 320 a day. What is a "fair wage" in each of these plants? Is it the same for the highly skilled man who forms cups with hand tools as for the man who mass produces them at 20 times the first man's rate?

If the advocate of "fair wages" begins with the assumption that eight dollars an hour is a fair wage for the man using hand tools, it is clear that each cup must sell for no less than four dollars—just to cover labor costs. But charging any such price for handmade cups obviously is out of the question if superior cups from the nearby competing plant are offered, shall we say, at one dollar each.

If consumer choice is to be a determinant of the price of cups, then it appears that this hand craftsman—for the job he is doing—may not be able to earn more than a couple of dollars an hour. Were he to insist on more from his employer, he'd obviously price himself out of that job. This, of course, would leave him the alternative of seeking employment elsewhere—possibly at the more highly mechanized plant in the next block.

Within an economy of open competition, it seems reasonable that any person should be free to choose from among various

available employment opportunities. But if all interested parties
—including employers and consumers—are to be equally free to
choose, then it is clear that the employee may not arbitrarily set
his own "fair wage" and demand a job at that rate. Nor can an
employer arbitrarily maintain for an appreciable time a "fair
wage" that is much higher or lower than is indicated by the
competitive situation. If he tries to pay more than is justified by
the productivity of his workers and tools, he must face bankruptcy. And if he pays much below the prevailing level in that
area, his workers will quit.

If freedom of choice is to be respected, then the only fair wage
is one determined by the purely voluntary process of competitive
bargaining in a free market.

One may deplore the plight of the poor fellow in the un-
mechanized plant; how will he use his skills? Indeed, it is unfortunate if he lacks the modern equipment to make his efforts
most productive. But to suggest that he should receive more than
is reflected in the price consumers will voluntarily pay for cups
is to reject the ideal of competitive private enterprise, to turn
away from freedom and to accept Marxian philosophy. That
would be saying in effect that *need,* and not productivity or consumers' choice, determines wages; and that once a person starts
work at a certain job, he has a vested interest in that job and a
right to receive more than he can earn in it. We may decry the
decisions of consumers in the marketplace if they reject the high-
priced product of the hand-skilled employee, but the only substitute arrangement is to deny the consumer's right of choice by
law, forcing him or some other taxpayer to subsidize the particular craftsman. No one can have a *right* to such an arbitrary
"fair wage," unless someone else is *compelled to pay it.*

So a "fair wage" is not something static which anyone can
pick out of the air or arbitrarily define. It is not a fixed amount
for every employee, but a figure that varies with each person and
situation. The physical strength and technical skill of the employee may be highly important factors; but from this simple
illustration it is clear that neither these, nor the man's *needs,*
can be the sole determinants of wages. The most important single factor—assuming consumers' choice of this product—is productivity which proceeds from investment in tools. When this

truth is recognized, it wholly displaces the fallacious idea of a right to a "fair wage."

—C. W. ANDERSON

51

"Women are at a disadvantage in the marketplace."

We live in an exciting time for women. More than ever before, they are achieving their goals, from fulfillment in the home to the apex in business, the sciences, and the professions, and many successfully combine family and careers.

The denial of legal rights, along with the force of tradition, once made virtual slaves of women. They couldn't own property, couldn't enter the professions, couldn't vote, and sometimes weren't even accountable for their offenses against others, which were, instead, referred to their "owners." Categorical discrimination was institutionalized by the power of law, and reflected the prejudice, if not arrogance, of the lawmakers. Through the ages, this prejudice resulted in human tragedies, injuring the self-image and mental health of those affected, and depriving the human race of almost half the available, but untapped, human creativity.

One of the avenues of advancement for victims of discrimination has been the opportunity for them to form their own businesses and institutions when they were barred from the existing ones. Black- and Jewish-owned and operated colleges, hospitals, and businesses come to mind, such as Tuskegee Institute in Alabama, Provident Hospital in Chicago, Brandeis University in Massachusetts, and Johnson Enterprises in Chicago, to name a few. Ironically, or perhaps it would be more accurate to say "predictably," many of these have failed even though they've received government help, while others have been enormously successful far beyond the dreams of their founders, without ever asking for or receiving state aid. In recent years women, too, have begun to take this route. The Women's Bank in Denver,

Colorado, is an example of a women-founded and operated institution, in contrast to the women's colleges of the last century, which were primarily founded and operated by men.

Opportunities still exist for entrepreneurs, and women are no longer barred from the marketplace. However, the marketplace is less accessible and less free than it once was because of government's expanded role in the economy, and women, as well as men, are the victims. The hindrances are well known to freedom champions: oppressively high taxes, excessive regulation, and restrictive licensing, among others. Economic freedom is surely womankind's greatest need.

Through necessity, women have been brilliantly resourceful in the face of barriers, and their solutions have been as individual as themselves.

"Individual" is a key word, for it is as individuals that women have gained their greatest successes. History is replete with stories of women who have distinguished themselves in what were for their times unconventional endeavors. The facts of history prove what women can do, individually and in groups.

Those with brains and talent do not necessarily have the stamina, courage, and aggressiveness to forge ahead in the face of discrimination. These are the people who usually turn to political solutions. But, let's consider a few of the reasons why legislation against discrimination creates more problems than it solves.

Affirmative Action is the angry stamp of impatient feet, and a brandished fist that smacks too much of revenge. Affirmative Action stigmatizes women because it gives the sanction of law to the myths about women which have been so damaging to them. It denies that women are capable of competing on an equal basis and therefore, they must have a "handicap," an artificial advantage to make up for what they lack.

Affirmative Action focuses on results rather than on the equal right to compete. It demands that unqualified people be hired if, as in the area of our concern, they happen to be women, while highly qualified candidates for jobs are rejected. In other words, it amounts to reverse discrimination. Men have every reason to feel bitter about laws that favor women, and women should understand that bitterness very well.

Barry R. Gross, who discusses reverse discrimination from a philosophical point of view, succinctly states the essence of the case against reverse discrimination as it applies to blacks. It is, he says, "an attempt to correct one sort of injustice by producing another."[1] He rightly points out that those who are to benefit from such a policy are not the original victims, and those who will suffer from it are not the original perpetrators of the crime. In seeming contradiction, however, Gross views reverse discrimination as an abuse of an otherwise well-intentioned policy. Well-intentioned it undoubtedly is, but surely any policy that mandates a double standard is an abuse in itself.

Finally, and most important, Affirmative Action opposes our national commitment to freedom. Women's place in the United States has seldom been consistent with the principles on which our country was founded, but that's no excuse to continue the hypocrisy. To rectify past wrongs by turning to the quick fix of discriminatory legislation is to flirt with totalitarianism. Ultimately, that means an exploitation that is all-encompassing and unalterable for everyone. As Milton and Rose Friedman have so aptly put it: "A society that puts equality—in the sense of equality of outcome—ahead of freedom will end up with neither equality nor freedom. The use of force to achieve equality will destroy freedom, and the force, introduced for good purposes, will end up in the hands of people who use it to promote their own interests."[2]

Women don't need Affirmative Action, or set-asides, or any of the laws that demand special privileges for them. They're not in their present straits because they've been denied special privileges, but because others have had special privileges over them. Victory gained at the expense of others is no victory at all. Recent gains for women have come about more from the propagation of ideas and a reasoned call for justice than from discriminatory legislation. And yet, at the first signs of progress in human affairs, a clamor arises for laws to speed the process.

Passing laws which favor women, however, has not caused, and cannot cause, fully formed female geniuses to erupt spontaneously into being like Hydra's heads.

How ironic, and even tragic, that women have released themselves from bondage to their fathers, brothers, husbands, and sons only to find themselves in bondage to the state. And in the latter, they find common ground with men, for the enemy that stands in the way of both sexes is Congress, and Congress' counterparts on the local scene.

Today, we have thousands of state and federal programs and regulatory agencies, and hundreds of thousands of government workers whose primary responsibility is to tell other Americans—men and women alike—what Congress and state and local governments have said may or may not be done. As a result, we have become polarized into self-seeking factions that, like jealous children, clamor for the attention and favor of an all-powerful parent, pushing their brothers and sisters out of the way as they grab at the apron strings of the state.

How much better for men and women to unite in a fight for freedom instead of fighting each other. Wise women, like wise men, perceive that to the extent that we have become a collectivist society with inefficient and wasteful central planning, we are less free. A look at just a few of the ways in which collectivism adversely affects us, as human beings and as men and women, should convince us that we must not wait until we hit rock bottom before we dig out the root cause of our discontent.

For example, one woman's need for child care is another woman's opportunity. That's a simple truth, until government enters the picture. What could be more efficient and mutually advantageous than for the woman who elects to stay home with her offspring also to take care of the working woman's child for a fee? It's a proven system that is entered into voluntarily by both parties. Everyone is satisfied, or the deal's off. Although there are no statistics available, it is believed that very large numbers of small-scale versions of this system exist. Others who need day care depend on relatives, and some couples work split schedules so that one or the other is always home to care for the children.

Licensed day care centers are another story. Restrictions vary across the country, but their grand design seems to be to put day care entrepreneurs out of business. Typically, permits are costly and complicated; one's house and yard must be a certain size according to the number of children; health and safety rules are unreasonable, exceeding what exists in most homes;

specific routines must be followed; and much more. Regulations multiply, more people are needed to enforce them, day care operators give up, and in many cases children are left home alone in spite of the regulators' declared concern for child welfare. The larger day care centers also find it difficult to hang on under these conditions, and their fees rise accordingly. When this happens, it is then proclaimed that there is a shortage of day care, and we end up with government filling the void. We all know what that means.

In the meantime, the unlicensed homes go underground, perhaps accepting fewer children, which deprives those who need them. There is no need to go into all the ramifications of this familiar series of events common to many of our endeavors, except to answer the frequently expressed fear that unlicensed homes are unsafe. There is no more reason to fear unlicensed homes than licensed ones. Experience has shown that sacrosanct governmental agencies cannot be relied upon to verify the safety of a day care home. Only a caring, responsible parent can do that to his or her own satisfaction, unless we are to become like children ourselves, unable to investigate and make judgments.

Resourceful women who want to start businesses in their homes—computer technicians, seamstresses, caterers, hairdressers, and others—face the same problems as day care operators. If the government finds out about that one-chair beauty shop in your basement, you're doomed.

Humble beginnings have had a way of burgeoning into empires, as Mrs. Fields of Mrs. Fields Cookies can tell you. But, larger capitalists, men and women who've built their enterprises from the ground up, assuming all the risks, responsibilities, hard work, and long hours that are involved, discover sooner or later that they're not operating profit-making enterprises for themselves, their employees, and stockholders so much as they have become an arm of the government, and are operating social agencies to promote the general welfare. They must serve as the government's accountants and tax collectors, not only contributing monetarily to their employees' Social Security, but also taking care of the paperwork at their own expense. They must contend with OSHA, EPA, DOE, FTC, ICC, and on and on endlessly in a veritable minefield.

Economic freedom is the crux of the matter. Assure economic freedom for women, and with brains, hard work, determination, and imagination women will catch up. But, not overnight. Their victories will be the building blocks of reform, leading to a renovation in many hearts and minds that will gradually overcome the prejudices of centuries.

Women will become tough enough to face discrimination with the dignity and courage of free people who know their own worth. They will face the fact that some people will never give up their prejudices, but they will know that the power of discrimination to injure is lessened in a climate of freedom. And, they will understand that we can't all be leaders and successful entrepreneurs no matter how smart we are. These are facts of life for men as well.

Working in a market that is free, career women will more easily find safe, dependable, affordable child care; the equal pay for equal work situation will resolve itself; and imbalances according to race, sex, and national origin will tend to adjust. Women will become captains of industry and leaders in the sciences.

Making choices and assuming responsibility for our lives, while often difficult, are the privileges of a free people. The outcomes of our choices, good or bad, enable us to grow and mature. We become stronger and wiser because of them.

Women have everything to gain from focusing their efforts on reforms that emphasize freedom, rather than on legislation that restricts others. Why should they waste their energies and resources calling upon Congress to rectify real or imagined wrongs when their precious liberty is at stake?

—JEAN L. BAKER

1. Barry R. Gross, *Discrimination in Reverse: Is Turnabout Fair Play?* (New York: New York University Press, 1978), p. 93.

2. Milton and Rose Friedman, *Free to Choose* (New York: Harcourt Brace Jovanovich, 1980), p. 148.

52

"Employees often lack reserves and are subject to 'exploitation' by capitalist employers."

It is frequently argued that an employee is at a bargaining disadvantage when he seeks a favorable employment contract because he has less of a reserve to draw upon than does an employer. It is said that the employee needs bread for his family's supper, whereas the employer needs nothing more urgent than a new yacht. The effect of such dramatization is to draw attention from the subject of the employer-employee relationship. The employee wants the use of tools and managerial services, and the employer wants the worker's services so that together they may create something useful in exchange for bread, yachts, or whatever else either of them may choose to buy with his part of the product.

It is true that some employees have little except their weekly wages as a buffer against bill collectors. And if the loss of a week's wages is that serious to an individual, it may be a sign of insufficient personal planning or, for some other reason, a preference against trying to make a living by self-employment. Thus, a worker is in this sense dependent upon job opportunities created by others. But in a competitive society, a person is not bound to continue working for others, nor is he bound to depend upon any one employer for an opportunity to work. Some employees, of course, prefer not to change jobs; free men have that choice. Unless competition has been strangled by coercive intervention, employers will be competing against one another for the productive services of employees. This competition between employers for an employee's productive capacity is the thing that constitutes the employee's reserve, just as the reserve value of capital depends upon the competition for the use of that capital.

Compare, for a moment, the dollar value of an employee's

reserve with a reserve fund of capital. For instance, let us assume that a person finds regular employment for a period of forty years at an average weekly wage of $600. For a nonworking person to draw a comparable income from a trust fund—assuming that it earns interest at the rate of 4 percent and that the principal also is to be used up over the period of forty years—an original capital investment of over $600,000 would be required. The fact is that a person who is willing and able to work does have a kind of reserve—in a sense, a better reserve than is available to the man who has nothing except money or capital. Robinson Crusoe could have salvaged the ship's silver, but as a nonworking capitalist, he would have starved. According to the story, he saved his life by digging into his reserve capacity to work.

This same principle applies in our own kind of a complex society where each of us depends more or less upon exchange for his livelihood. If a man owns a million dollars, yet refuses to offer it in trade, he may go hungry, just as an employee may be faced with hunger if he refuses to turn his services to productive use. The market does not automatically guarantee subsistence to those who stop producing and trading while waiting for a better opportunity to present itself. An employee who chooses not to work may properly complain that he has no other means of support, but he ought to confine his complaint to the person who is solely responsible for his sad plight—himself. No one else has any right to make him work, nor any moral obligation to support him in his voluntary idleness.

The employee who wants to sit until an employer comes forth with a more attractive job offer may say that he doesn't have the reserve to enforce his demand, but what he means is that he doesn't have control over other employees who are willing to accept the jobs which are offered.

The true nature of the employer-employee relationship may be understood by those who see that individuals are involved—two individuals—each of whom owns and controls something of value. Their bargaining is to determine a satisfactory exchange rate for what each has voluntarily offered.

The employee is an individual who has a right to offer his services for exchange—a right which is or ought to be recognized by the employer. Labor, thus voluntarily offered by any person, is a form of property—his property—and he may offer it as a marketable commodity. If a man voluntarily offers his services for sale, that doesn't make him a slave. It is simply an expression of his right to his own life.

—PAUL L. POIROT

53

"Temporary workers are bad for the economy."

Interventionists say that people who work for temporary employment firms, and the businesses that hire them, are harming the economy. The truth is the opposite. Temporary employment contracts are good for business and for workers, especially when the alternative is unemployment.

In a free-enterprise economy, employers prefer to keep employees on a full-time basis because this is an economical arrangement. But when labor costs rise, employers may not be able to hire full-time employees. Seasonal changes in production schedules and a variety of interventions in the market make the temporary employment contract an essential part of modern business life.

Temporary jobs save on search costs for employees. If an employee needs a job quickly, he is spared the cost of searching for a permanent position and instead lets a labor-entrepreneur discover useful places for him to work. The business also saves on search costs. Instead of placing ads, he can call up an agency and get a temp right away.

Between 1982 and 1990, this kind of mutually beneficial exchange made the market for temporary employees grow ten times faster than overall employment. In 1992, 20 million people worked as temporaries, and more than 90 percent of firms in the United States used temporary employees.

One reason the temp market has grown so fast is the rising labor costs imposed by intervention. In the United States, employment decisions to hire or not hire, to promote or not promote, or to retain or to fire are second-guessed by bureaucrats. The temporary work industry allows businesses to avoid this kind of illegitimate scrutiny. If business had more autonomy, there would be less need for temporary agencies. It's no accident that the first modern agency, Kelly Girls, was founded in response to the heavy labor controls of the New Deal and World War II.

In the beginning, temps served a relatively limited market. The agency's phone rang when an employee got sick or an odd job needed to be done. Today they serve as essential support staff because they help avoid the costs imposed by government intervention. Even simple interventions like overtime rules have fueled the market; for decades, hiring temps has proven more effective than paying overtime to regular employees.

Businesses are willing to pay more per hour for temps than for full-timers because, in return, they get what ought always to be the case: the freedom to hire and fire.

The main opponents of temps are labor unions, who do not like the competition that temps give to their members. In many social democracies—Sweden, Greece, and Spain, for example—unions have succeeded in placing restrictions on the market. Laws mandate that temp employment must be full-time and include benefits that government forces businesses to provide.

It is to be expected that people bent on centrally controlling the economy would oppose the temp market. They portray it as a remnant of the Industrial Revolution, when employees were supposedly exploited. These people place a higher value on permanency rather than freedom. But as Soviet citizens learned, that is a bad bargain. The temporary market, far from being harmful, is a valuable and essential tool for avoiding the horrible consequences of the mixed economy.

—LLEWELLYN H. ROCKWELL, JR.

54

"Labor is not a commodity."

Throughout most of recorded world history, and even today in some of the more primitive societies, human beings have been and are treated as animals fit only to serve as slaves under the lash of a master.

No civilized person wishes to condone such savagery. A person is not a commodity; each individual is priceless—his worth not to be measured or expressed in dollars, or gold, or things. The laborer as such is not a chattel to be sold and bought, owned and controlled by others. Yet, one frequently hears serious debate as to whether labor is a commodity—whether the services a laborer renders should be priced in market fashion according to the forces of supply and demand.

Apparently, many persons still believe in the old "iron law of wages" propounded in error by some of the earlier economists. It seemed to them, at the dawn of the Industrial Revolution, that wages in general could never rise above that bare level at which wage earners could subsist and reproduce their kind. On the basis of that fallacy, Karl Marx advocated political revolution and compulsory communism as the only chance for workers to receive "the full produce of their labor."

Marx was intelligent enough to recognize that human labor is a scarce factor of production, but he could not or would not see that labor is only one of the costs of production. He seemed to take for granted that somehow someone would accumulate savings and make them available in the form of tools and other capital for use by workers, whether or not a return were allowed on such investment. Nor would Marx recognize that what attracted workers into the factory system was the opportunity they found there to improve their level of living—an opportunity for progress by their own free will and choice. All he could see was that poverty still existed at the middle of the nineteenth century—and he urged revolution.

In reality, though, a free market was, and is, the only escape of workers from feudal poverty and serfdom, their only opportunity for progress. Yet Marx and his followers, by confiscating private property, would destroy the market mechanism for price determination and voluntary exchange, and with it all hope for relief of poverty.

It is the free market and competition among employers for the services of wage earners that make workers independent of arbitrary discretion on the part of the employer. Within broad limits set by what consumers are willing to pay for finished products, a wage earner is free to shop around for the job opportunity of his choice. "What makes the worker a free man is precisely the fact that the employer, under the pressure of the market's price structure, considers labor a commodity, an instrument of earning profits.... Labor is appraised like a commodity not because the entrepreneurs and capitalists are hardhearted and callous, but because they are unconditionally subject to the supremacy of the pitiless consumers."[1]

It is the prospect of profit from employing laborers of given skills that drives businessmen to compete and bid wage rates up to the limit consumers will allow. If present entrepreneurs ignore such profit opportunities, then others will enter the business—perhaps some of the wage earners themselves. To say that labor is a commodity in this situation simply means that the individual wage earner is free to shop around and sell his or her services to the highest bidder—or free to be self-employed or unemployed if no bid is suiting.

In this connection, it should be clear that the worth of every person's service is similarly determined, whether as a strictly unskilled laborer or the most highly skilled artist, teacher, minister, butcher, baker, lawyer, engineer, business executive, or whatever. The value of any work depends upon the highest bid acceptable to the worker in the free market.

The seller of services, of course, is not free to compel consumers to pay prices high enough to cover every conceivable wage demand. But, short of government compulsion in such forms as minimum wage laws, unemployment compensation, and the like, no one has such power over consumers.

So, the wage earners' alternatives are to sell their services at market rates, as other scarce factors of production are priced in a market economy, or to work under the decree of a dictator of one kind or another.

The wage earner himself is no more a commodity than is the farmer whose labor results in a bag of potatoes. But the farmer should be free to sell either his labor or his potatoes; and so should every wage earner be free to offer his services as a commodity. Laborers or others who argue that labor is not a commodity would thus deny freedom of exchange, which is the economic method—and the only one—that assures the laborer true and full value for his services.

—PAUL L. POIROT

1. Ludwig von Mises, *Human Action* (New Haven, Conn.: Yale University Press, 1949), pp. 605–629.

55

"Labor unions are too powerful today, but were useful in the past."

To believe that labor unions actually improve the lot of the working people is to admit that the capitalist economy fails to provide fair wages and decent working conditions. It is to admit that our free economy does not work satisfactorily unless it is "fortified" by union activity and political intervention.

The truth is that the unhampered market economy allocates to every member the undiminished fruits of his labor. It does so in all ages and societies where individual freedom and private property are safeguarded. It did so 1,900 years ago in Rome, in eighteenth-century England, and in nineteenth-century America.

The reason great-grandfather earned $5 a week for 60 hours of labor must be sought in his low productivity, not in the absence of labor unions. The $5 he earned constituted full and fair payment for his productive efforts. The economic principles of the free market, the competition among employers, and a man's mobility and freedom of choice assured him full wages under the given production conditions.

For ages past, wages were low and working conditions primitive because labor productivity was low, machines and tools were primitive, and technology and production methods were crude when compared with today's. If, for any reason, our productivity were to sink back to that of our forebears, our wages, too, would decline to their levels and our workweek would lengthen again no matter what the agents of labor unions would say or do about it.

In a free market economy, labor productivity determines wage rates. As it is the undeniable policy of labor unions to reduce this productivity, they have in fact reduced the wages and working conditions of the masses of people although some privileged members do benefit at the expense of others. This is true especially today when the unions enjoy many legal immunities and vast political powers. And it also was true during the eighteenth and nineteenth centuries when our ancestors labored from dawn to dusk for low wages.

Through union rates, work rules, and a variety of coercive measures, labor unions merely impose higher labor costs on employers. The higher costs reduce the returns on capital and curtail production, which curbs the opportunities for employment. This is why our centers of unionism are also the centers of unemployment.

True enough, the senior union members who happen to keep their jobs do enjoy higher wages. But workers who can no longer find jobs in unionized industries then seek employment in non-unionized activity. This influx and absorption of excess labor, in clerical occupations, for instance, tends to reduce their wages, which accounts for the startling difference between union and nonunion wage rates. It gives rise to the notion that labor unions do benefit the workingmen. In reality, the presence of the non-unionized industries hides the disastrous consequences of union policy by preventing mass unemployment.

The rise of unionism during the past century is a result of the fallacious labor theory of value. It teaches that all profit, rent, and interest had to come out of the "surplus value" unfairly withheld from the workers. Labor unions are the bitter fruit of this erroneous theory, with a long record of violence and harm of workers far more grievous than the alleged evils the unions were supposed to rectify.

—HANS F. SENNHOLZ

56

"Without legislation, we'd still have child labor and sweatshop conditions."

Prevalent in the United States and other industrialized countries is the belief that without governmental intervention, such as wage and hour legislation, child labor laws, and rules concerning working conditions for women, the long hours and grueling conditions of the "sweatshop" would still exist.

The implication is that legislators, in the days of Abraham Lincoln, for instance, were cruel and inconsiderate of the poor—no better than the caricatured factory owners of the times who would employ men and women and children at low wages, long hours, and poor working conditions. Otherwise, had they been humanitarians, legislators of a century ago and earlier would have prohibited child labor, legislated a 40-hour week, and passed other laws to improve working conditions.

But the simple truth is that legislators of past generations in the United States were just as powerless as Mao Tse-tung or Stalin or Castro were to wave a wand of restrictionist legislation and thereby raise the level of living and abolish poverty among the people. If such a miracle were possible, every dictator and every democratically chosen legislator would "push the button" without hesitation.

The reason that women and children no longer find it necessary to work for low wages under poor conditions from dawn to dusk six days or more a week is the same reason that strong healthy men can avoid such onerous labor in a comparatively free industrialized society: surviving and earning a living are made easier through the use of tools and capital accumulated by personal saving and investment.

In fiction, the children of nature may dwell in an earthly paradise; but in the real life of all primitive societies, the men and women and all the children struggle constantly against the threat of starvation. Such agrarian economies support all the people they can, but with high infant mortality and short life spans for all survivors.

When savings can be accumulated, then tools can be made and life's struggle somewhat eased—industrialization begins. And with the growth of savings and tools and production and trade, the population may increase. As incomes rise and medical practices improve, children stand a better chance of survival, and men and women may live longer with less effort. Not that savings are accumulated rapidly or that industrialization occurs overnight; it is a long, slow process. And in its early stages, the surviving women and children are likely to be found improving their chances as best they can by working in factories and "sweatshops." To pass a law prohibiting such effort at that stage of development of the society would simply be to condemn to death a portion of the expanding population. To prohibit child labor in India today would be to condemn millions to starvation.

Once a people have developed habits of industry and thrift, learned to respect life and property, discovered how to invest their savings in creative and productive and profitable enterprise, found the mainspring of human progress—then, and only then, after the fact of industrialization and a prosperous expanding economy, is it possible to enact child labor laws without thereby passing a death sentence.

A wise and honest humanitarian will know that a death sentence lurks behind every minimum-wage law that sets a wage higher than some individual is capable of earning; behind every compulsory 40-hour-week rule that catches a man with a family he can't support except through more than 40 hours of effort; behind every legislated condition of employment that forces some marginal employer into bankruptcy, thus destroying the job opportunities he otherwise afforded; behind every legal action that encourages retirement at age 65.

Rarely in history has there been an advanced industrial society able to afford as much labor legislation and related socialistic measures as constitute the present laws of the United States. Never in history have a people lifted their level of living by passing such laws. Whether the present level of living can be maintained under such laws seems highly improbable, for such restrictions are fundamentally sentences of death—not gifts of life.

Men can take children and women out of "sweatshops" as fast as they can afford it—as fast as better job opportunities develop—as fast as the supply of capital available per worker increases. The only laws necessary for that purpose are those which protect life and private property and thus encourage personal saving and investment.

To believe that labor laws are the cause of improved living and working conditions, rather than an afterthought, leads to more and more "welfare" legislation. And the ultimate effect is not a boon to mankind but a major push back toward barbarism.

—Paul L. Poirot

VI. THE HEALTH-CARE MARKETS

57

"The government should provide free medical care."

If government ever does to health care what it's done to the post office, we'll be well down the road to contracting the national illness known as "socialized medicine." With so many regulations already, it's arguable that we're halfway there now. We'll know we've reached the end of that road when doctors become federal employees and medical care is "free."

What's wrong with socialized medicine? A friend put it more concisely than I've ever heard it before. His name is Dr. Roberto Calderon and he's a radiologist in Managua, Nicaragua.

Dr. Calderon didn't just answer the question with exotic theories. His insight is derived from a decade of experience, from a time when the Marxist Sandinistas ran his country and tried to put the state's bureaucracy in charge of almost everything. He saw socialized medicine from the inside and argues forcefully that "it doesn't work" for the following five reasons:

1. The patient can't choose the doctor. The bureaucratic process makes this important assignment. After all, he who pays the piper must call the tune. There's little room for free choice, for shopping around, for switching from one doctor to another, when medicine has to go by the book. Too much freedom for the patient makes life difficult for the bureaucrats; they have more than enough paperwork to deal with already.

2. The doctor can't choose the patient. Assignments are assignments, doc. Referring a patient to another doctor is an unnecessary complication, an evasion of responsibility, and it messes up the system. Because medical services are made "free" by the state, demand for them goes up, which means that every doctor is probably overbooked and overworked as it is. So the orders are, just get the job done whether you like the patient or are suitable for him or not.

201

3. The doctor gets paid at the end of the month regardless of what or how well he did. Even an eighth-grader understands why this is a prescription for high cost and poor performance. What on Earth is it that makes socialists think that people work harder and better for some faceless bureaucracy than they work for themselves?

4. The patient doesn't get consoled. Dr. Calderon told me that it was common in Sandinista Nicaragua for patients to complain that "the doctor hardly speaks to me; he just says to sit there and be quiet." Ever since the Hippocratic Oath was written, it has been regarded as an important, even vital, role of the healer to provide comfort, reassurance, and a positive mental attitude to the sick. This gets lost when doctors, in effect, become short-order cooks in an uncompetitive, state-run medical soup kitchen.

5. The patient doesn't get well. That's exactly the way Dr. Calderon put it, but he really meant that far too many patients under socialized medicine are "chronically sick" as a direct consequence of the previous four points.

Additionally, socialized medicine inevitably means that the right equipment or medicines or physicians aren't available at all or just aren't at the right place at the right time. People go on waiting lists to have operations performed, and not a few of them die before they ever get to the head of the line.

If Dr. Calderon is right, as experience bears out in Nicaragua and a number of other countries where medicine has become a state monopoly, the only consolation the patient gets from all this is that he won't get a bill in the mail. His taxes and the taxes of everybody else pick up the tab. All this agony is for "free."

All things considered, I think I'd rather find another solution for whatever ails medical care than putting the government in charge of it.

—LAWRENCE W. REED

58

"Health care is 'unique' and should not be left to the market."

There are, within the field of science, laws known to be certain and consistent. For instance, no one disputes the Law of Gravity, and human activity is undertaken with the understanding that "what goes up must come down." Students of elementary economics also learn that there are certain laws governing the marketplace. Economies consistent with these laws have been exceedingly more successful than those that aren't. One only has to look at the failed Soviet economy to observe the consequences of ignoring basic economics.

Even with the fall of the Soviet Union as case in point, some economic experts still insist that the production and distribution of certain goods and services, like health care, falls outside the abilities of the market, and that government action is necessary to correct these deficiencies. This assertion is tantamount to Sir Isaac Newton proclaiming the Law of Gravity applicable to everything except skydiving.

Critics contend that health care is not a commodity and therefore not subject to normal economic laws of competition governing the supply of goods and services. They assert that health care is unique, therefore requiring a significant governmental role to correct for these failings of the market. Daniel Callahan, medical ethicist and author of *What Kind of Life?* agrees, asserting that in health care "... the market cannot efficiently and effectively do what is necessary." He contends that government must be involved in health care, "... if there is to be any sustained drive to meet health care needs in a reasonably efficient way. No more than we can afford to organize private armies and fire brigades can we any longer depend upon private medicine and private financing to take care of us adequately."

Others contend that health care is too fundamental a good to be left to the market. This is a fallacious contention. The same argument can be made for food, clothes, or housing, certainly goods that are extremely important to the well-being of consumers, yet their production and distribution are predominantly left to the market. Food could certainly be judged more important even than health care, yet we've left that industry primarily to the marketplace and have fed not only ourselves but a large share of the world. If such reasoning is to be consistent, then a significant expansion of government regulation into most of the economy should be undertaken on the assertion that government control would be superior. But the failed experiences of those countries that have done precisely that promotes caution in adopting similar policies.

Some health-care experts believe that consumers do not have the ability or knowledge to choose the best quality health-care services for themselves, contributing to another sort of market failure. This amounts to what has been called by some a "plantation mentality," that consumers need to be told what to do by the government or else they will make the wrong choices. Consumers lack a basic understanding of many of the services they contract for, but this does not prevent them from enlisting the aid of an auto mechanic, appliance repairman, or attorney on a daily basis. Consumers compensate for a lack of knowledge by asking friends for recommendations or consulting consumer publications. Most consumers shop around, receiving price quotes and asking what kind of service will be provided. The process is similar with medical care. If a person needs a doctor, he generally asks friends or relatives for a recommendation, or his family doctor if he needs a specialist. If a special procedure or operation is recommended, many patients will obtain a second opinion.

Regardless of the process involved, decisions on health care will ultimately have to be made by someone. In a market system choices are made by the consumer according to his individual needs and desires. In a non-market system, the choices are made by bureaucrats, who would need omnipotent knowledge to understand the specific needs of every consumer. John Goodman and Gerald Musgrave comment on this dilemma in their book *Patient Power,* "If choosing a physician is complex, choosing a politician who will appoint a bureaucrat to choose the physician is even more complex." The farther removed the decision-making process from the consumer, the less likely the appropriate and most effective and efficient choices will be made.

Before labeling aspects of the economy "unique," politicians and government officials must analyze the failures of previous economic controls and the outcome of other countries' interventionary policies. Failure to comprehend basic laws of economics, and live by them, disrupts the provision and consumption of goods and services across the economy, health care included. Adherence to them benefits both the interests of consumers and providers of health care. The economic "laws" that govern the marketplace are consistent, and valid for all areas of the economy—without exception.

—TERREE P. WASLEY

59

"For safety's sake, government must regulate the market for medical products."

Americans traveling in many foreign countries are surprised to discover that they can freely purchase drugs available in the United States only by prescription. If they become ill and require medical treatment, they may be helped—indeed, their lives may be saved—by drugs or medical devices that no one, not even physicians, may legally purchase in the U.S. market. Such experiences cause some travellers to wonder whether the strict controls exercised over the sale of medical goods in America really improves our health care.

The great majority of Americans now living have never experienced a free market for medical goods. Most believe that government alone should have the power to decide which drugs and medical devices may be sold. People tend to think that without the government's protective supervision, the market would be taken over by bogus medicines and phony devices because ordinary consumers lack the knowledge to distinguish the helpful from the hurtful.

This belief is curious, because people usually do not view similar markets in the same way. Even though most of us know very little about electrical or automotive engineering, we do not fear that sellers will deliver hazardous electrical appliances or dangerously designed cars. We rely on independent, private evaluators of products, like Underwriters' Laboratories and the Consumer's Union, as well as the Better Business Bureaus and the manufacturer's reputation for high quality. We understand that producers have strong incentives to deliver good quality products. Otherwise they will lose customers or, in extreme cases, face product liability lawsuits.

Why can't a free market for medical goods work as effectively as other markets? The answer is that it can and, despite the heavy-handed controls now exercised by government, already does work to a considerable degree.

Take medical devices, for example. The buyers of these heavily regulated goods are usually knowledgeable professionals such as doctors, hospital technicians and administrators, and paramedics. These buyers do not rely on government to screen products and provide essential information. Instead, they utilize information provided to them through the market, including such privately published sources as the *Health Devices Alerts,* the *Journal of Emergency Medical Services,* and *Clinica: World Medical Device & Diagnostic News.*

Similarly, doctors and pharmacists purchasing medicines and other medical supplies do not rely on the government for information. Instead, they turn to manufacturers' representatives and privately published sources such as the *Medical Letter on Drugs and Therapeutics* and *M.D. Buyline.* For many years the American Medical Association operated a certification program in which worthy products could gain the association's seal of acceptance. Private hospital committees now evaluate drugs for placement in their institutional formularies.

But what about ordinary consumers? If they were free to purchase without restriction, wouldn't they be easy targets for quack doctors and snake-oil peddlers? No. No more often than consumers fall victim to fraud in other markets where complex and potentially dangerous goods are traded. Before 1938, when Americans could purchase any medicine they wanted without a doctor's prescription, many patients purchased only the medicines prescribed by their doctors. Others relied on alternative sources of information, including trusted family members and neighbors who had used the product. The pre-1938 free market for medical goods worked about as well as the markets for oven cleaners, lawn mowers, and ladders—that is, although consumers sometimes harmed themselves by misusing the products, doing so was the exception rather than the rule.

Since 1938, however, the U.S. Food and Drug Administration (FDA) alone has decided what medical goods may be sold in the United States. Paternalistic to the core, this government agency ostensibly aims to protect us from ourselves. The FDA requires that every medical good marketed in the United States first establish its safety and efficacy to the agency's satisfaction by undergoing rigid, elaborate, expensive, and time-consuming testing procedures. Getting over these hurdles may cost hundreds of millions of dollars and take a decade or longer. As a result, drugs and devices commonly become available to consumers abroad years before they are permitted to be sold here—in fact, despite successful use elsewhere, some *never* gain FDA approval.

Doesn't this careful government screening save lives? Sadly, the answer is "no," at least not when one considers its negative as well as its positive effects. Of course some lives are saved when goods that might cause serious adverse side effects are kept off the market. But studies by leading authorities such as pharmacologist William Wardell of the University of Rochester and economists Henry Grabowski and John Vernon of Duke University indicate that the lives saved number far fewer than the lives lost because access to life-saving drugs and devices was delayed. Ironically, the government that supposedly saves us from ourselves has been responsible for *at least* tens of thousands of premature deaths and untold avoidable suffering. Beta-blockers alone, which the FDA kept off the American market for a decade, might have saved 10,000 lives a year.

Besides slowing the admission of new products to the market, the FDA's regulations have discouraged companies from developing products in the first place. When the costs of complying with government testing requirements are added to the costs of research and development, then, given the long delays before the government permits the products to be sold, many potentially useful products become unprofitable to develop. Studies by Grabowski and Vernon and other economists have established that the FDA's more stringent and extensive testing requirements authorized by Congress in 1962 caused the rate of innovation to plummet in the drug industry. In recent years a drastic reduction of FDA approvals of new or improved medical devices has had a similarly discouraging effect on product innovation and improvement.

By submitting to government controls over vital medical goods, Americans have experienced immense unnecessary harm. While taking credit for saving lives, the FDA has, on balance, probably caused more American deaths than the Korean and

Vietnam Wars combined and subjected the population to enormous unnecessary suffering. A government that cannot be trusted to deliver the mail promptly or keep the roads in repair certainly cannot be trusted with our health and our very lives. Until Americans come to understand the actual consequences of the government's sham protection and demand to be freed from its malignant paternalism, the deadly toll will continue to mount.

—ROBERT HIGGS

60

"National health care is working in Canada."

Since 1971, all of Canada's provinces have provided universal hospital and physician insurance. The federal government contributes part of the cost and the provinces are responsible for the rest. Canadians have free choice of hospitals and doctors and pay virtually nothing directly. A mixture of taxes pays for the system, usually income, payroll, or sales taxes. Residents over age 65 receive services without paying premiums, as do individuals and families without sufficient resources. Total premiums contribute about 20 percent of the health insurance budget.

Compared to the United States, new technology is less available to patients in Canada. For example, in the United States there are 2,000 magnetic resonance imaging machines (MRI); in Canada, only 15.[1] The entire province of Newfoundland, with a population of 579,000, has just one CAT scanner, while the city of Tucson, Arizona, with a similar population, has eleven.[2] Seattle, Washington, population one-half million, has more CAT scanners than British Columbia with three million residents.[3]

Because of the lack of available technology, the government controls the type and frequency of many diagnostic tests. A person complaining of headaches doesn't immediately receive a CAT scan and may have to wait several weeks for one. In Newfoundland, an "urgent" Pap smear, used to detect cervical cancer, routinely takes two months.[4]

Many experts agree that Canada has held its costs down in part by limiting the number of certain procedures such as coronary bypass surgery and angiograms. In Ottawa, a heart patient can expect to wait for four months for a coronary bypass operation.[5] In Toronto it can take up to a year.[6] Canada has only 11 heart surgery facilities, one for every 2.3 million residents, according to the AMA. In the United States there are 793, one for every 300,000 people. Certainly, long waiting lists for medical care seems inconsistent with the ideal of national health care (that everyone receive quality care).[7]

A shortage of hospital beds in Canada is increasingly becoming the norm. In September, 1989, it caused officials of Princess Margaret Hospital, one of the nation's best cancer facilities, to announce that they would take no new patients for six weeks.[8] In Brampton, Ontario, Thomas Dickson, head of surgery at Peel Memorial Hospital says, "we don't have enough beds. We sometimes have to cancel surgery for lack of beds."[9]

In Canada, physicians don't fare any better than patients. There are caps on doctors' incomes. In Quebec, when a general practitioner's gross quarterly income (before taxes and overhead) reaches the U.S. equivalent of $37,102, the government will pay him or her only 25 percent of the usual fee for the rest of the quarter.[10]

According to Dr. William Goodman, a specialist in Toronto who has been on strike since 1986, "the bureaucratic establishment of mandatory norms for doctors and hospitals is rapidly leading to a government-directed, assembly-line, civil-service type of practice. Computers run by non-medical, politically appointed medical administrators are progressively replacing medical judgment. Canadian medical bureaucrats now make the decisions on what care shall be made available, not individual patients in concert with their personal physicians."[11]

Some physicians, fed up with the system, have either quit the practice of medicine or emigrated to the United States. Dr. Goodman remarks, "The emigration or early retirement of many of our best physicians have [sic] left large gaps in the medical, hospital, and university hierarchies."[12]

The answer for many patients, frustrated over the lack of available treatment, has been to go to the United States. Canadians are allowed to buy insurance policies to cover care in the United States. Since 90 percent of Canadians live within 100 miles of the American border, it's no problem for them to drive to a dozen or more major American cities. This allows them an escape route from the rationing and waiting lines in their homeland. *Hospitals* magazine reported that in the first five months of 1989, half of the patients receiving lithotripsy (a technique to

212 / *Clichés of Politics*

treat kidney stones) at Buffalo General Hospital were Canadians.[13] Michael Billett, who founded Windsor Cardiac Emergency Care Center after he was forced to go to the United States for his own heart surgery, said his organization helped 600 patients get to the United States for surgery in 1990. And, at the Cleveland Clinic, approximately 100 Canadians get heart surgery every year.[14]

Proponents of nationalized health-care systems claim that Canada spends much less than the United States on health care, using data that compares health care spending of the two countries relative to their Gross National Product (GNP). In 1967, both countries spent relatively the same amount of their GNP on health care, approximately 6 percent. By 1971, when the main components of Canada's national health-care system were in place, both countries were spending a little above 7 percent. In 1987, Canada's national health expenditures as share of GNP were 9 percent, compared to the U.S. at 11 percent.[15]

Comparing the health-care spending of the two countries solely on GNP is misleading and inaccurate. Success in attaining cost control in health-care spending is not a reflection of a better system but of faster GNP growth. The Health Insurance Association of America (HIAA) conducted a study that compares health-care spending in Canada and the U.S. for the period 1967-1987.[16] The results showed almost parallel rates of increase in health spending for both Canada and the United States.[17]

Pro-Canadian forces state that one of the main reasons Canada has achieved lower health-care costs than the United States is because the system is more efficient and has less administrative costs due to a centralized bureaucracy. They assert that government monopolies can reduce overhead and do not incur the marketing costs found in our system. However, students of economics know that, in the long run, all monopolies become increasingly inefficient due to the lack of pressure to compete, and, as a result, extremely costly to operate. When accurate cost comparisons are made, such as the HIAA study, the savings attributed to the Canadian system vanishes, making any efficiency arguments invalid. In addition, the bureaucratic costs incurred due to tax collection and the redistribution of tax monies for health care are not usually included in Canadian cost estimates.

Another problem within the Canadian system is one that contributes to rising health-care costs in the United States—that patients contribute little or nothing to the cost of their care. This "little or no" deductible or co-pay policy leads to increased demand for services, resulting in spiraling costs, and out-of-control government budgets and private market costs. However, in countries with national health-care budgets determined by political process, the increasing demand for cheap services outgrows the supply of government funds, resulting in chronic shortages, deficiencies, and rationing of medical services and supplies. Price controls, rationing, and waiting lists do put a lid on health-care spending, but at what cost to patients?

An interesting fact not often reported in the American press is that a bill passed in 1990 (Bill C-69) substantially cut and will eventually eliminate the federal contribution to health care in Canada. It is gradually reducing transfer payments from Ottawa to the provincial health plans, and will cause the death of the Canadian national health plan within the decade. Apparently, national health care is not working in Canada.

—TERREE P. WASLEY

1. Lee Smith, "A Cure for What Ails Medical Care," *Fortune,* July 1, 1991, p. 44.

2. Data on Newfoundland from Michael A. Walker, "Neighborly Advice on Health Care," *The Wall Street Journal,* June 8, 1988. Data on Tucson from Daniel Anavy, M.D., Nuclear Medicine Department, St. Joseph's Hospital, Tucson, Arizona.

3. Don Feder, "The High Cost of National Health Insurance," *Human Events,* June 15, 1991.

4. *Ibid.*

5. Michael Malloy, "Health, Canadian Style," *The Wall Street Journal,* April 22, 1988.

6. Feder, "High Cost."

7. The Fraser Institute in Vancouver, British Columbia, published the first comprehensive, scientific survey of waiting lists in the Canadian health system. The average waiting time for the 20 least available treatments in British Columbia ranged from six weeks for a D & C to 33 weeks for septal surgery. A child's tonsillectomy requires a wait of 14 weeks, and a hysterectomy is delayed for 16 weeks. Some 522 children are waiting for a tonsillectomy, and 206 women are waiting for a hysterectomy. Additional information on various procedures and waiting periods can be found in Steven Globerman and Lorna Hoye, "Waiting Your Turn: Hospital Waiting Lists in Canada," *Critical Issues Bulletin* (Vancouver, B. C.: Fraser Institute, May 1990).

8. Michael Specter, "Health Care in Canada: A Model With Limits," *Washington Post,* December 18, 1989.

214 / Clichés of Politics

9. Malloy, "Health, Canadian Style."

10. "The Crisis in Health Insurance: A Look at the Canadian Alternative," *Consumer Reports,* September 1990, p. 614.

11. William E. Goodman, M.D., "Canadian Medicare: A Road to Serfdom," Association of American Physicians and Surgeons, pamphlet no. 1012, August 1990, pp. 9, 11.

12. *Ibid.,* p. 9.

13. Stuart A. Wesbury, Jr., "Doctors After Hours," *The Washington Post,* March 18, 1990, p. B3.

14. John Goodman, "Wrong Prescription for the Uninsured," *The Wall Street Journal,* June 11, 1991.

15. Edward Neuschler, "Canadian Health Care: the Implications of Public Health Insurance" (Washington, D.C.: The Health Insurance Association of America, June 1990).

16. *Ibid.*

17. The U.S. per capita growth in health-care spending rose from approximately $700 in 1967 to approximately $1,600 in 1987. In Canada the rate rose from approximately $600 in 1967 to $1,500 in 1987.

VII. THE AGRICULTURAL INDUSTRY

61

"Government should support agriculture— the backbone of America."

Agriculture is inherently risky because of unfavorable weather and unpredictable market conditions. Thus, it is said, government intervention is beneficial because it enables farmers to cope with uncertainty and effectively compete in the market-place—at home and abroad. This assertion is countered below on two grounds. First, farm programs are shown to persist not because they are in the "public interest" but because of the political clout of milk, sugar, and other agricultural interest groups. Second, government's attempt to stabilize agriculture is thwarted by information and incentive problems inherent in the political process.

The federal government long has been heavily involved in U.S. agriculture. Numerous Roosevelt New Deal programs, including price supports, credit subsidies, food stamps, and other subsidized food programs, were enacted during the Great Depression more than 50 years ago. Spending on these programs, which totaled some $65 billion in fiscal 1993, has been increased over time despite fundamental changes in economic conditions.

There is a vast gulf between the rhetoric and the reality of government farm programs. Consider the reality of the following group of clichés:

"Farm programs are beneficial to the public at large."

If farm programs were abolished, taxpayers would benefit and consumers would be able to purchase many food products at prices much lower than those now paid. For example, import quotas are used to raise domestic sugar price to almost double the world price level.

"Farm subsidies are necessary to assist small farmers."

Farm programs in reality provide most of the benefits to large farmers. The USDA (U.S. Department of Agriculture) con-

217

cedes that two-thirds of government payments go to the wealthiest 15 percent of U.S. farmers and that the average income of commercial farmers is 25 percent higher than of the average U.S. family.[1] Moreover, the average small farmer derives virtually all disposable income from sources outside the farm.

"Government farm programs make farming more profitable."

Farm programs provide only transitional gains and do nothing to increase the long-run profitability of farming.[2] Expected benefits of higher product prices received by farmers are quickly incorporated into higher prices of land, allotments, and other farm assets. Therefore, only those who own specialized farm assets when product prices increase benefit from government programs because later entrants find that expected gains from government subsides are offset by higher costs.

"Government can reduce uncertainty at no cost to taxpayers."

It is argued that markets can be stabilized at no cost to consumers by setting a price floor at the competitive market level. The reality is that there is no way government planners can determine before a crop is planted what the market-clearing price will be. Moreover, information about supply and demand conditions is unlikely to be assessed as accurately by government officials as by market participants, whose own money is on the line. However, even if government officials *could* determine future market conditions, they are likely deliberately to set price above the competitive level in seeking votes (or other political favors).

In short, the reality is that government farm programs distort resource use and frequently *increase* rather than reduce market instability. Indeed, much of the instability in agricultural markets can be traced to government policies, including inflationary monetary and fiscal policies, subsidized credit, and trade restrictions.

If farm programs benefit the few at the expense of the many, why have they lasted for a half century? First, the political process often gives louder voice to small groups when benefits are highly concentrated and costs widely diffused. For example, benefits of the sugar program, on average, amount to more than $200,000 per year for each domestic producer of sugar and sugar substitutes. In sharp contrast, with sugar consumption averaging less than 100 pounds per person annually, program cost to the average U.S. family is no more than $100 per year. Thus, it is not surprising that sugar interests rather than consumers perennially win the political battle when the sugar program is debated in Congress.

Second, the political process is oriented toward the short run. Politicians prefer programs in which benefits are conferred on constituents in the short run and costs occur in the long run—preferably after the next election! However, elimination of any farm program is likely to impose short-run costs. Elimination of the sugar program, for example, would have an immediate adverse effect on sugar interests.

Third, legislators have incentives to overspend because the federal budget—like the sea or the air, which no one owns but many have access to—is a common property resource. This leads to "pork barrel" spending because the benefits are received by people within the district, but the costs are borne by taxpayers throughout the United States. Thus, local voters, realizing that federal money not spent locally is likely to be spent elsewhere, place pressure on even the most conservative members of Congress to "bring home the bacon."

Is government intervention necessary to assist and stabilize agriculture? The competitive market process is capable of coordinating economic activity in agriculture, as evidenced by the fact that more than half of all U.S. farm goods are now produced and marketed largely on the basis of market signals. Moreover, as the dependence of U.S. agriculture on international trade increases, domestic programs that reduce the competitiveness of U.S. farm products are increasingly counterproductive.

In short, government intervention in agriculture is explained by "government failure" rather than "market failure." Indeed, it is only through the market that the nation's agricultural resources can be used most effectively and the interests of farmers, consumers, and taxpayers best be served.

—E.C. Pasour, Jr.

1. William A. Niskanen and Stephen Moore, "How to Balance the Budget by Reducing Spending," *Policy Analysis* No. 194 (Washington, D.C.: The Cato Institute, April 22, 1993), p. 19.

2. E.C. Pasour, Jr., *Agriculture and the State: Market Processes and Bureaucracy* (New York: Holmes and Meier, 1990), chapter 12.

62

"The government should stabilize agricultural markets."

Agricultural industries, beset by vagaries of weather and crops, produce highly variable outputs, resulting in fluctuating prices. These, in turn, have led to industry calls for the government to step in and "stabilize" agricultural markets (on behalf of consumers, of course), calls the government has been most willing to heed. However, the result is "stabilization" of prices far above what the market would generate, as government controls pick consumer pockets for producers, while preventing those market responses capable of mitigating the problem.

One area in which this government "stabilization" on behalf of producers is most blatant is agricultural marketing orders in the citrus industry. These marketing orders create grower cartels, and enforce them with the full power of the government.

They establish producer administrative committees, with representation based on size (resulting in Sunkist's domination to the extent that a 1982 Small Business Administration report stated, "The Lemon Administrative Committee's annual marketing policy statement originates at Sunkist"). The committee is empowered to set weekly quotas restricting how many fresh oranges and lemons each grower can sell. Despite the official price stabilization rationale, which implies that growers are incapable of rationally marketing their crop without government help, the actual effect of this output restriction is to boost fresh citrus prices. What cannot be sold fresh must rot, or be "dumped" in far less lucrative markets for juice, exports, or by-products.

Unfortunately, this "market stabilization" does not achieve its stated goal. Studies have found that lemon prices vary more than those for other fruits without marketing orders (e.g., grapefruit and limes, and Florida oranges, whose markets are hardly chaotic). Summer lemon prices can be double the winter prices

221

because sales are sharply curtailed during the peak demand months of summer (and because Sunkist has kept shrink-wrap technology from extending the effective selling season for lemons).

Even a 1981 study by the United States Department of Agriculture, whose existence depends on the continuation of many such anti-consumer policies, found that marketing orders actually increased price fluctuations by hindering the use of forward contracts in futures markets, long established mechanisms for reducing price volatility. A 1982 Office of Management and Budget (OMB) study came to similar conclusions. These studies so threatened Sunkist's grip on the citrus market that the company lobbied Congress into prohibiting OMB from conducting future reviews of marketing orders' effects.

Defenders of marketing orders dispute charges of massive waste. However, wasting large percentages of these crops has been a common result. Orange growers have been forced to sell as by-products or let rot up to 40 percent of their crops, and the number for lemons has approached 75 percent. (In 1983, for instance, only 60 percent of the orange crop was allowed to be sold fresh, and more lemons were dumped than sold fresh to American consumers.)

Currently, little fruit is left to rot. However, that is only because fruit which cannot be sold fresh will be sold to some other, less valuable use, as long as the price received exceeds the harvesting costs. (Why, as one comedian put it, today you can find lemon juice in everything but lemonade.) But much of its value is still wasted by such sales to lower-value markets.

Marketing order defenders also argue that they don't reduce sales, because production has greatly increased. But production is not the same as the amount sold fresh, when sales are heavily restricted. In fact, it is only because marketing orders prevent growers from selling more fresh fruit that they are willing to accept lower prices for the third of their sales that typically go to other markets (they wouldn't voluntarily sell for $10 in one market if they could get $20 elsewhere).

Marketing orders increase fresh citrus prices by 30 to 40 percent. This fact is overshadowed by the public relations effort of the industry when arguing that ending marketing orders would cause drastic losses to producers—ignoring completely that such market restrictions now deny consumers the benefits of lower prices. Further, this argument would mean that one could never undo any government policy that ripped off consumers, since it would harm those now benefiting from the policy.

Even exporting excess citrus production at depressed prices is seen as beneficial rather than wasteful. The net difference in prices between what the fruit would fetch fresh in the United States and in, for example, Japan (which imports despite a 40 percent tariff on oranges) is nothing but waste. But cartel members point only to the export earnings that result, equivalent to claiming that selling a $15,000 domestic product to Japan for $9,000 generates $9,000 in benefits to Americans, instead of a $6,000 loss.

Marketing orders actually increase the waste by stimulating production. The high prices for fresh fruit that they cause, together with quotas based on production shares, encourages growers to raise more fruit that will have to be dumped in order to get the right to sell more fresh (for lemons, at a ratio of as much as four dumped to every one sold fresh). These raised prices have also led to an aberration in the market where despite this country's high production and exports, citrus imports are attracted to the United States, displacing American sales at the same time American fruit is forced into less valuable markets.

If a private group tried to cartelize this industry at consumer expense, they would fail because they would have no way to enforce their restrictions or keep out competitors. Market pressures would destroy the attempt. So, as many industries do, citrus producers have recruited government away from its legitimate goal of defending property rights and voluntary contracts to become their instrument of regulatory plunder. Once again, behind the rhetoric of government kindness in overcoming alleged "market failures," we see nothing but an organized attempt to use its coercive power to steal.

—Gary M. Galles

VIII. THE ARTS, MEDIA, AND EDUCATION

63

"We can rely on the media to bring us an unbiased political outlook."

How reliable are the print and electronic journalists who report on the nation's political affairs? Can we expect them to bring us an unbiased political outlook despite their personal views and preferences? And if not, what can be done to correct the problem?

The subject of media bias is, and should be, a troubling issue for devotees of liberty. At stake is the First Amendment, which still stands as a singular beacon in a world that seethes with interventionism and statism. No person of libertarian principles should ever want to join hands with those who would use media bias as a pretext for undermining press freedom only to use coercive measures to promote their own political biases. So the libertarian answer is to understand media bias and then deal with it in constructive and peaceful ways.

The first step in understanding media bias is to concede that leading print and electronic journalists do not *knowingly* distort facts to mislead the public deliberately or to advance a political agenda. Despite a few notorious examples, such as the NBC "Dateline" fiasco with GM's pickup trucks, intentional dishonesty is not the rule.

What does happen is that most reporters and editors share a mind-set that influences how news is selected, worded, and presented. In today's world, they are conditioned to accept a great deal of interventionism as necessary and inevitable. Perhaps without news people even realizing it, routine reportage may even reflect an interventionist bias. And since government at all levels is heavily involved in economic and social matters, these everyday news stories may reflect and advance political opinions. A recent news article in Toledo, for example, emphasized the fact that an "unlicensed roofer" had been working on a building that caught fire. This implied a connection between occupational licensing and fire safety that does not necessarily exist.

The same mind-set prevails when problems arise in unregulated businesses and industries. The news stories will invariably point out the fact that the enterprise is unregulated or will favorably quote public officials who express a need for regulation to avoid similar problems in the future. This has the political effect of endorsing regulation in the news columns without supplying additional commentary or reasons that such control is either unnecessary or even counterproductive.

Media political bias also grows out of the needs of the organizations. Large newspapers and broadcast enterprises are profit-seeking businesses with a primary interest in protecting their own commercial advantages and opportunities. Like most major corporations, news and broadcast organizations have come to terms with invasive government involvement in their business and even accept it as the way things should be. While the First Amendment gives the media organizations considerable discretion and leeway in news coverage and editorializing, they are regulated in countless other ways. The news organizations must remain profitable while dealing with numerous federal and state regulatory bodies. And like major corporations in other lines of business, they are attacked and threatened by interest groups who enlist politicians as their allies. All of this has a role in shaping the presentation of news.

Reporters and editors, though professing independence and a devotion to the truth, will not often bear down too heavily on any issue that threatens the survival of their own organizations. This is most noticeable in the long-term failure of major newspapers to protest and overturn the licensing of the broadcast media. Good reporting and commentary in the print media could have helped avert the increasing efforts the government is now making to control and shape TV programming. This is possible only because of broadcast licensing. But large news organizations have held back on their opposition in tacit recognition of the fact that licensing and regulation are also commercial disadvantages for their largest competitors for advertisers' dollars.

Much is made of the obvious liberal bias shared by most of

today's influential journalists. As explained in "The Media Elite," an important 1986 study,

> Today's leading journalists are politically liberal and alienated from traditional norms and institutions. Most place themselves to the left of center and regularly vote the Democratic ticket. Yet theirs is not the New Deal liberalism of the underprivileged, but the contemporary social liberalism of the urban sophisticate. They favor a strong welfare state within a capitalist framework. They differ most from the general public, however, on the divisive social issues that have emerged since the 1960s— abortion, gay rights, affirmative action, *et cetera*. Many are alienated from the "system" and quite critical of America's world role. They would like to strip traditional power brokers of their influence and empower black leaders, consumer groups, intellectuals, and ... the media.[1]

Because it's hardly a secret that this bias exists, it sometimes becomes an issue in national elections when journalists are suspected of being too hard on certain candidates while giving their favorites a "free ride." This could sometimes happen, but the more disturbing bias is the ongoing news treatment journalists give to issues and groups they like while ignoring facts and arguments that might be detrimental to their pet causes.

Are there any workable answers? In a country that values press freedom, can anything be done to offset the problem of biased reporting? It can, if critics of the practice retain respect for liberty, fair-mindedness, and even a sense of humor. It's also important to remember that while we can't always rely on the popular, mass media for an unbiased political outlook, we can find additional facts and opinions in the great variety of publications that are available to us. In other words, where liberty of the press is maintained and protected, the problem of media bias will be self-correcting. Here are several points to keep in mind:

1. *The media professionals have their own critics within the profession.* No matter what issue is involved, there are a number of journalists and columnists who will always come forth to ex-

plain where coverage has been wrong, biased or inadequate. Though some are arrogant in their bias, most journalists are still sensitive to even the slightest hint that they've been less than professional in their coverage.

2. *Biased reportage offers critics and opponents the opportunities to present their own views.* People complain about biased reporting, but this also gives them the opening to present their own views in "Letters" or political speeches and articles. It can sometimes even be a political advantage to be treated unfairly by a newspaper or TV reporter.

3. *Where there is press freedom, alternate voices and viewpoints will always appear, achieving a following proportionate to the level of dissatisfaction with popular media.* In the U.S. media, this has been amply demonstrated by the astonishing rise of Rush Limbaugh as a conservative spokesman. His success is almost without parallel in American history. Hated by some and adored by others, Mr. Limbaugh has obviously tapped into the intense feelings large numbers of people have about the way their views are treated by the general media. It doesn't reflect on Mr. Limbaugh's personal abilities to say that his popularity is a "market response" to an unmet need that was already there. And where there is freedom in the information marketplace, spokespersons will always arise to fill such unmet needs.

4. *Media coverage is only part of the processes which deal with our political outlook.* Though it's often said that newspapers control political events, this does not always turn out to be true. There are any number of local political actions, for example, which are defeated even though supported by the single newspaper in the town. This is especially true with tax issues, where a few people distributing circulars overturn a proposal that may have had the support of the community's top leaders. It's also important to remember that citizens passing out circulars are also "media," and that this is an expression of First Amendment rights.

5. *Be wary and skeptical of what you read and hear in the mass media. But be more on guard against those who would use your discontent to destroy liberty.* In the commercial field, consumer dissatisfaction with some products and services became the pretext for destroying a great deal of personal freedom under

the guise of regulation. This was a far worse bargain for the public than a few customers might have been getting in the marketplace. Today, ...any of us are unhappy with the media, which works in the marketplace for information and ideas. While we cannot rely on the media completely for an unbiased political outlook, we can rely on our own common sense and love of liberty to deal constructively with the media bias. If there's a good general understanding and acceptance of liberty, there will also be sufficient checks and balances in the information marketplace to correct any amount of biased coverage.

—MELVIN D. BARGER

---

1. S. Robert Lichter, Stanley Rothman, and Linda S. Lichter (Bethesda, Md.: Adler & Adler, Publishers, Inc., 1986), p. 294.

64

"Public finance of the arts advances a nation's culture."

It is often argued that government subsidies of the arts, such as those which go to fund symphony orchestras, operas, dances, museums, and theater productions, advance culture. This position is responsible for the creation of the National Endowment for the Arts and is illustrated by many proponents in numerous ways. For example, in an essay by Maya Angelou entitled, "Arts and Public Policy," she stresses that art should be removed of all "shackles" because art helps people to "stand erect." Furthermore, this pride helps people to survive the trials and burdens of life. Ms. Angelou says:

> The strength of the black American to withstand the slings and arrows and lynch mobs and malignant neglect can be traced directly to the art of literature, music, dance, and philosophy which we inherited and which, despite significant attempts to eradicate them, remain in our communities today.[1]

Her point is clear. She believes that government should subsidize the arts so as to free black American artists from the "shackles" which limit their ability to express themselves. But two questions arise: What is it that shackles the black American artist (or any artist for that matter) and why does it take government subsidies to eliminate the shackles?

To examine these questions we need to consider the nature of government action and the nature of art. There are several criteria for judging any action, such as the efficiency and fairness of the action, but since Ms. Angelou focuses on fairness, let's consider whether or not government subsidization of the arts actually does lead to greater justice.

To examine this issue we must first consider what a subsidy

is and how it is funded. Government subsidies must come from government funds which are ultimately raised through some form of taxation. Taxation always involves forcing citizens to part with some of their material possessions in order to fund government programs. Thus those who must pay for subsidies to artists no longer have a choice and are effectively "shackled" by the plan to pay for something they may or may not want. The only freeing component of Ms. Angelou's argument is that the artist is now free to offer up something in the name of art in order to participate in the largess created by enslaving taxpayers to the subsidy program. If slavery is unjust, such a plan must fail its test of fairness and should be rejected on those grounds alone.

This leaves us to examine the nature of art itself and what our goal is in its consumption. The best statement we have found of art's goal is from Leonard Peikoff. He says that the goal of art is, "not to prove but to show—to concretize whatever sense of life the artist has, whether it be true or false."[2] Art can take the human emotion felt from a problem and concretize it so that people gain a better understanding of one another and of their various experiences in life. Art has been described as a mirror of society—a mirror in which we can see our reflection; but for it to have value, it must communicate.

Art can educate and illuminate, but to do so it must communicate. The artist attempts to communicate to others by concretizing emotion so that the consumer can gain a better understanding of a particular dilemma, situation, or emotion. The communication can be intergenerational or intragenerational. It can be interracial or intraracial. In any case the consumer seeks to benefit from a better understanding through the consumption of the art, but only the consumer of the art is in the position to tell whether or not a particular effort actually communicates some meaningful message.

Given a definition of art and its goal, let's consider another question: What government policy will best allow art to provide meaningful communication between the artist and the consumer of art? The answer should be obvious. Since the consumer is the only one who can judge whether or not significant communication has taken place, only the consumer is in a position to choose.

Government subsidies eliminate this choice and allow artists to choose what they will produce whether or not the result actually communicates anything significant for the audience.

The argument for letting the forces of the free market control art is clear. With so much ambiguity surrounding the arts it seems more than reasonable that it is up to each individual to decide the type of, quantity of, and quality of art he or she will consume. Furthermore, that consumption will be based on the benefits gained by the consumer, who alone is in the position to assess the merit of the message received from the artist. Any advancement or exaltation of culture will be a result of effective communication of some truth which has not previously been seen.

Does the artist have an important message for society? If so, let him attempt to communicate his message through his art. If the message is getting through, then he will know as people respond to his work, but the government can never force the communication which gives art its value. In a completely free market all discussion of artistic standards which should be employed is moot. Each individual chooses what is and is not valuable as well as what is and is not offensive.

Criticism over allowing market forces to decide which art succeeds and which fails really stems from unsuccessful artists who speak without being heard. Frustrated by the lack of consumer response, these individuals, aided by those few consumers wishing to have their consumption subsidized, have sought and gained relief by lobbying Congress to gain a captive audience. In reality they seek to "free" themselves by enslaving others. True freedom is never gained in this way.

Someone might wish to argue that this would tend to stifle innovation in the arts, but this argument is very weak. If the artist is truly interested in the message he hopes to take to the masses, then he will continue to look for new ways to communicate that message. Hopefully, if the message is true and not false, someone will eventually listen. Even a true message which has gone unheard does not give occasion for government subsidies. It should be obvious to everyone that even a captive audience forced to listen may not hear the real message. Thus this argument fails. It is futile to attempt to force people to hear a message, even an important one. Greater alienation between the artist and the consumer of art is the only thing that can result from such a program.

—PAUL A. CLEVELAND AND BENJAMIN L. CRAWFORD

1. Andrew Buchwalter, ed., "Arts and Public Policy," *Culture & Democracy* (Boulder, Colo.: Westview, 1992), p. 29.

2. Leonard Peikoff, *Objectivism: The Philosophy of Ayn Rand* (New York: Penguin, 1991), p. 438.

65

"Government grants are required to perpetuate the arts."

Who is an artist? How can this person be discovered and aided? And how can we be assured that real art will be found and preserved for the benefit of all humanity and posterity?

The way some groups have it, artists are an endangered species that may die out unless special help and attention are given them. This view seems to be generating the pressure to make supporting the arts a necessary and important function of government. Americans are being especially berated for not supporting more lavish government grants to the arts. While many European governments support artists and art enterprises, there's been less enthusiasm in the United States. Until just recent decades, artists of all kinds were viewed as an independent breed that didn't really want anybody's direction or help.

But a major turning point came with the establishment of the National Endowment for the Arts (NEA) in 1965. This soon became a $180-million-a-year industry with federal support. Influential voices continue to demand increases in NEA funds along with more subsidies for the arts by state and local governments. And the persistent argument is that the arts will falter and die without this federal help and much more in the future.

The free-market answer is that the arts should be supported by individuals and private organizations using voluntary, peaceful means and processes. This is particularly important for all branches of the visual and performing arts because such issues as freedom of speech, belief, and expression are also at stake. In a free society, it is necessary for governments to maintain the same neutrality toward the arts that they're supposed to show toward religion and the press. People in the visual and performing arts require a wide range of freedom in their pursuit of full self-expression. There is almost no justification for governments to shut down a play, ban a book, interfere with a concert, or forbid the display of a painting or a photograph.

But if artists are to be free from government coercion, they must not make the fatal error of looking to government for support of any kind while still expecting artistic freedom. There's been much argument about this in recent years, with artists crying censorship when certain elected officials objected to what they considered obscene exhibits under NEA sponsorship. But it's unavoidable that artists receiving government grants must toe a certain political line or expect political reactions to their work.

Whether they admit it or not, artists who receive government aid have become hirelings of the state and must be subjected to some political control. Even if it's not stated, the acceptance of the grant implies a contractual agreement to comply with a number of politically directed guidelines. In practice, for example, government grants to the arts are sometimes distributed in such a way as to favor certain minority groups. Though many view this policy approvingly, it is a political purpose, not an artistic one. Were the grants being made solely to preserve the best artistic expression, they would be made exclusively on merit.

But the main question here is whether the arts will be perpetuated under the free-market system. The answer is that liberty is indispensable for the creation and preservation of good art. Most of the art now being produced is being done by individuals working alone or by commercial enterprises devoted to such efforts. Much of the art from the past ages also has been produced by individuals, sometimes against intense government opposition. At the same time, a great deal of fine art is purchased as investments or collectibles by individuals and organizations, and as a result gets close protection and care. With rare exceptions, the dealers and owners of artistic works are more likely to preserve it than the various bureaucratic organizations that work under government control.

We should also note that there is strong disagreement about the definition of real art. This is a field that is loaded with opportunities for sham, fraud, and pretense. Time and again, elite groups have decided that certain people are great artists while completely shunning or even denouncing others whose works and performances are popular with the public. Look into these controversies, however, and you discover that even the elitists are not of one mind as to what comprises real talent or good art. Many of them are likely to be unfairly critical of rivals and inhospitable to artists whose work does not meet their own standards. Given the divided nature of the art world itself, it's hard to believe that any government body can pick out the real winners and losers among artists.

There is also a myth to the effect that great artists whom posterity will honor are likely to be mistreated in their own time. If we neglect federal support of the arts, this argument goes, we will be condemning another van Gogh or Mozart to a wretched existence. But it's not clear that NEA officials even know how to nurture a future van Gogh or Mozart, let alone select one from among the thousands of contenders who display signs of early talent. We also have to face the fact that many talented artists, past and present, have personal problems which cause their troubles. In fact, it would be hard to find a group of people less willing to work under the restrictions and guidelines which should follow government aid and control.

In general, the market itself will always prove to work best in perpetuating the arts. Artists of all kinds are better treated and more handsomely rewarded in a flourishing free-market economy than under any kind of government-sponsored system. It is probable that there are more art-related occupations and profitable outlets now than ever before in history. In the United States alone there are many people in the performing and visual arts who earn six figure incomes, while others work in fields that allow sufficient leisure time to pursue the arts. At the same time, the colleges and universities are great sponsors of art-related activities. Another function of the commercial market has been to develop new technologies and systems that enhance artistic expression: electronic amplifiers in music, vast improvements in sound systems and motion pictures, better materials for painters and sculptors, more efficient printing methods.

But even if the market falters or is suppressed for a time, the arts will survive, and there's no need to fear for the future of art or individual artists. The human impulses to express in various art forms run deep and have a long history. Art is truly part of humanity's soul, not its government, and will prevail in its own way and through its own channels. It's all part of human existence and our upward, ongoing progress.

—MELVIN D. BARGER

66

"We ought to have sex education in the schools."

This has been a very divisive issue of late. Some parents want very much for their children to be fully educated, and they see learning about human sexuality as crucial to the well developed person. Others are equally vociferous—but on the other side. In their view, such matters should be left to the home or to the church, or not discussed at all.

How can such disputes be resolved? Well, there are two and only two ways to accomplish this; all others are simply combinations and permutations of these polar cases.

The first method is the use of physical force. The matter is decided by a dictator, or by a democratic election of the entire populace, or by a school board or a mayor or a city council or a parent-teacher association. However it is determined, the decision is enforced upon the losers. Whichever way it goes, we either have sex education in the schools, or we do not. One group, either the opponents or the proponents, must of necessity be dissatisfied.

The other method is called the free enterprise system. Here, there is no such thing as public schools. All are private. Each one determines its own policy on this issue. In some, sex education is totally banned. In others, it forms the central focus of the entire learning experience. In most cases, this subject plays a more intermediate role.

Under such circumstances, everyone can be satisfied. Parents can patronize the schools that most nearly reflect their own views on the matter. Given dozens—if not hundreds—of educational enterprises in each city, there is little doubt that all tastes on the spectrum can be accommodated.

Let us now consider an analogy. Instead of considering the

proposition "We ought to have sex education in the schools," let us contemplate "We ought to have pizza in the restaurants."

Were this question solved in the manner presently used for sex education, our system would be very different. Most restaurants would be run by the government. All citizens would be forced to pay for these public restaurants, whether they used them or not. Those who patronized private ones would have to pay twice: once in fees for meals, and then again through taxes. People, moreover, would be assigned to the public restaurant located nearest to them.

As to the pizza question, all public restaurants would either stock this foodstuff, or they would not. There could be no such thing as restaurants specializing in different cuisines, and people sorting themselves out according to their tastes. Thus, either the pizza lovers, or the pizza haters, would be disappointed.

The point is, the market is almost infinitely flexible compared to government. And this holds true even when a free market in education is compared to educational socialism. In addition, the profit and loss system of free enterprise tends to weed out those entrepreneurs who cannot satisfy their customers. Let a business firm supplying elementary school services answer the sex educational question in a way at variance with a parent, and that is one customer gone to patronize a competitor. In contrast, the state educational bureaucrats have very little incentive to satisfy the demands of their captive audience; if the parents don't like the policy, it is just too bad for them: they must continue to pay their school taxes in any case.

The proof of this contention is that there simply *is* no "pizza in restaurants" issues now bedeviling society. The very idea is ludicrous. But the reason we have escaped this particular vexation is that the market functions, in large part, without our appreciation or even knowledge. The best way to answer the challenge of sex education in the schools is to privatize the entire industry, and allow each parent to decide this issue for him or herself.

There is the objection that schooling is too important to be left to free enterprise, and that the government must therefore take it over.

It is certainly true that education is crucial to living a good life. The ignorant man is only half alive. But food, too, is important. And if we have found a way to feed people—efficiently and affordably—without emulating the Soviet system of collectivized farms, restaurants, grocery stores, and so on, surely we can do so with regard to education as well.

We conclude that the way to address the issue of sex education (as well as other seemingly intractable issues such as school busing, prayer in the schools, and debates over educational philosophy) is to allow the market to function. It is the most productive and moral economic institution known to man; surely it can suffice in this particular case.

—WALTER BLOCK

IX. FOREIGN TRADE AND THE WORLD ECONOMY

67

"International trade is different and thus requires government management."

"I am for free commerce with all nations." So said Thomas Jefferson in a letter to Elbridge Gerry in 1799.

"We must compete, not retreat," said President William Jefferson Clinton in 1993 on behalf of international trade.

But early in his term the U.S. Commerce Department found firms in 19 foreign countries guilty of "dumping" steel on the U.S. market, of allegedly selling steel here at prices less than those at home. The Department imposed provisional tariff duties of up to 109.22 percent. The imposition had the effect of an overnight foreign steel embargo. It also had the effect of worsening the competitive position of American steel-consuming industries such as the manufacturers of pipe, autos, and refrigerators.

Such two-faced language of managed trade is of course par for Washington. It reflects some attempt to cloud the language of negotiations in what economist Milton Friedman calls Washington's "iron triangle" of legislators, officials, and special interests (including big business). Friedman argues that when a foreign government subsidizes its export goods, it inadvertently subsidizes the consumers of those countries importing those goods—a gift that should hardly be declined. Consumers should be "free to choose," i.e., consumers should be in charge of whatever they buy, regardless of the source of the goods. This is the meaning of the phrase, consumer sovereignty, used so extensively by W.H. Hutt and Ludwig von Mises.

Managed trade, on the other hand, puts the iron triangle in charge, with PAC (political action committee) money holding the legislators in line. So of course deciphering Beltway circumlocution in and out of trade isn't easy; interventionists don't always say what they mean or mean what they say.

My point is that managed trade ignores the logic of competition, whether that competition is foreign or domestic. It ignores the gain of geographic division of labor, and hence of trade itself. Trade only proceeds when it is mutually advantageous to both buyer and seller.

Ostensibly for international commerce, managed trade dwells on the need for "reciprocity." It argues that one country's tariff reductions are conditional on its trading partners taking like action. This indeed is the whole tit-for-tat idea of the Geneva-based organization, the General Agreement on Tariffs and Trade (GATT), which has spent some eight years trying to get its so-called Uruguay Round of tariff reductions approved. Reciprocity or managed trade thereby gives but lip service to the wisdom of comparative advantage. Or as Adam Smith put it in *The Wealth of Nations:*

> If a foreign country can supply us with a commodity cheaper than we ourselves can make it, [we had] better buy it of them with some part of our own industry, employed in a way in which we have some advantage. The general industry of the country will not thereby be diminished, but only left to find out the way in which it can be employed with the greatest advantage.

Yet once big business did stand foursquare for free trade, no strings attached—i.e., for wide-open international competition, *unilateral* free trade if need be, complete consumer sovereignty, the consumer free to choose. Reciprocity was not a ploy.

The place was Britain. The time was the 1820s, 1830s, and 1840s. On the statute books were the Corn Laws of 1815 imposing high duties on grain imports so as to maintain the landed gentry's income after the Napoleonic Wars had ceased along with French armed interference with British trade. The Corn Laws placed a heavy peacetime burden on the workers and the poor, sharply driving up the price of bread and keeping them in many cases on the verge of starvation.

Into this picture stepped two successful Manchester textile businessmen and free traders—John Bright and Richard Cobden. Both entered Parliament to fight the free trade battle directly. Both sustained and advanced the aim of the Anti-Corn

Law League, a quite different nineteenth-century counterpart to today's protectionist or managed trade interests. The League's aim was to repeal the Corn Laws outright, with no "if's, and's, or but's." The League published pamphlets by the ton. It agitated the media of its day on behalf of unilateral, free trade.

John Bright was especially articulate as he toured the country arguing for free trade: "Give us this day our daily bread," he said, meaning bread unencumbered with steep subsidies in each expensive loaf. He attacked the landowners as *"Corn*servatives," who were scornful of the common good, attentive to only their class interest, controlling Parliament so as to keep foreign grain out and their rents up. He held protectionism invited retaliatory tariffs against English manufactured exports while depriving the poor of cheap bread.

The League published free trade arguments, sometimes in the form of rhymes, such as:

While the burden remains on our backs,
  Let the shout for repeal ne'er relax,
Till, like Jericho's wall, Protection shall fall,
  And give us our loaf without the tax.

And:

Free trade will be the link to bind
  Each nation to the other;
'Twill harmonize the rights of man
  With every fellow brother.

Inadvertently the League-Bright-Cobden assault on protectionism gave rise to new thinking, a new school of economics—the Manchester School, a group of businessmen and economists who argued for not only free trade but the idea of laissez faire: the idea that the state should interfere as little as possible in economic affairs.

But the decisive argument in the debate over free trade came not in rhetoric but in the form of a fungus, a blight that attacked the potato crop in America in 1843 and soon spread to Europe and especially to Ireland. The resulting Irish Potato Famine—potatoes were the main staple in the Irish diet—was compounded by the soaring price of bread. In all, some 240,000 Irish perished by starvation or malnutrition-induced disease, and a vast migration began leaving Ireland for America, Australia, and Canada.

Prime Minister Robert Peel, shocked by the turn of events, pushed for repeal of the Corn Laws; and on June 26, 1846, his repeal measure became law. *Unilaterally.* No managed trade. Reciprocal tariff reductions on the part of Britain's trading partners were neither asked nor received. Thus did Britain enter a remarkable era of free trade, industrial expansion, and higher living standards—including those of the workers and the poor. Indeed, Britain became the world's number one economic power in the nineteenth century.

Unilateral free trade. Consumer sovereignty. Quite a contrast with the managed trade advocates of today.

—WILLIAM H. PETERSON

68

"America consumes too much of the world's resources."

In a recent year, a United Nations report listed the United States as consuming 115,540 kilowatt hours of energy per person per year. At the same time, each person in the tiny central African nation of Burundi was using up just 120. My guess is that the average American is still consuming about a thousand times as much energy as the average Burundian.

Is that something we should feel guilty about? Does Burundi use less energy because America uses too much? Is world energy a fixed pie, with America greedily hogging more than its quota at the expense of the Burundis of the planet? Would Burundi be better off if America impoverished itself?

These are questions that came to mind when I read a statement in a newspaper by a man who claims to be a conservationist. Referring to the United States, he was quoted as saying, "When 7 percent of the world's population uses 40 percent of its energy, that's a disgrace." He thinks "greed" is the explanation.

Energy, by the way, isn't the only thing of which America consumes more than its share of world population. We also eat more than 7 percent of the world's potato chips and broccoli. We enjoy more than 7 percent of the world's indoor plumbing, hearing aids and baseballs. We operate more than 7 percent of the world's autos, buses, trucks, minivans, tractors, hang gliders, tricycles, and skateboards. We read more than 7 percent of the world's books and listen to more than 7 percent of all lectures and speeches. And maybe we even put up with more than our share of nonsense, too.

Apparently, it never occurred to the critic that America consumes more because it produces more. That's right—more than 7 percent of the world's potato chips, baseballs, skateboards, and countless other things. If we didn't first produce, we wouldn't have it to consume or to trade for what we really wanted.

It is not a disgrace that Americans consume 40 percent of the world's energy, if in fact that's the correct number. Rather, it is a tribute to our ingenuity, creativity, productivity, our talent for putting God-given abilities to work. If we restricted our energy consumption to just 7 percent of the total supply, our lives would be shorter, less healthy, and a lot more painful. There would be fewer of us, and not just by choice.

Moreover, the rest of the world would be worse off, too: Nobody prospers when his neighbors, mentors, or trading partners self-destruct. If anything is to be lamented, it's whatever causes Burundi to produce and consume so abysmally little of just about everything. I doubt that "greed" has anything to do with it.

Are things like clean highways, conservation, recycling, less waste, and more efficient use of resources worthwhile? Of course they are.

But that doesn't mean we have to treat bits of garbage as priceless treasures. It doesn't mean that spending a dollar to save a dime makes sense. It doesn't mean that the planet, the surface of which we've only begun to scratch, is about to run out of resources. It doesn't mean that our capacity to create, innovate, and think our way to new heights of technology and achievement has suddenly come to an end. And it certainly doesn't mean that we should hang our heads in shame because we have shown the world how to go from Model T's to space shuttles in less time than most peoples have taken to get from dirt paths to gravel roads.

The world's problems are plentiful enough without anyone making it his duty to manufacture more. That America consumes more than 7 percent of any particular moment's available energy is one of the biggest non-problems anybody could possibly waste his time on.

—LAWRENCE W. REED

69

"In order to develop, Third World countries need foreign aid."

The view prevails that in order to develop, Third World countries require foreign aid. This is a self-refuting myth. If foreign aid—the transfer of money from wealthy to poor countries—were necessary for development, no development could *ever* have occurred since at one time everyone was poor and, thus, there were no countries from which aid could have been transferred. That some countries developed, therefore, belies the notion that foreign aid is necessary for development.

But if foreign aid is not necessary for development, doesn't it at least facilitate it? The historical record is clear. Far from aiding, foreign aid is more likely to harm the very people it was officially intended to help.

A 1986 World Bank study concluded that the Bank-funded enterprises "represent a depressing picture of inefficiency, losses, budgetary burdens, poor products and services and minimal accomplishment." Other World Bank studies admitted that fully 75 percent of its African agricultural projects, totalling billions of dollars, had failed, that nearly 60 percent of its projects around the world were either "complete failures" or had "serious shortcomings," and that 60 percent of those projects judged to be successes were not sustainable after completion. And in a 1989 report, the Agency for International Development (AID), which administers United States foreign aid, acknowledged that all too often aid resulted in dependency rather than development and that even where growth occurred, "development assistance, overall, has played a secondary role." Of the scores of countries receiving U.S. assistance, AID was able to cite just three success stories: Japan, South Korea, and Taiwan. Yet, even these are doubtful. Japan is a case of reconstruction, not development. The task facing Japan in the late 1940s was the relatively simple one of rebuilding a developed economy ravaged by war, not the far more complex problem of stimulating development. And the impressive economic performances of both Taiwan and South Korea began only *after* large-scale economic aid was discontinued.

One reason foreign aid has been disastrous is that, by its nature, it generates perverse incentives that make sustained growth all but impossible.

Micronesia is a case in point. When it became a U.S. trust territory in 1945, private investment was outlawed and Micronesians were given free clothes, food, and other supplies. Many local farmers and businessmen went bankrupt, and the incentive to work was undermined. As productivity plummeted, Micronesia became entangled in a vicious circle: the more the economy declined, the more aid it received; and the more aid it received, the more the economy deteriorated. Between 1947 and 1985 this territory of fewer than 150,000 people received $2.4 billion in aid. Agricultural output declined by over 50 percent and imports of foods that had been produced locally rose five-fold. One public official complained that "We have no technicians, no plumbers, no electricians ... because the U.S. Government just handed us everything and didn't ask us to do anything for ourselves."

The point is not that Micronesians are lazy. It is that they responded rationally to the incentives facing them. By rewarding nonproductive behavior at the expense of hard work, by driving local producers out of business, foreign aid not only resulted in eliminating skills from the local population, it also retarded the development of those attitudes—thrift, industry, and self-reliance—that are essential for development.

If foreign aid is counterproductive, why does it continue? Again, one must look at the incentives.

The aid "industry" is a lucrative business, with hundreds of vice-presidents, directors, and outside consultants earning well in excess of $100,000 a year, excluding lucrative fringe benefits. But aid workers have little interest in eliminating the poverty they are officially employed to combat. On the contrary, the more poverty means larger budgets. True, those acting in the market may not have any more inherent interest in serving others. But, it is the genius of the market that it correlates self-interest and service to others. Doctors may have an interest in spreading rather than curing disease, but any doctor who did so would quickly find himself with empty waiting rooms and a dwindling income. In contrast, since foreign aid comes not from voluntary purchases on the free market but from government tax revenues, aid workers are able to benefit themselves without having to serve others.

Moreover, aid agencies are supposed to disburse money, not make it. Consequently, promotions depend more on meeting or exceeding lending targets rather than worrying about the soundness of loans, as commercial banks must do. And since it is easier to meet one's quota with a handful of big loans than with many small ones, the incentive is to "lend big, lend fast." This often redounds to the benefit of special interest groups in the First World. Typically, more 80 percent of all aid money distributed to the Third World is actually spent in the First World in the form of purchase orders. It is hardly surprising that many large corporations are the biggest proponents of foreign aid.

And finally, since aid does not go directly to the poor but is channeled through government rulers, who divert part of it into their own pockets, dispensing aid on the basis of need gives Third World rulers a vested interest in keeping their own subjects poor. The poorer the country, the more aid the rulers receive; the more a country develops, the less money they get. It is hardly surprising that some of the wealthiest individuals in the world, whose fortunes are in the billions of dollars, are rulers of some of the world's poorest countries.

By rewarding indolence and penalizing thrift and hard work, foreign aid undermines the acquisition of those attitudes that are necessary for economic development. And by politicizing the economy, it replaces the free market process by which individuals can become wealthy only by serving others with a process in which some become wealthy at the expense of others.

In short, foreign aid is in fact foreign harm.

—DAVID OSTERFELD

70

"Industrialization assures progress in undeveloped countries."

In government circles in nearly every "underdeveloped" nation of yesterday and today, there is a fixed idea that the economic salvation of the country lies in industrialization.

Among outstanding examples have been Egypt with its zeal for dams and India with its mania for a government steel mill. But examples can be found everywhere. In the early 1960s I met a typical one on a visit to the Argentine. Argentina imposed a practical prohibition on the import of foreign cars in order to create a home automobile industry that not only assembled cars but made the parts for them. Some of the chief American and foreign producers had established plants there. But it was then estimated that it cost about two-and-a-half times as much to make a car in the Argentine as it would to import one. Argentine officials were apparently not worried about this. They argued that a local automobile industry "provides jobs" and sets the country on the road to industrialization.

Was this really in the interest of the Argentine people? It certainly was not in the interest of the Argentine car buyer. He had to pay, say, about 150 percent more for a car than if he were permitted to import one without duty (or by paying a merely nominal revenue-raising duty). Argentina diverted capital, labor, and materials to car manufacturing—resources that could have otherwise been used far more efficiently and economically (by producing more meat, wheat, or wool, say, to buy automobiles rather than to make them).

The effect of all government-forced or subsidized industrialization is to reduce overall efficiency, to raise costs to consumers, and to make a country poorer than it otherwise would be.

But the authors of import prohibition might reply with a

form of the old "infant industries" argument that played such a large part in our own early tariff history. They may contend that once they can get an automobile industry established, they can develop the domestic know-how, skills, efficiencies, and economies that would enable an Argentine automobile industry to be not only self-supporting but capable of competing with foreign automobile industries. Even if this claim were valid, it is clear that a protected or subsidized industry must be a loss and not a gain to a country as long as the protection or subsidy has to be retained.

And even if a self-supporting motorcar industry were finally established, it would not prove that the losses in the period of hothouse growth were justified. When the conditions are in fact ripe in any country for a new industry capable of competing with the equivalent foreign industries, private entrepreneurs will be able to start it without government subsidies or prohibitions on foreign competition. This has been proved again and again within the United States—for example, when a new textile industry in the South competed successfully with the long-established textile industry in New England.

There is another fallacy behind the industrialization mania. This is that agriculture is always necessarily less profitable than industry. If this were so, it would be impossible to explain the prosperous agriculture *within* any of the industrialized countries today.

A popular argument of the industrialization-at-any-cost advocates is that it is impossible to point to a purely agricultural country that is as wealthy as "industrialized" countries. But this argument puts the cart before the horse. Once a dominantly agricultural economy becomes prosperous (as the early United States) it develops the capital to invest in domestic industries and therefore rapidly becomes a country of diversified production—both agricultural and industrial. It is diversified because it is prosperous rather than prosperous because it is diversified.

It is the great superstition of economic planners everywhere that only they know exactly what commodities their country should produce and just how much of each. Their arrogance prevents them from recognizing that a system of free markets and free competition, in which everyone is free to invest his labor or capital in the direction that seems to him most profitable, must solve this problem infinitely better.

—HENRY HAZLITT

71

"Foreign imports destroy jobs."

It seems so obvious. Everyday we see on the streets autos made in Germany and Japan. Our stores are filled with clothes made in Taiwan and shoes sent from Portugal and Hungary. If they were all made here instead, just think of all the jobs that American workers could have! If we could only keep foreign imports from invading our country, couldn't we cut our unemployment rate to zero in an instant?

The Constitution of the United States allows the government to restrict foreign imports. Article I, Section 8, gives Congress the power to "regulate commerce with foreign nations." So we have tariffs and quotas on steel and textiles and peanuts and a myriad of other products. Why not impose even more restraints and put all Americans back to work?

The flaw in that argument is something that most of us don't see. About 12 percent of our Gross Domestic Product is composed of goods bought by foreigners. So, suppose we do stop buying goods from Germany and Japan, Hungary and Taiwan. Where will the people there get the dollars they need to buy goods from us? After all, they are probably not inclined to paper their walls with small pictures of George Washington, so the dollars we send to foreigners are used here to buy, for instance, U. S. grain or planes or videotapes of American films. If we stop buying foreign products, we will destroy jobs for American wheat farmers, aerospace engineers, and movie producers.

Besides, if our government imposes restrictions on our purchases from abroad, what may foreign governments do? Retaliate! They can play the same game—and they do. Not too long ago, when we threatened to limit imports of wearing apparel from China, the Chinese replied that if we took such action they would repay us in kind, by cutting back on their imports of American soybeans. When we told the European Community that we wanted less of their pasta products, they told us that they would get by with fewer of our walnuts and lemons. Tit for tat!

Does that mean we should respond to all foreign trade barriers against our products by setting up barriers of our own? In late 1992, President Bush threatened to impose huge tariffs on French wine and other products in an effort to spur progress on the negotiations to reduce tariffs multilaterally under GATT, the General Agreement on Tariffs and Trade. The ploy worked, but we can't be confident that it always will. The response may even be further escalation, just like in an arms war. In the meantime, our cost of living is driven up, our standard of living falls, and consumers face fewer choices in the marketplace when foreign goods are kept out.

Even if there is no foreign retaliation or refusal to buy our products in response to trade barriers we impose, our tariffs and quotas can hurt workers in other American industries. What happens when we protect the jobs of workers in our steel industry by keeping out foreign steel? Chrysler, Ford, and General Motors will now find that they must pay higher prices for steel than BMW, Volvo, and other foreign rivals. That puts them at a competitive disadvantage and reduces jobs for our automobile workers.

In *Economics in One Lesson* Henry Hazlitt pointed out that the "art" of economics consists of being able to detect *secondary effects* of government policies. That is not always easy to do, particularly in the case of trade barriers. For example, in one case a number of years ago involving limits on imports of foreign shoes, a study indicated that the barriers might protect about 20,000 jobs for workers who produced shoes; but because the restrictions on shoe imports would drive up shoe prices and reduce shoe sales, about 12,000 jobs might be lost for people who work in stores selling shoes.

If import restrictions are so counterproductive, then why did the framers of the Constitution include a clause allowing them to be imposed? Was this simply a sad lapse in an otherwise brilliant document? The reason for allowing trade barriers seems to have been to provide a source of revenue for the federal government in the form of tariffs. After all, there was still a huge debt incurred during the Revolutionary War that needed to be repaid, and under the Articles of Confederation the central government had been utterly hamstrung in its efforts to raise revenue.

We should also realize that jobs are sometimes lost here for reasons other than foreign imports. For example in recent years Americans have been eating more chicken and less beef for nutritional reasons. Cattle ranchers have been hurt by the change. Supermarkets have been putting groceries in plastic bags rather than paper ones, and the workers in paper bag plants have seen jobs disappear. These changes in taste and technology have not had anything at all to do with imports. If we protect our workers who lose jobs because Americans decide to buy more foreign products, then what about protecting workers from losing jobs in domestic cases? Why not protect local jobs from the trade competition of neighboring cities?

Finally, think about what the wonders of technological improvement have wrought. People have invented cars, boats, planes, and trains; we've constructed truly marvelous highways and bridges. All these have helped speed the passage of goods around the world, making us all better off and delighting us with the variety that other people can produce. In the face of all these improvements, don't efforts to impose artificial barriers to trade in the form of tariffs and quotas seem downright stupid? But the special-interest groups who enlist the government to erect these barriers are not stupid; they rely on our ignorance of the true impact of trade barriers. We must recognize the fallacies in the arguments and reject their requests. Leaving people free to trade wherever they wish increases their opportunities to achieve their maximum well-being.

—RUSSELL SHANNON

72

"A balance of trade deficit hurts the domestic economy."

Most people shrewdly care about how they earn their incomes and spend and save their money. But they commonly have little interest in or familiarity with the flow of spending and investing between people in this country and those of other nations. And their impressions of this flow—summarized in the balance of payments—stem from journalists and politicians.

May the saints preserve us! Through innocence and deviousness, journalists and politicians have spread many untruths about the balance of payments. Note some of the error and nonsense.

It is not true that *international* transactions dominate the United States economy. The tail of world trade does not wag the domestic economy dog. The exchange and investment transactions recorded in the balance of payments are big, but they are still only a modest portion of our enormous total economy. Even after rising considerably from the mid-1960s to 1980, today's exports and imports of merchandise each represent less than 10 percent of gross domestic product (GDP).

It is not true that the balance of payments is *unbalanced.* The balance of payments is a double-entry accounting record of transactions between U.S. residents and the rest of the world. Essentially, one side of this record summarizes all the dollar payments people in our nation make to foreigners, and the other side shows how foreigners use these dollars. In one way or another, foreigners do use every dollar we pay to them, so both sides of the accounting record are necessarily equal: the balance of payments always balances.

It is not true that only *merchandise* buying and selling is recorded. There is more to the balance of payments than the "balance of trade" in goods. Many additional things are included.

Each of these categories almost always is unbalanced, but all of them together balance. Imports of merchandise have long exceeded merchandise exports, but this "deficit" is matched by "surpluses" in such things as services, investments, and investment income.

It is not true that an ideal trade pattern consists of *balanced* merchandise trade with every other nation. Whether or not total trade is balanced, we naturally have big imbalances with some countries and small ones with others, and some of those imbalances are net imports and others net exports.

It is not true that *importing goods* is irresponsible or a reflection of weakness. Individuals, households, and firms do benefit by buying things. When some of those things are made abroad, we benefit from use of foreign resources and foreign production. The gains from trade stem from what we get (imports), not from what we give (exports).

It is not true that big deficits in merchandise trade during the 1980s, which hit peaks in 1986 and 1987, stemmed from a *binge of U.S. buying* from abroad. The proportion of GDP spent on merchandise imports is now virtually the same as in 1979, and that ratio varied little in the intervening years. The proportion of GDP represented by merchandise exports also is now almost what it was in 1979, but the export ratio fell greatly in the mid-1980s, and then recovered. Our imports were consistently maintained as our economic health continued in the 1980s; but exports fell when the rest of the world economy weakened.

It is not true that our imports are solely for direct *consumption*. Some of what we import today makes us more productive tomorrow. More than 40 percent of current merchandise imports consist of industrial materials and capital goods—an investment proportion which has persistently grown since 1980.

It is not true that *importing capital* is undesirable. Borrowing, like spending, can be done well and wisely, making efficient use of obtained resources. Our early history of robust economic growth is a reflection in part of prolonged, sensible capital importation before World War I. Not only can capital inflow be beneficial, sometimes it is inevitable: an import balance of goods and services trade is necessarily financed (balanced) by foreign investment here. If we buy $100 of foreigners' goods and services but they use only $90 of their receipts to buy our goods and services, then the $10 they keep are invested in U.S. assets. The $10 deficit in our balance of goods and services trade is then matched by a $10 inflow of capital.

It is not true that the substantial net capital inflow of the 1980's was simply a large *increase in U.S. borrowing* from foreigners. The net inflow reflected also a precipitous fall in our lending to foreigners. The world in general, including U.S. residents, had found this economy to be a relatively attractive place in which to invest. During the '80s, foreign capital flooded here, and American capital largely stayed here.

It is not true that federal *budget deficits* have been largely and increasingly financed by borrowing abroad. The proportion of the federal debt now held by foreigners—about 13 percent—is smaller than it was in the late 1970s.

We need not go into a tizzy over our international accounts. Trade is trade, and investment is investment, whether the traders and the investors are residents of the same country or are geographically separated by political boundaries. International trade and investment—when left to private individuals seeking economic gain rather than manipulated by agents of the state—are natural and useful extensions of the domestic economy. If we work and save and invest and manage much and well, and if we maintain open markets in which free people can use their resources as they think best, we will prosper—and the balance of payments will take care of itself.

—WILLIAM R. ALLEN AND WILLIAM DICKNEIDER

X. RESOURCES AND
THE ENVIRONMENT

"Government is the key to protecting the environment."

When it comes to "environmentalism," it's presumed by many that government is the only game in town. At least that's the message of radical environmentalists, who see private enterprise as the villain and the public sector as the white knight.

That perspective is being challenged by a growing number of scientists and public policy scholars advancing what is known as "progressive environmentalism." To them, government has largely failed at the role of protector and, in fact, is quite often playing the role of despoiler. Progressive environmentalists believe that the best way to protect the environment is to empower private, property-owning individuals. What's yours you take care of, but what belongs to "everybody" nobody takes care of.

A report from the National Center for Policy Analysis in Dallas, entitled "Progressive Environmentalism: A Pro-Human, Pro-Science, Pro-Free Enterprise Agenda for Change," is full of examples that make the point:

The U.S. Forest Service uses taxpayer money to build roads (eight times the total mileage of the U.S. Interstate Highway System) into ecologically fragile areas in the Rocky Mountains and Alaska, so that loggers can cut down trees.

The Bureau of Land Management has subsidized the destruction of three million acres of wildlife habitat by using huge chains, which uproot everything in their path, in order to create more grazing land for livestock.

While the federal government owns only 4.7 million acres of wetlands and has encouraged the destruction of private wetlands, about 11,000 private duck clubs have managed to protect from five to seven million acres of wetlands from destruction.

Private individuals and organizations and even for-profit companies have acted to save a wide range of animals endangered by state bounties and vegetation threatened by counter-productive government policy. It's a story that's seldom told by the radical environmentalists and other Big Government types.

Similar examples are provided in a 1991 report from the Pacific Research Institute for Public Policy Research, entitled "Free Market Environmentalism" by Terry L. Anderson and Don R. Leal:

In England and Scotland, where there are property rights to fish in certain rivers and streams, private voluntary associations have been formed to fiercely protect these rights against the threats of over-fishing and pollution. Usually, rivers and streams have no private owners (they're "public property") and thus few real protectors or defenders.

Because there are no well-defined property rights in U.S. coastal waters, virtually every major species of commercially valuable marine life is being over-fished and stocks are being depleted. But at privately owned or leased oyster beds and private salmon fisheries, studies show that the stocks are carefully maintained (because of the direct financial interest of specific individuals).

If you think about it, the core philosophy of progressive or free-market environmentalism makes a lot of sense. Most people don't pollute their own backyard, but they may toss a wrapper onto somebody else's, or even more likely, on to publicly owned roadsides. And on a grand scale, we are now finding out that in those countries where government has had complete control of the environment (such as Eastern Europe or the former Soviet Union when they were Communist), ecological disaster is the normal order of things.

In this era of heightened interest in environmental protection, let's not jump to the conclusion that more government with its expensive bureaucracy is always the answer. The progressive environmentalists are trying to tell us that appropriate incentives within the framework of free markets and private property would get the job done a lot better.

—LAWRENCE W. REED

74

"Private enterprise leads to pollution."

Before we can determine whether or not this statement is true, we have to define our terms.

Pollution is relatively easy. This refers to a private property border crossing: waste matter is transported from one person's holdings to that of another, either directly of indirectly. It is important that we interpret pollution in this manner, otherwise it can easily be confused with something that superficially resembles it but is actually quite different, namely waste disposal. In the latter case, the by-products of the processing of goods or services are retained by the firm which created them. It disposes of them without negatively impacting others' rights. In this case there is no "spillover" effect, nor "externalities" affecting third parties.

The definition we are considering here, then, is a legal, not a physical one. As far as chemical analysis is concerned, it is impossible to distinguish pollution from waste disposal. In both cases, the waste material may well consist of identical chemical compounds.

The simplest example of pollution using this terminology is when Mr. Jones dumps his garbage on Mr. Smith's front lawn. That would be a case of direct pollution. The indirect version occurs when there is an intermediary between Jones and Smith, such as the air, or water. Here, Jones first incinerates his refuse, and prevailing winds carry the same material over to Smith, his lawn, and his lungs. Alternatively, Jones could dump this material into a river, negatively impacting Smith who lives downstream and is forced to use the now polluted water for drinking, irrigation, and washing.

Non-polluting waste disposal occurs when baseball fans leave the stadium littered with peanut shells and beer cans. There is no "border crossing" in this case, since ticket prices reflect the cleanup costs. The management voluntarily disposes of the detritus. Another example would be hiring a maid to clean one's home. There may be garbage strewn all over the place, but this is not pollution; the maid has agreed to do the cleaning for the owners.

What, then, is a private enterprise? This is not a system where government grants special privileges (subsidies, protection from competition) to business concerns. Far from it. On the contrary, free enterprise is a system based firmly on the premise of private property rights. Trespassing and theft are absolutely incompatible with the free market system. The market is the concatenation of all voluntary trades (employment, barter, purchase, rental, sale, etc.) between mutually consenting parties. Under pure and unadulterated laissez-faire capitalism, the only function of government is to protect person and property against physical attack from outsiders.

We are now ready to put these two elements together. Pollution, we have seen, is in effect a bombardment, an infringement of one person's rights by another. But the essence of private enterprise is precisely to prevent such goings on. It can therefore be stated, without fear of contradiction, that private enterprise does not lead to pollution. But this way of putting matters is far too understated. Actually, "market pollution" is a contradiction in terms. To the extent that there *is* private enterprise, there cannot *be* pollution; it is against the law. To the extent that pollution exists, this is *prima facie* evidence that the legal underpinnings of capitalism have been breached; that the law of trespass is not being upheld; that private property rights are not being defended. Pollution is a trespass or border crossing; the sole function of a free enterprise government is to prevent this (and other) violations of property rights. Therefore, the two are entirely incompatible.

Now it is of course true that many countries, in many areas of the world, in many time periods, have been *considered* to be based on free enterprise principles, and yet suffered from pollution. This only attests to the inaccuracy of language.

Let us consider one such example, the United States in the nineteenth century. Up until approximately 1830, the courts had based their decisions in "nuisance cases" (we would now call them environmental litigation) on a reasonably close approximation to a free enterprise legal system. If a farmer could show that the railroad engine was spewing forth sparks and setting his haystacks on fire, he could collect damages. If the housekeeper complained that factory fumes were dirtying the clean laundry she hung on her clothesline, she would typically be granted a cease and desist order. Injunctions were invariably granted to downstream users victimized by upstream waste dumping.

Under these conditions, it was clear that manufacturers had to take into account third party effects. There were strong incentives to use cleaner burning but more expensive anthracite coal instead of the dirtier but cheaper high sulfur variety; to install smoke prevention devices; to engage in research and development aimed at abating nuisances. There was even an "environmental forensics" industry in the making, dedicated to determining guilt for pollution. And when all else failed, the railroad, the factory owner, and the "upstreamer" could pay their victims to the latter's satisfaction, thus converting pollution into waste disposal, and "internalizing" the externalities.

But in the 1850s and thereafter, a new philosophy began to permeate the legal fraternity. It was determined that the "public good" required economic progress. In the view of an increasing preponderance of judges, this could only be attained by supporting manufacturing. So when the aggrieved victim of pollution next appeared before the bench, they said, in effect, "Our primary goal is to facilitate a rising GNP. In order to do so, we must give carte blanche to polluters. Your selfish private property rights are in the way of the greater good for the greater number, and must be swept aside."

Under this conditions, all market-oriented environmental incentives came to an abrupt halt. Previously, environmentally sound acts resulted from both selfishness and benevolence. Now, only the latter could operate, the one that Adam Smith saw as far less reliable. After all, why should the profit-seeking firm use clean fuel, or worry about smoke prevention, when it was not legally responsible for damages? The few businessmen who did so in any case, on moral grounds, put themselves at a competitive disadvantage; they became more liable to bankruptcy.

The resulting environmental crisis was due not to free enterprise, but to its very opposite.

—WALTER BLOCK

75

"Only government is farsighted enough to protect resources for future generations."

Many people think that private companies and individuals are shortsighted and interested only in immediate profits. They feel that the private sector cannot be entrusted with the protection of natural resources for future generations. In their view, only the government is independent and objective enough to give up short-term rewards from exploitation in favor of long-term protection of natural resources.

This view explains the creation of the U.S. Forest Service early in the twentieth century. Because private loggers were cutting down many forests, influential people, including President Theodore Roosevelt, feared a "timber famine." The Forest Service was to be a public agency that would manage the government's forests for the long term. Later, a prominent natural resource economist, Harold Hotelling, warned in the 1930s that the world's natural resources could be depleted for personal gain and urged government control of natural resources.

But these views are wrong on two counts: Private companies and individuals act in a more farsighted way than many people think, and governments act in a shortsighted way.

The nature of private property forces companies and individuals to take the future into account. If people are self-interested, as economic theory assumes, they will use their property to attain greater personal wealth. Since the value of property today depends on the future returns from that property, actions that reduce future returns lower its current value. So owners who want to maximize their wealth have an interest in assuring that those future returns continue. This leads, in general, to good stewardship.

This incentive for stewardship exists even for the assets of companies managed by officers with a short-term horizon (that

272 / Clichés of Politics

is, those who don't expect to be around when their decisions affect profits). Current stock prices reflect the knowledge available to people in the market. Stockholders seeking to increase their wealth incorporate information about the future effects of decisions into the price they are willing to pay for a company's stock. If corporate actions appear to increase a firm's future value, the stock price will rise; if actions are likely to reduce future value, the price will fall.

Although stockholders usually want to preserve the value of their assets, some individuals or companies may prefer to consume resources now, even though it means reducing the value of their assets. The market allows others who disagree to act on their own opinion. Someone who thinks that a resource (say, a forest or copper mine) will be more valuable in the future may buy it, to save the resource or invest in it to produce more in the future. Historically, these conservation and investment activities have worked well. As far as we know, no non-renewable resource has ever actually disappeared. To the contrary, investments in conservation and new sources have driven down the prices of most minerals over time (after adjusting for inflation).

Those who invest to supply resources for the future are often speculators. They provide for the future in a way similar to the way that distributors who buy fruit and vegetables in Florida for resale in New England provide for New Englanders.

In contrast to the private sector, where markets and capital values force consideration of the future, government officials typically have no market signal as to how their decisions affect the future, and little incentive to consider impacts on future voters. However altruistic their feelings toward future generations, such altruism is normally swamped by current political realities.

For politicians, the pressure to be re-elected often gives them a two- or four-year horizon. To stay in office, politicians have to think about rewarding voters now. Otherwise, competitors who want their job will do so. Voters and politicians, unlike market investors, have no market price changes to signal the future benefits and costs of current actions and, without personal wealth at stake, no reason to scrutinize decisions for their potential impacts. Since resources that are government owned are not traded in a market, their capital value is seldom known. When governments do sell off the future, reducing the value of the nation's assets entrusted into their care, generally no one's the wiser.

But don't voters look toward the future? Yes, but they are unlikely to carefully monitor the actions of politicians. Voters as a group control government, but at election time an individual's vote is never decisive. The voter who carefully weighs the issues will be unable to cast the winning ballot. He or she is forced to share the costs (and share any benefits) of the group's voting decisions. Unable to decide an election, a voter has little incentive to seek detailed information. It is more in the interest of a voter to carefully research and weigh decisions such as which car to buy than which candidate to vote for, since the individual decision on which car to buy is always decisive. So voters remain far more ignorant about government than they are about decisions that involve their own assets. Policies with short-term, visible benefits will be popular, even when future costs are high.

One sign of the resulting shortsightedness in government is the poor maintenance of much of our nation's infrastructure—its roads, bridges, subways, and water systems. This poor maintenance is widely recognized. George Peterson of the Urban Institute, for example, points out that "if public officials have to choose between trimming maintenance or trimming current services, or between cutting back expenditures and laying off public employees, there is a built-in bias against capital preservation." He points out that the consequences of deferred maintenance may not show up for four or six years, "which is a political lifetime."

Another example of the government's failure to provide for future generations is the tendency for governments to pay a large portion of public employee wages in the form of unfunded pensions—costs that can be placed on future voters. Private pensions are much less often underfunded, in part because pension obligations show up instantly in stock prices.

When it comes to preserving natural resources, the story is the same. While it may look as though the government is preserving the environment for the future—as in 1964 when Congress passed the Wilderness Act—it is actually responding to the demands of strong contemporary political constituencies. When we look at what the government is doing to manage or protect the land that it has set aside, the story is often quite different. Concern about future generations is frequently low on the list of priorities, since political realities control government.

—RICHARD L. STROUP AND JANE S. SHAW

XI. PHILOSOPHICAL AND
ETHICAL PERSPECTIVES

76

"Private enterprise panders to greed and selfishness."

Private enterprise, or capitalism, is often attacked on the grounds that it encourages a number of character traits that are incompatible with moral and religious values. Political intervention with private markets is then justified on the grounds that politicians, governmental bureaucrats, and liberal elitists are good people with pure motives whose interference with the market not only reflects their moral superiority but will inevitably benefit the masses. The errors in this last claim are addressed elsewhere in this book. It is important at this point to challenge the thoughtless equating of capitalism with greed and selfishness.

If we take our cue here from the Christian tradition, the Bible clearly does condemn *selfishness*. But the catch is that selfishness should never be confused with the quite different characteristic of *self-interest*. When Jesus commanded us to love our neighbor as ourself (Matthew 22:39), he gave implicit approval to self-interest. When a person is motivated by selfishness, he seeks his own welfare with no regard for the welfare of others. But when a person is motivated by self-interest, he can pursue his welfare in ways that do not harm others; in fact, one of the things we can learn from a careful study of market economics is how one person's acting out of self-interest can produce consequences that benefit large numbers of other people.

There is nothing sinful in caring about what happens to one's family or oneself. In fact, the New Testament condemns those who lack such concern (1 Timothy 5:8). Since the kinds of voluntary exchanges that characterize the market are mutually beneficial, selfishness is not an *inherent* feature of capitalism. People who exchange on the basis of market principles engage in activities that benefit themselves and others. The conditions of any free market oblige people to find ways of helping themselves at the same time they help others, whether they do this consciously or not.

The market is an instrument that enables people to attain individual goals in a voluntary, nonviolent way. It is difficult to see how the pursuit of individual goals, which the market makes possible, is equivalent to selfishness. It requires a great deal of question-begging to equate even the pursuit of monetary profit with selfishness. Since profit can be a means to other ends, it can be used for selfish or for altruistic purposes. The market only reflects the value of the people who use it. The pursuit of goals, even profits, is not selfish *per se*. Moreover, the less fortunate members of a society cannot be helped by the productive members until the economic system produces at least enough to go around. The free market makes private and public charity possible in this way.

The claim that the market panders to greed is also false. A proper understanding of the operation of the market will show how the market, in fact, *neutralizes* greed. One may lust after the property of another all he wants. But as long as the rights of the second party are protected, the greed of the first individual cannot harm him. Greed can never harm another person so long as his rights are protected under the constraints of a true capitalist system that prohibits acts of force, fraud, and theft. If a man is going to satisfy his greed within a market system of rights, he is going to have to offer others something that they want in exchange. His greed must lead him to a product or service which others are willing to barter for. Thus, every person in the market system who wishes to succeed must be conscious of others. Each must ask himself what other people want and how he can best service those wants.

But contrast all this with the totally different situation that exists in economies where representatives of the state intervene in market processes. Within socialist and interventionist economies, men and women motivated by greed and selfishness need not attend to the wants and desires of the people from whom they seek to gain advantage. All such a person needs to do is bribe one or more government officials who will reward his bribe by giving him special consideration.

But greed that operates within a market system involves a paradox. The market is one area of life where concern for the other person is required. Instead of pandering to greed, the market mechanism allows natural human desires to be satisfied in nonviolent ways. The alternative to free exchange is violence and coercion, both trademarks of socialist and interventionist economies.

—RONALD H. NASH

77

"I prefer security to freedom."

Giving up freedom for security is a little like choosing to be beheaded rather than to die from natural causes—there is some solace in knowing when and by whose hand the axe will fall, but once executed the deed is difficult to undo.

Happily, the choice between security and freedom is a less dismal one than of the manner of one's demise, although its importance is no less grave. In fact, to an extent there is no choice between freedom and security at all, since realizing maximum personal freedom in a civil society actually requires giving up some measure of personal autonomy. (By "security" we usually mean protection against dangers that may be actual, potential, or perhaps completely unknown. "Freedom" refers to the ability of a person to exercise the right to make choices voluntarily, in the absence of coercion and compulsion.) Thus, for example, to secure the most personal freedom, we must recognize the conditional and strictly limited authority of some (e.g., police) to use coercion and compulsion against persons or groups who use or threaten aggression.

Beyond these limits, however, there does exist a trade-off. It may include the promise of complete protection against danger in return for total loss of autonomy, or, more commonly, of a partial sacrifice of freedom in exchange for some perceived security.

It would be a mistake to dismiss the plight of those who find themselves in such desperate circumstances that they believe giving up some or all of their freedom is the most effective solution to their problems. For many, bondage may appear to be the only alternative to destitution. Those in less dire need may still believe the loss of some freedom worth the promise of more protection against hunger, disease, and ignorance. To them, tax-funded food, medicine, and education represent a viable middle ground between slavery at one extreme, and what they regard as the "freedom to be poor" at the other.

Nevertheless, opposing such sentiments, no matter how sincere, are two facts: Freedom is far easier to lose than to regain; and surrendering freedom promotes insecurity.

Freedom is easier to give up than to get back. Why should this be? To begin with, choosing less freedom means sacrificing the very right itself to choose. While there is a certain sense in which we "choose" even at gunpoint ("Your money or your life!"), it is not one we normally identify with genuine choice. Thus, giving up freedom means forfeiting the right to make real choices, including the choice to recover one's freedom. Unlike risk and return in a business investment, the trade-off between freedom and security in society does not occur in proportionate increments. Once citizens have given the state the authority to make their decisions for them, the state is usually loath to relinquish that authority even when that is the best action for its citizens, since that would hamper the pursuit of its own, rather than its citizens', interests.

Sacrificing freedom for security ultimately renders all citizens less secure. First of all, becoming dependent on someone else merely substitutes one kind of insecurity for a more insidious kind. In the context of political choice, greater "security" means placing more power over our lives in the hands of those who work for the state. Decision-making, in the face of the same dangerous and uncertain world, comes to rest with persons other than ourselves. These persons, however, are highly unlikely to know better than each of us what our unique problems, abilities, and goals are. But if public authorities know less than we do about facts relevant to each of us, how can we be confident that they will make better choices for us than we would ourselves, even if they are kind and benevolent rulers? (We can well imagine, of course, how they would behave were they not kind and benevolent.) Having surrendered our freedom, we would bear less individual responsibility for our lives, but this would do little or nothing to bolster our personal security. Like so-called "social justice," absolute security is a mirage. We are secure only insofar as we are free to exercise the effort and creativity needed to meet life's challenges.

Secondly, the preference for security over freedom will usually result in declining freedom and expanding government. One important reason for this is that when the state protects select persons or groups against a hazard that confronts everyone in society, this forces the unprotected to bear a larger proportion of the hazard and renders them even less secure. As the security of the unprotected diminishes, their demand for state-sponsored security for themselves (with the accompanying loss of freedom) becomes stronger and more justifiable. Thus, for example, a state program that guarantees a minimum income to the non-working means that at least some workers must pay for it out of their own non-guaranteed incomes. Those who feel the extra burden most acutely will have a clear incentive to demand that the state extend the guarantee (or something like it) to themselves, also. Yet, if the state meets this demand, any remaining uncovered workers would suffer even greater insecurity. In this way, an escalating demand for security drives the growth of government and the decline of freedom. The ultimate outcome of this process, as we have seen, is not genuine security at all but its opposite.

Let us escape the chopping block while we still can.

—Sanford Ikeda

78

"Society is to blame, not I."

In some 63.7 percent of all interviews in my office as Dean of Wabash College, the person across the desk is there to tell me who's to blame. And in 99.6 percent of the cases where that is the question, the answer is the same: *He* isn't.

Now if these were just simple cases of prevarication, we could all shake our heads at the loss of the old Yes-Father-I-chopped-down-the-cherry-tree spirit and turn to some other problem, such as the danger presented to the stability of the earth by the build-up of snow on the polar icecaps. But the denial of responsibility is rarely that simple, and herein lies the story.

Today's George Washington, on the campus and elsewhere, says, "Yes, I chopped down the cherry tree, *but*—"and then comes 10 to 90 minutes of explanation, which is apparently supposed to end in my breaking into tears and forgiving all, after which he goes home to sharpen his little hatchet.

The little Georges of today say, "Yes, I chopped down the cherry tree, but let me give you the *whole* story. All the guys over at the house were telling me that it's a tradition around here to cut down cherry trees. What's that? Did any of *them* ever actually cut down any cherry trees? Well, I don't know, but anyway there's this tradition, see, and with all this lack of school spirit, I figured I was really doing the school a favor when I cut down that crummy old tree."

Or it may run like this: "Now this professor, see, told us to collect some forest specimens; he may have told us what trees to cut, but, frankly, I just can't understand half of what he says, and I honestly thought he said cherry tree. Now actually I wasn't in class the day he gave the assignment and this friend of mine took it down and I can't help it if he made a mistake, can I? Anyway, if the callboy had awakened me on time, I'd have made the class and would have known he said to get leaves from a whortleberry bush."

So far we have run through the simpler cases. Now let's move to more complex ones. In this one, little George says to his father, "Yes, Dad, I cut down the cherry tree, but I just couldn't help it. You and Mother are always away from home and when you are home all you do is tell me to get out of the house, to go practice throwing a dollar across the Rappahannock. I guess I cut down the tree to get you to pay a little attention to me, and you can't blame me for that, can you?"

These can get messy. Here's another. In this one, young George has hired himself a slick city lawyer who has read all the recent books on the sociology of crime. The lawyer pleads G.W.'s case as follows: "It is true that this young man cut down the tree, marked exhibit A and lying there on the first ten rows of the courtroom seats. Also, there can be no question but that he did it willfully and maliciously, nor can it be denied that he has leveled over half the cherry trees in northern Virginia in exactly the same way. But is this boy to blame? Can he be held responsible for his actions? No. The real crime is his society's, and not his. He is the product of his environment, the victim of a social system which breeds crime in every form. Born in poverty [here we leave the George Washington example], raised in the slums, abused by his parents," and on and on. The lawyer closes by pointing a finger at me and saying dramatically, "You, Dean Rogge, as a member of the society which has produced this young monster, are as much to blame as he, as much deserving of punishment as he." The boy gets off with a six-month suspended sentence and I am ridden out of town on a rail.

I do want to refer to just one other possibility. In this one, the lawyer calls as a witness an eminent psychoanalyst who, as a result of his examination of the young man, absolves him of all conscious responsibility for the crime, in testimony that is filled with the jargon of that semi-science, hence obscure, hence somewhat pornographic. It turns out that the cherry tree is a phallic symbol and the boy's action an unconscious and perverse response to the universal castration complex.

Far-fetched? Not at all. As Richard LaPiere writes in his book, *The Freudian Ethic:*

The Freudian doctrine of man is neither clear nor simple, but those Freudians who have turned their attention to the criminal have derived from it a theory of the criminal act and a prescription for social treatment that anyone can understand. It is, they hold perfectly natural for human beings to violate the law—every law, from the law that governs the speed of motor vehicles to that which prohibits taking the life of another human being.

The Freudian explanation of crime absolves the individual from all personal responsibility for the criminal act and places the blame squarely upon the shoulders of an abstraction—society. Modern society is especially hard upon the individual, since it imposes upon him so many and often contradictory restraints and at the same time demands of him so much that does not come naturally to him. His criminal acts are therefore but a symptom of the underlying pathology of society, and it is as futile to punish him for the sins of society as to attempt to cure acne by medicating the symptomatic pustules.

Where does all this leave us? Who's to blame? Well, nobody, or rather everybody. The Freudian Ethic has eliminated sin (and, of course, that means that it has eliminated virtue as well).

Personally, I can't buy it. I cannot accept a view of man which makes him a helpless pawn of either his id or his society. I do not deny that the mind of each of us is a dark and complex chamber, nor that the individual is bent by his environment, nor even the potentially baneful influence of parents. As a matter of fact, after a few months in the Dean's Office, I was ready to recommend to the college that henceforth it admit only orphans. But as a stubborn act of faith I insist that precisely what makes man is his potential ability to conquer both himself and his environment. If this capacity is indeed given to or possessed by each of us, then it follows that we are inevitably and terribly and forever responsible for everything that we do. The answer to the question, "Who's to blame?" is always, "Mea Culpa, I am."

This is a tough philosophy. The Christian can take hope in the thought that though his sins can never be excused, he may still come under the grace of God, sinner though he be. The non-Christian has to find some other source of strength, and believe me, this is not easy to do.

What does all this have to do with our day-to-day living, whether on or beyond the campus? Actually, it has everything to do with it. It means that as students we stop blaming our teachers, our classmates, our parents, our high schools, our society, and even the callboy for our own mistakes and shortcomings. It means that as teachers and college administrators we stop blaming our students, the board of trustees, the oppressive spirit of society (and even our wives) for our own failures.

As individuals it means that we stop making excuses to ourselves, that we carry each cherry tree we cut down on our consciences forever. It means that we say with Cassius, "The fault, dear Brutus, is not in our stars, but in ourselves." This is a tough philosophy, but it is also the only hopeful one man has yet devised.

—Benjamin A. Rogge

79

"All people should perform some type of national service."

What is national service? There have been different versions of the idea, some advanced by socialists, some even by conservatives. The basic notion is that once people reach young adulthood, following their having obtained all sorts of benefits from society free of charge, they ought to be grateful and return the favor, show their gratitude, and do service for those who sacrificed for them. But there is more. Since so much of what past generations have done benefits those who live in the present, it is only fair that members of the latter group should leave contributions to subsequent generations.

Yet although some of this has the air of good sense, it is in fact all nonsense. The worst aspect of the proposal, from a moral point of view, is to treat unsolicited gifts as if they could mandate compensation. No one who without request gives another something of value has any claim to be paid for this. Where is the respect for choice here? Is this not, in fact, a cruel hoax whereby one makes another beholden to oneself? If this were legitimate, we could embark on enslaving generations of human individuals, by merely giving them things of value they may not want at all and have shown no inclination of wanting to obtain at a cost to them.

An equally important realization is that if those in the past who left certain values to us did not have sufficient reason to do this, they would have done other things. Is it even imaginable that Shakespeare, Dante, Rembrandt, Hugo, Newton, or Chopin labored so as to leave us indebted to them, to call forth within us a sense of gratitude and obligation toward future generations? Or did they rather accomplish their innumerable artistic, scientific, and other feats because, well, they had their own reason; they wanted to do it quite apart from something as indeterminate as hoping for some kind of reciprocity? The latter is clearly the case, if only because we all know we have no control over what those in the future will do, how they will assess our contributions, and how important it will be to them.

All in all, the very idea that people's doing things for others leaves these others with enforceable obligations is morally cynical and largely silly (not that one or two people might not have set out to invent something or to research some facts with this in mind). It makes better sense to surmise that those who created the values of one's culture expected rewards, if any, from those who were around them and with whom they could discuss terms. The rest they did because they had good reason, apart from what others, especially members of future generations, would do "in return." I don't write or help my children with their homework or assist a student in my class or lend a hand to a friend with his moving or job-seeking with the anticipation of some payback, or placing a burden on the beneficiary. What I do in these respects is to be, as it were, largely its own reward. And the rest I am paid for by those who knowingly contracted with me to deliver to them some of what I can produce.

It is also extremely puzzling how national service would determine just how much benefit one has reaped from the contributions of people who came before those who are to do service. Why two years? Suppose I have gained enormously from the works of some people in the past—I personally, for example, have had some of the most wonderful times in my life while reading W. Somerset Maugham, watching Fred Astaire and Ginger Rogers dance, hearing innumerable blues and jazz singers belt out their tunes, listening to the vitality of the great composers, and taking in the paintings, sculptures, and architecture of great artists throughout the world. (I often wish I could express to them my pleasure with their accomplishments, and now and then try to pen some little ode to their creativity.) Am I to understand that my national service will compensate for this? No way—the benefits I have enjoyed cannot be compensated, and one can only hope that those who provided them had a reasonably rewarding life through making these wonderful things. There is no way for some bureaucrats or politicians to tell what it has been worth to me to encounter these great creations. There is no way to put a price on it at all, and to pretend to do so is an insult to the good name of the creators.

No, the national service idea is a ploy, once again, to extract unpaid work from unsuspecting and gullible folks, another type of involuntary servitude. Moreover, as with other attempts to allocate resources through central (even if democratically assisted) planning, national service is a wasteful way to give direction to human works. Who is able to tell better than human beings in free negotiations among one another in a marketplace what service should be provided where in the culture? Who has the God-like omniscience to tell that a sizable group of young adults should work, say, in Manhattan soup kitchens rather than assist scientists in finding intelligent life in outer space? What system of assessment will guide the national service dream—the advice of philosophers, sociologists, economists, psychologists, and city planners?

National service is another idea that breeds a kind of tragedy of the commons—most groups would naturally wish to reap the benefits they imagine such service could provide; but because this service is largely to be rendered without regard to a market price, there will be no end of abuse and overuse of it. Innumerable projects of little if any discernible public worth will be undertaken. All those Works Progress Administration projects of the New Deal Era, hailed by some enthusiasts as great contributions to our culture, have no *measurable* value at all since they were not produced via the method of free exchange, the only reasonably reliable way to know what value goods and services, including education, science and the arts, have for human beings. This is not because there are no common values we share but because they are rare, and the rest are highly particularized, specialized, and even individualized. What is of real, objective value to me may not be to you. It is like medicine—despite some general "do's and don't's," the details are highly diversified, depending on the patients.

So national service is a bad idea because (a) no one may morally be put under an obligation without first having the chance to consider whether to assume it (thus parents are wrong to think that children owe them, unless they went way beyond the call of their self-assumed duty and the child had the option to say "no"); (b) those who have left us with much to enjoy in life presumably had their good reasons, apart from any attempt to put us under some obligation, to make their contributions and collect their just rewards in their own lifetime; (c) to assess the value of both what benefited us and what our own work may be worth, is impossible due to the great diversity of human beings; and (d) the process would unleash the familiar tragedy of the commons, in this case stemming from the perception that the universal service is a kind of public good available for all to draw benefits from.

Of course national service can seem like a fine idea when we live in a welfare state. In such an environment of massive government spending, the citizenry may more readily accept the notion of repayment of public benefits handed to them by previous generations. What about, for example, the free public primary, secondary, and higher education "we" gave to "them"? What of the free beaches, roads, museums, hospital care, and all other goodies provided in the welfare state?

This is all a great fraud, though. If, as defenders of the welfare state argue, we all have this coming to us, why ask for payment in terms of national service and other contributions? And what made the idea of giving us all these goodies legitimate anyway? So now it can be used to justify subjecting us to involuntary servitude? Indeed, the welfare state itself comes in for severe criticism in part because it leads to this confusion between what government services we ought to have in the first place— e.g., the competent protection of our rights to life, liberty, and property (for which all we owe is the fee that pays the service)— or all these welfare handouts which, it turns out, aren't handouts at all but involuntarily acquired debts. So welfarism won't help justify national service.

Good deeds toward others should be their own reward, at any rate, not to be done in anticipation for compensation. Let's leave the process of reciprocal benefit to good will or explicitly formulated terms of exchange.

—TIBOR R. MACHAN

80

"If government doesn't relieve distress, who will?"

President Grover Cleveland, vetoing a congressional appropriation of $10,000 to buy seed grain for drought stricken Texans, may have given us all the answer we need to this cliché:

> The friendliness and charity of our countrymen can always be relied upon to relieve their fellow-citizens in misfortune.... Federal aid in such cases encourages the expectation of paternal care on the part of the government and weakens the sturdiness of our national character, while it prevents the indulgence among our people of that kindly sentiment and conduct which strengthens the bonds of a common brotherhood.

No doubt many of the congressmen who voted this appropriation were sincerely asking, "If the federal government does not save these poor Texans, who will?" President Cleveland had only to veto the measure and write an explanation. But we private citizens have no power beyond reason and suasion. What, then, might we have said? This would be one honest answer: "I am not clairvoyant and, thus, do not know *who* will relieve these people. However, I do know that Texans acting on their own initiative and with their own resources will take care of themselves better than they will be taken care of by any number of politicians imitating Robin Hood and applying the theories of Karl Marx."

The question, "If government does not relieve distress, who will?" is illogical. No one can ever answer, *who* will? Thus, the cliché maker wins his implied point without a struggle—unless one lays claim to clairvoyance or exposes the fakery of the question.

Every reader of these lines can prove to himself, by reflecting on personal experiences, that the relief of distress is an unpredictable event. Time after time, each of us, with no preconception, has observed distress and then taken steps to relieve it—with his own income!

Prior to the nineteen thirties, before the federal government assumed responsibility for "relief," no one could have foretold *who* would come to whose rescue; yet, since 1623, there is no record of famine or starvation in this country. Among a people where the principles of freedom were more widely practiced and government more limited than elsewhere, there has been less distress and more general well-being than history had ever recorded. Societies saddled with bureaucracy have no record of coming to the aid of free societies; it has always been the other way round.

Charity is a personal virtue. When government does not undertake police grants-in-aid—"relief"—millions of adults stand as guardians against distress. Their available charitable energy is totally at work observing distress in its neighborly detail, judging and coming to the rescue with the fruits of the labor of each charitable person. And on occasions of major disaster, there has been a voluntary pooling of individual resources, often extravagant.

What happens when government takes over? Charity gives way to politics. Funds coercively collected are dispensed to individuals according to group, class, or occupational category. This has no semblance of charity; it is the robbery of Peter to pay Paul. Further, when government constructs a feeding trough and fills it with fruits forcibly extorted from the citizenry, it creates new claimants and aggravates the problem it set out to solve.

It is not only the so-called "relief" projects that are based on the same tired cliché, but most other cases of government intervention in our society: "If the government doesn't do the job, who will?" If the government doesn't level mountains and fill valleys, drain swamps and water deserts, build highways over waters and seaways over land, send men to the moon and promise the moon to mankind, and a thousand and one other projects—if the government doesn't do these things, that is, force taxpayers to do them, who will? And more often than not the answer is that probably no one in his right mind would ever think of doing such things—at his own risk, with his own money. Eventually, a time might come when some ingenious person would see a way to do one or more of these jobs, in hope of profit, and would take the chance. But there is no way to determine in advance who that pioneer might be. The most that can be done is to leave men free, for only among free men do pioneers emerge.

Freedom affords every opportunity, in charitable enterprises or on the market, for the best—not the worst—to rise topside.

—LEONARD E. READ

81

"From each according to his abilities, to each according to his needs."

As a teacher in private and public schools, I found that the socialist-communist idea of taking "from each according to his abilities," and giving "to each according to his needs" was generally accepted without question by most of the pupils. In an effort to explain the fallacy in this theory, I sometimes tried this approach:

When one of the brighter or harder-working pupils made a grade of 95 on a test, I suggested that I take away 20 points and give them to a student who had made only 55 points on his test. Thus each would contribute according to his abilities and—since both would have a passing mark—each would receive according to his needs. After I juggled the grades of all the other pupils in this fashion, the result was usually a "common ownership" grade of between 75 and 80—the minimum needed for passing, or for survival. Then I speculated with the pupils as to the probable results if I actually used the socialistic theory for grading papers.

First, the highly productive pupils—and they are always a minority in school as well as in life—would soon lose all incentive for producing. Why strive to make a high grade if part of it is taken from you by "authority" and given to someone else?

Second, the less productive pupils—a majority in school as elsewhere—would, for a time, be relieved of the necessity to study or to produce. This socialist-communist system would continue until the high producers had sunk—or had been driven down—to the level of the low producers. At that point, in order for anyone to survive, the "authority" would have no alternative but to begin a system of compulsory labor and punishments against even the low producers. They, of course, would then complain bitterly, but without understanding.

Finally I returned the discussion to the ideas of freedom and enterprise—the market economy—where each person has free-dom of choice and is responsible for his own decisions and wel-fare.

Gratifyingly enough, most of my pupils then understood what I meant when I explained that socialism—even in a democ-racy—would eventually result in a living death for all except the "authorities" and a few of their favorite lackeys.

—THOMAS J. SHELLY

82

"If we don't get our share of government money, someone else will."

Over and over again, in city council meetings, in the deliberations of county commissioners, or in the state legislatures, one hears the assertion that if one's own governmental body does not take its share of federal money or state grants, then some other municipality, city, or state will take that share for themselves. Headlines in papers now regularly tout lawmakers who get millions for local or state projects, whether the project be a jogging path, library addition, community house, or bridge. Seldom does a local improvement occur without being reported as having been made possible by federal or state dollars, and with the politicians proudly reporting that the local citizenry has done well to take the governmental grants rather than let others grab them.

This tired cliché of interventionism is really several fallacies rolled into one. First, those who argue for participating in governmental handouts claim that citizens are only obtaining tax monies that they themselves have paid in. That is what is meant by getting "their share." Naturally, as the redistributive state has grown larger and larger, citizens feel more and more justified in trying to get part of the governmental largesse. If the truth be known, no local officials calculate what their citizens have actually paid in taxes in order to set a limit upon what they will accept in governmental grants. In fact, politicians are now commonly found priding themselves in the huge "windfalls" their local districts are getting compared to those obtained by their predecessors in office or by other contiguous districts. There is no longer any pretense of trying to get even, that is, to garner grants equal to taxes paid out. The mentality is one of a victim who has had his pocket picked now taking up picking pockets himself and not caring how much he takes from *his* victims.

A second false component of the cliché is the idea that such grants come from government. Ultimately, of course, no governments—federal, state, or local—can distribute monies unless they first obtain them from citizens through taxation or, in some cases, borrowing. In actuality, such grants are the last step of the redistributive process in which government has already seized from others the valuable resources it "gives," and has taken out its own cut to cover the administrative costs of redistribution. So, for example, this means that if Moline, Illinois (hypothetically speaking) obtains a federal grant to help build a jogging path, many other people in towns like Decatur, Georgia, and Jackson, Michigan, and Hartford, Connecticut, as well as people in tens of thousands of boroughs, cities, and hamlets across the United States will have fewer dollars to spend on their own recreation. A governmentally (state) financed library addition in Erie, Pennsylvania, will mean that other Pennsylvania citizens in Sharon, Harrisburg, King of Prussia, and Waynesburg will have less money to purchase their own books and newspapers. What is a gain for some is a loss to others. One really wonders whether citizens could be made to understand this by changing the wording on commemorative plaques which usually grace the sites of these public improvements. For example, wouldn't Moline voters be less likely to support the project if the plaque at the entrance to the jogging track read: "This Moline Public Jogging Track was made possible by the sacrifices of our fellow citizens in Decatur, Georgia; Jackson, Michigan; Hartford, Connecticut; and a host of unnamed others who have less that we might have more"?

What is needed is for citizens to urge their political representative to forgo the enticements of grants from various higher levels of government. Then, they should support that representative in his efforts to campaign against the redistribution which continues. If Moline gives up its jogging track (which should after all be supported by joggers, not the general citizenry), and then explains the reasons, others may be convinced to follow suit. The question is a moral one at root. Although we have suffered a decline in the application of fundamental moral principles to public life, there is no reason that, by explanation and persistence, the pendulum cannot swing away from the "dun my brother" outlook. But such an effort can only be begun when someone says, "If we don't take this governmental grant then we will have spared our fellow citizens' pockets, have done the right thing, and may have started a movement away from the morass of redistributionism in which we find ourselves."

—JOHN A. SPARKS

83

"The more complex the society, the more government control we need."

Argued a college president at a seminar: "Your free market, private property, limited government theories were all right under the simple conditions of a century or more ago, but surely they are unworkable in today's complex economy. The more complex the society, the greater is the need for governmental control; that seems axiomatic."

It is important to expose this oft-heard, plausible, and influential fallacy because it leads directly and logically to socialistic planning. This is how a member of the seminar team answered the college president:

"Let us take the simplest possible situation—just you and I. Next, let us assume that I am as wise as any president of the United States who has held office during your lifetime. With these qualifications in mind, do you honestly think I would be competent to coercively control what you shall invent, discover, or create, what the hours of your labor shall be, what wage you shall receive, what and with whom you shall associate and exchange? Is not my incompetence demonstrably apparent in this simplest of all societies?

"Now, let us shift from the simple situation to a more complex society—to all the people in this room. What would you think of my competence to coercively control their creative actions? Or, let us contemplate a really complex situation—the 255 million people of this nation. If I were to suggest that I should take over the management of their lives and their billions of exchanges, you would think me the victim of hallucinations. Is it not obvious that the more complex an economy, the more certainly will governmental control of productive effort exert a retarding influence? Obviously, the more complex our economy, the more we should rely on the miraculous, self-adapting processes of men acting freely. No mind of man nor any combination of minds can even envision, let alone intelligently control, the countless human energy exchanges in a simple society, to say nothing of a complex one."

It is unlikely that the college president will raise that question again.

While exposing fallacies can be likened to beating out brush fires endlessly, the exercise is nonetheless self-improving as well as useful—in the sense that rear guard actions are useful. Further, one's ability to expose fallacies—a negative tactic—appears to be a necessary preface to accenting the positive influentially. Unless a person can demonstrate competence at exploding socialistic error, he is not likely to gain wide audiences for his views about the wonders wrought by men who are free.

Of all the errors heard about the "bargaining tables" or in classrooms, there is not one that cannot be simply explained away. We only need to put our minds to it.

The Foundation for Economic Education seeks to help those who would expose fallacies and accent the merits of freedom. The more who outdo us in rendering this kind of help, the better.

—LEONARD E. READ

Authors and Editor

William R. Allen is Professor of Economics Emeritus at the University of California, Los Angeles.

C.W. Anderson was Manager of the Employers' Association of Milwaukee.

D.T. Armentano is Professor of Economics at the University of Hartford and author of *Antitrust and Monopoly*.

Charles W. Baird, a contributing editor of *The Freeman,* is Professor of Economics and Director of The Smith Center for Private Enterprise Studies at California State University, Hayward.

Jean L. Baker, based in the Chicago area, writes regularly for national and local trade, travel, and business publications.

Melvin D. Barger was a business writer associated with Aeroquip Corporation and Libbey-Owens-Ford Company for over 30 years. He is now a writer-consultant in Toledo, Ohio.

K.L. Billingsley is a media fellow of the Pacific Research Institute in San Francisco, California.

Walter Block is Professor of Economics at the College of the Holy Cross, Worcester, Massachusetts.

Cecil E. Bohanon is Professor of Economics at Ball State University, Muncie, Indiana. His articles have appeared in the *American Economic Review, Social Science Quarterly,* and other professional journals.

Gregory B. Christainsen is Professor of Economics at California State University, Hayward. He has lectured and consulted in more than 30 countries.

Paul A. Cleveland is Assistant Professor of Finance at Birmingham-Southern College, Alabama.

Benjamin L. Crawford is an economics student at Birmingham-Southern College, Alabama.

W.M. Curtiss (1904–1979) was a member of the senior staff of The Foundation for Economic Education from its beginnings in 1946 until 1973, serving as Executive Secretary and as Director of Seminars.

William Dickneider is a curriculum coordinator at Junior Achievement, Inc.

John Fiske was a nineteenth-century American philosopher and literary critic.

Gary M. Galles is Associate Professor of Economics at Pepperdine University, Malibu, California.

Henry Hazlitt (1894–1993) served as a trustee of The Foundation for Economic Education from its founding in 1946. Mr. Hazlitt was a noted economist, author, journalist, reviewer, and editor.

Robert Higgs, a contributing editor of *The Freeman,* is the author of *Crisis and Leviathan.* He has taught at the University of Washington, Lafayette College, and Seattle University.

John Hospers, a contributing editor of *The Freeman,* is Professor of Philosophy (emeritus) at the University of Southern California, and the author of numerous books, including *Introduction to Philosophical Analysis.*

Sanford Ikeda is Assistant Professor of Economics at the State University of New York at Purchase.

Matthew B. Kibbe is a Republican Budget Committee Associate, U.S. House of Representatives, and former Director of Federal Budget Policy, U.S. Chamber of Commerce. His articles and reviews have appeared in *The Wall Street Journal* and *The Washington Times,* among other publications.

Tibor R. Machan, a contributing editor of *The Freeman,* is Professor of Philosophy at Auburn University and the author of *Capitalism and Individualism: Reframing the Argument for the Free Society.*

James E. McClure is Associate Professor of Economics at Ball State University, Muncie, Indiana. His articles have appeared in *Economic Inquiry* and *Public Choice.*

Richard B. McKenzie is a professor in the Graduate School of Management at the University of California, Irvine, and an adjunct fellow at the Center for the Study of American Business in St. Louis. He is the author of *What Went Right in the 1980s.*

W.C. Mullendore (1892–1983) was the Chairman of Southern California Edison Company.

Ronald H. Nash is Professor of Philosophy and Theology at Reformed Theological Seminary in Orlando, Florida. Among the books he has edited or written are *Poverty and Wealth* and *Beyond Liberation Theology.*

Gary North is president of The Institute for Christian Economics in Tyler, Texas.

Edmund A. Opitz, a contributing editor of *The Freeman,* served as a member of the staff of The Foundation for Economic Education from 1955 until his retirement in 1992. He is the author of the book *Religion and Capitalism: Allies, Not Enemies.*

David Osterfeld (1949–1993) was Professor of Political Science at Saint Joseph's College in Rensselaer, Indiana. His most recent book was *Progress Versus Planning.*

E.C. Pasour, Jr. is Professor of Agriculture and Resource Economics at North Carolina State University and author of *Agriculture and the State.*

William H. Peterson, a contributing editor of *The Freeman* and Heritage Foundation adjunct scholar, taught most recently as the Lundy Professor of Business Philosophy at Campbell University.

304 / Clichés of Politics

Paul L. Poirot served as Managing Editor of *The Freeman* from its acquisition by The Foundation for Economic Education in 1956 until his retirement in 1987.

Leonard E. Read (1898–1983) established The Foundation for Economic Education in 1946 and served as its president until his death. Mr. Read was the author of numerous books and articles.

Lawrence W. Reed is president of the Mackinac Center for Public Policy, an educational and research organization located in Midland, Michigan.

Llewellyn H. Rockwell, Jr., is founder and president of the Ludwig von Mises Institute at Auburn University.

Benjamin A. Rogge (1920–1980) was Dean and Professor of Economics at Wabash College in Indiana and long a trustee of The Foundation for Economic Education.

Murray N. Rothbard (1926–1995) was the S. J. Hall Distinguished Professor of Economics at the University of Nevada, Las Vegas. He was the vice president for academic affairs at the Ludwig von Mises Institute, and the editor of the *Review of Austrian Economics*.

Dean Russell, an economist and retired college professor, is a former staff member of The Foundation for Economic Education.

John Semmens is an economist at the Laissez Faire Institute, an Arizona-based public policy research organization.

Hans F. Sennholz was Chairman, Department of Economics, Grove City College, Pennsylvania, until his retirement in 1992. Since that time he has been the president of The Foundation for Economic Education.

Russell Shannon is Professor of Economics at Clemson University, South Carolina. He specializes in the subjects of international trade, and comparative economic systems.

Jane S. Shaw is a senior associate of the Political Economy Research Center in Bozeman, Montana.

Thomas J. Shelly, now deceased, was a high school teacher in Westchester County, New York.

Mark Spangler is the senior financial officer of a manufacturing company located near Philadelphia, Pennsylvania. He is a former staff member of The Foundation for Economic Education.

John A. Sparks is Chairman of the Department of Business Administration, Economics, and International Management at Grove City College, Pennsylvania. He is also editor of *Vision and Values* and a principal in the law firm of Bogaty, McEwen and Sparks, P.C.

Richard L. Stroup is a senior associate of the Political Economy Research Center in Bozeman, Montana. He is also Professor of Economics at Montana State University.

Kyle S. Swan is a member of the staff of The Foundation for Economic Education.

Joan Kennedy Taylor is the editor of *Free Trade: The Necessary Foundation of World Peace* and the author of *Reclaiming the Mainstream: Individualist Feminism Rediscovered.*

Terree P. Wasley is an economic consultant specializing in health care, tax, and federal budget issues. She is the author of *What Has Government Done to Our Health Care?*

Index

Adams, John, 62
Advertising, 158–159
Affirmative Action, 181
Affluent society, 145
Africa, 251
Agrarian economies, 197
Agriculture, 19, 58–60
  agricultural markets, 221–223
  exports and imports, 223
  foreign aid and, 252
  government support of, 217–220
  and prices, 218
  profitability of, 218, 255
Airline industry, 84–86
Alabama, 130–131
Allen, William R., 115–117, 260–262
American Council of the Blind, 12
"American competitiveness," 172
American Indians, 59
American Medical Association, 207
American Revolution, 121, 259
Anderson, C.W., 177–179
Anderson, Terry L., 266
Angelou, Maya, 232
Anti-Corn Law League, 246–247
Antitrust laws, 155–157
Argentina, 254
Armentano, D.T., 155–157
Arrow, Kenneth J., 52
Articles of Confederation, 30
Arts, public finance of, 232–235,
  236–239
Automobile industry, 254
Ayau, Manuel, 105

Baird, Charles W., 9–11, 30–32
Baker, Jean L., 180–185

Balance of payments, 260
Bankers and regulators, 80
Barbarism, 46
Barger, Melvin D., 38–41, 227–231,
  236–239
Bastiat, Frederic, 113
Beta-blockers, 208
Better Business Bureaus, 206
Bias in media, 227–231
Big business, 61, 160–162, 245, 246
Bill of Rights, 16, 23, 30, 62
Billett, Michael, 212
Billingsley, K.L., 112–114
Black Americans, 232
Blame, 283–286
Block, Walter, 240–242, 267–270
Bohanon, Cecil E., 18–21, 163–165
Böhm-Bawerk, Eugen, 63
Brady, Nicholas, 80
Brandeis, Justice Louis, 76
Brandeis University, 180
Bright, John, 246, 247
Broadcast licensing, 228
Broken window parable, 133–134
Buckley, William F., Jr., 112
Budget deficits, 115–117, 262
Bureau of Land Management, 265–
  266
Bureaucracy, bureaucratic manage-
  ment, 35, 36, 39, 55, 91, 108, 132,
  143, 211, 212, 277, 289
Burger, Chief Justice Warren, 47
Bush, George, 171

Caesar, 103
Calderon, Roberto, 201–202
Callahan, Daniel, 203

Canada, national health care in, 210–214
Capital accumulation, capital investment, 26, 128, 191, 196
Cartel agreements, 156
Carter, Jimmy, 116
Carter Administration, 82
CAT scanners, 210
Censorship, 42–44
Central planning, 36, 46, 255, 289
Character, 291
Charity, 291
Child care, 183–184
Child labor, 66, 196–198
China, 19, 127, 257
Christainsen, Gregory B., 135–137
Christianity, 285–286
Citrus industry, marketing orders in, 221–223
Civil rights, 3, 27–29
Civil Rights Act (1964), 27–28
Civil Aeronautics Board, 84
Class warfare, 124
Clayton Act, 155
Cleveland, Grover, 291
Cleveland, Paul A., 130–132, 232–235
Clinton, William J., 112, 171, 245
Cobden, Richard, 246, 247
Coercion, 46, 51, 78, 90–91, 119, 138, 237, 240, 279, 280
Collectivism, 183
Common ownership, 294–295
Compassion, 174, 197
Competition, 37, 84, 155–156, 163, 165, 172, 177, 186, 192, 203, 219, 245–246
Competitive private enterprise, 122
Complexity of society and economy, 299–300
Communism, 1, 294
Conservation, 249, 271, 272
Consumer's Union, 206
Consumers, 158–159, 164–165, 177, 204, 206
Consumption versus production, 112–113

Cooperation versus competition, 149–151
Corn Laws, 246
Corporations, government chartering of, 53
Corporations, size of, 160
Costs
  of exchanges, 42–43
  of labor, 189
Crawford, Benjamin L., 232–235
"Creature of the state" arguments for government regulation, 52–53
Credit Control Act (1969), 82
Curtiss, W.M., 58–60

Declaration of Independence, 9, 13, 23, 61
Defense expenditures, 116
Democracy, 30–32
Dependence, 176
Depository Institutions Deregulation and Monetary Control Act (1980), 80, 82
Deregulation, 84–86
Diagnostic medical tests, 210
Dickneider, William, 115–117, 260–262
Discrimination, 16, 28, 180, 181
Division of labor, 246
Doctors, 211, 253
"Dumping," 245
Dutch Revolution, 167

Eastern Europe, 1, 173
Economic controls, 75–79
"Economic democracy," 31
Economic freedom, 32
Economic growth, 43
Economic progress, 172
Economics in One Lesson, 258
Education, 59, 176, 240–242, 294–295
Egypt, 254
Emergency controls, 75–79
Emerson, Ralph Waldo, 62

Employer-employee relationship, 186–188
Employment Act of 1946, 77
Employment, 171–173, 174–176
Entitlements, 18, 20, 117
Entrepreneurs, entrepreneurship, 40, 158–159, 181, 255
Environment, 265–266
Environmental litigation, 269
Equal rights, 31
Equality, 17, 153, 182
Externalities, 267

Fact-finding, government role in, 90–93
Factory system, 191
"Fair wage," 177–179
"Fair profit," 152–154
Famine, 19, 102–103, 166
Farming, *see* agriculture
Farnese, Alexander, 167–168
Federal Aviation Administration, 52, 85
Federal deposit insurance, 83
Federal jobs programs, 171
Federal Reserve, 80, 82, 83, 88, 90
Federalist Papers, 30
Feudalism, 55
Fields, Debbie (Mrs. Fields Cookies), 184
Fine art, investment in, 237
First Amendment, 9–11, 13, 23, 32, 227
Fiske, John, 166–168
Food
  right to, 18–21
  prices, 217
Force, threat of, 23
Ford, Henry, 103
Foreign aid, 251–253
Foundation for Economic Education, role of, 300
Founding Fathers, 13, 16, 25
Franklin, Benjamin, 12
Free enterprise, alleged failures of, 87–89

Free market
  economy, 35, 62
  environmentalism, 265–266, 269
  for medical goods, 206–209
  and monopoly, 155
  and the poor, 118–120, 192
  in transportation, 85
Free market economics, contemporary relevance of, 163–165
Free Market Environmentalism (Anderson and Leal), 266
Free society, 32; importance of information in, 158
Freedom
  of choice, 201, 281
  and civil rights laws, 27
  of contract, 27, 28
  of experimentation and discovery, 46
  of exchange, 193
  and free choice, 145–146, 160–162
  guarantees of, 15
  individual, 230
  personal, 132
  versus security, 280–282
  of speech, belief, and expression, 236
  from want, 121–125, 126–129
  women and 180–183
Freudian Ethic, The (LaPiere), 284–285
Friedman, Milton, 182, 245
Friedman, Rose, 182

Galbraith, John Kenneth, 52, 112
Galles, Gary M., 221–223
Garn-St. Germain Act (1982), 80, 82
General Agreement on Tariffs and Trade, 246, 258
General Motors, 160–162
General welfare, 121
Gerry, Elbridge, 245
Gewirth, Alan, 52
Goodman, John, 204
Goodman, William, 211

Government
  "benefits," 49
  compulsion, 17
  "czars," 40
  deficit, 136
  and the environment, 265–266,
    271–274
  grants, 296–298
  growth of, 2, 38, 49–50, 282
  importance of limiting, 5, 38
  investment, 130–132
  intervention, 1, 37
  limited, 121
  planning, 43–44
  proper role of, 32, 268
  relief, 291–293
  size of, 61–64
  spending, 2, 97, 107–109, 116, 135–
    137
Grabowski, Henry, 208
Gravity, 203
Great Depression, 75, 76, 83, 87–89,
  217
Great Leap Forward (China),
  19
Greaves, Percy L., Jr., 1
Greed, 249, 277–279
Greenspan, Alan, 80
Gross domestic product, 260

Hayek, Friedrich, 36, 112–113
Hazlitt, Henry, 68–71, 133–134, 254–
  256, 258
Health care, 4, 9, 98, 201–202, 203–
  205, 206–209, 210–214
Health Insurance Association of
  America, 212
Higgs, Robert, 75–79, 206–209
Highway "user taxes," 142
Hippocratic Oath, 202
Hoarding, 167
Hollywood, 174–175
Hospers, John, 22–26, 102–106
Hotelling, Harold, 271
Housing, 65–67, 68–71
Human energy, 104

Human nature, 123
Hutt, W.H., 245

Ikeda, Sanford, 280–282
Importing capital, 261
Incentives, 20, 35, 36, 252, 294
Incomes, inequality of, 100–101
India, 197, 254
Individual choice, 30
Industrial Revolution, 46, 190
Industrialization, 197; in undevel-
  oped countries, 254–256
Industry, 100
Inequality of wealth and income,
  100–101
"Infant industries" argument in
  support of tariffs, 255
Inflation, 68, 70, 82, 88, 124
Information, 265; information mar-
  ketplace, 230, 231
Infrastructure, 141–144, 273
Intellectuals, 146
Internal Revenue Service, 91
International Emergency Economic
  Powers Act (1977), 77
Interventionism, 9, 27, 77, 91, 151,
  194, 227, 278, 292, 296
"Invisible hand," 163
Involuntary servitude, 175; via na-
  tional service, 289–290
Irish Potato Famine, 248
"Iron law of wages," 191

Japan, 47–48, 251
Jefferson, Thomas, 9, 12, 13, 97, 122
Jesus, teachings of, 45–46
Jobilism, 171
Jobs, 22–26, 133–134, 135–137, 171–
  173, 174–176, 184, 186; foreign
  imports and, 257–259; *see also*
  employment; labor; unemploy-
  ment
Johnson Enterprises, 180

Kelly Girls, 190
Kibbe, Matthew B., 35–37

Kirzner, Israel, 37
Knowledge, price of, 42
"Knowledge problem" (as posited by Hayek), 36, 91, 113

Labor
  child, 196–198
  as a commodity, 191–193
  contracts, 150
  government compulsion, 192–193
  government regulation of, 65–67
  legislation, 3, 197
  private sale of one's own, 31
  productivity, 194
  regulation, 66–67
  see also jobs, unemployment
Labor theory of value, 152–154, 195
Labor unions, 31, 63, 171, 190, 194–195
Laissez faire, 163, 247
Lane, Rose Wilder, 102
LaPiere, Richard, 284–285
Law, legislation, 47–48, 49–51
"Lawmakers," 48
Lawyers, number in U.S. compared with other countries, 47
Leal, Don, 266
Legal plunder, 12
Legal positivism, 11
Lenin, V.I., 2
Limbaugh, Rush, 230
Lincoln, Abraham, 107, 196
Lobbying, lobbyists, 61, 234
Locke, John, 12

Machan, Tibor R., 52–57, 174–176, 287–290
Madison, James, 12, 78, 99
Magnetic resonance imaging (MRI), 210
Majority rule, 30–32, 99
Man versus the State, The (Spencer), 24
Manchester School, 247
"Market failure" arguments for government regulation, 53

Marx, Karl, 35, 36, 46, 123, 178, 191, 201, 291
Matthew, Gospel of, 277
McClure, James E., 163–165
McKenzie, Richard B., 171–173
Media, 227–231
Medical care, *see* health care
Medical information, sources of, 207
Mercantilism, 171
Micronesia, 252
Middle Ages, 25
Military spending, 133
Mill, John Stuart, 52
Minimum wage laws, 67, 72, 197
Mises, Ludwig, 35–36, 39–40, 245
Money, 123, 149–150
Monopoly, 31, 155–157, 212
Morality, moral values, 45, 99, 154, 277, 287, 297
Mozart, Wolfgang, 238
Mullendore, W.C., 49–51
Murray, Charles, 66
Musgrave, Gerald, 204

Nader, Ralph, 52
Napoleonic Wars, 246
Nash, Ronald, 158–159, 277–279
National Center for Policy Analysis, 265–266
National debt, 110–111
National Emergencies Act (1976), 77
National Endowment for the Arts, 232, 236
National Labor Relations Act (NLRA), 31
National service, 287–290
Natural resources, 271
New Deal, 76, 190, 217, 289
New Testament, 277
New York City, 65
Newton, Isaac, 203
Nicaragua, 201–202
Nixon, Richard, 108
North, Gary, 42–44

Occupational licensing, 228
Opitz, Edmund A., 61–64, 145–146
Opulent State, 146
Orange industry, *see* citrus industry
Osterfeld, David, 251–253

Pacific Research Institute for Public Policy Research, 266
PACs, 245
Paine, Thomas, 104
Pasour, E.C., Jr., 217–220
Paternalism, 209
Patient Power (Goodman and Musgrave), 204
Peel, Robert, 248
Peikoff, Leonard, 233
Penney, J.C., 63
"People control," 72–74
Peterson, George, 273
Peterson, William H., 245–248
Plunder, 114, 119, 223
Poirot, Paul L., 15–17, 87–89, 110–111, 121–125, 138–140, 186–188, 191–193, 196–198
Political spending versus private spending, 145–146
Politicians, 2, 97, 107, 127, 205, 218–219, 272, 277
Pollution, 54, 57, 267–270
Poor, 118–120
Population control, 126–129
"Pork barrel" spending, 219
"Positive rights" argument for government regulation, 53–54
Postal delivery, 118
Poverty, poverty programs, 26, 104–105, 124–125, 126–127, 196, 252
Poverty, world, 126
Power, political, 122
Prayer in public schools, 242
Prescription drugs and medical devices, 206
Prices, price controls, 44, 68–71, 72–74, 166, 167, 213
Prices, price system, 123–124

Principles of the free market, 277–278
Private enterprise, 277
Private medicine, 203
Private property, 20, 29, 110–111, 192, 194, 271
Privilege versus right, 22
Privileges, special, 268
Production, 128
Production, problem of, 102–106
Productivity, 194, 250
Profit management versus bureaucratic management, 39–40
Profits, 150, 152–154, 278
Property rights, 15–17, 24, 166
Prosperity, economic, 26, 130–132, 133–134
Provident Hospital, 180
Public debt, 38–39, 97
Public goods, 27
Public needs, 145
Public officials, 38–41
Public services, government involvement in provision of, 53
"Public interest," 157
Public works programs, 174

Racism, 28
Rationing, 168, 211
Rawls, John, 52
Read, Leonard E., 118–120, 152–154, 291–293, 299–30
Reagan Administration, 80–81, 112, 171
Red tape, 58–60
Redistribution of wealth, 113, 124, 296, 298
Reed, Lawrence W., 12–14, 47–48, 100–101, 201–202, 249–250, 265–266
Regulation, government, 35–37, 52–57, 58–60, 75–79, 105, 137, 223
Regulation of banking, 80–84
Renaissance Tower, 130–131
Rent control, 68–71, 73
Resources, consumption of, 249–250

Responsibility, denial of, 283
Reverse discrimination, 28, 181
Rights
  to food, 18–21, 204
  human, 15–17
  of individual employees, 187
  to a job, 10, 22–26
  legal, 22
  moral, 22
  natural, 61
  nature and source of, 9–11
  positive versus negative, 11, 23–
    26, 56
  specious claims to, 5, 12–14
Road construction, 142
Robinson Crusoe, 187
Rockwell, Llewellyn H., Jr., 27–29,
  107–109, 149–151, 189–190
Rogge, Benjamin A., 283–286
Rome, 18, 19
Roosevelt, Theodore, 271
Rothbard, Murray N., 45–46, 90–93
Rule of Law, 61
Russell, Dean, 72–74, 160–162
Russia, 19

Sandinistas, 201–202
Savings and investment, 196
Savings and loan crisis, 80–83
Scarcity, 166
Schumpeter, Joseph, 173
Secondary effects of government
  policies, 258
Security, 4, 280–282
Seen and unseen, 133–134
Self-interest versus selfishness, 277
Semmens, John, 84–86, 141–144
Sennholz, Hans F., 80–83, 97–99,
  194–195
Sex education, 240–242
Shannon, Russell, 257–259
Shaw, Jane S., 271–274
Shelly, Thomas J., 294–295
Sherman Antitrust Act, 155
Siege of Antwerp, 167, 168
Slavery, 139, 280–281

Small Business Administration, 221
Smith, Adam, 86, 155, 157, 163–165,
  246, 269
Smuts, Robert, 66
Social liberalism, 229
Social Security, 1, 113, 138–140
Socialism, 1, 46, 87, 143
Socialized government, 110
Socialized medicine, 201–202
South Korea, 251
Sovereignty, individual versus
  state, 54
Soviet Union, 1, 43, 173, 203
Spangler, Mark, 1–5
Sparks, John A., 296–298
Special interest groups, 35, 131, 259
Special privileges, 182
Speculation, speculators, 166–168,
  272
Speech, freedom of, 23
Spencer, Herbert, 24
Spending, government
  cuts in, 107–109
  health care, 212–213
St. Germain, Fernand, 80
Stalin, 19
Standard of living, 65, 101, 103–104
State sovereignty, 54
Statistics, 90–93
Stewardship, 271
Stroup, Richard L., 271–274
Subsidies, 58–60, 70, 232–235, 236–
  239, 254
Sunkist, 221–222
Supply and demand, 191
Sutherland, Justice George, 15
Swan, Kyle S., 126–129
Sweatshops, 197, 198

Taiwan, 251
Talent, 100
Tariffs and quotas, 255, 257, 258
Taxes, taxation, 105, 115–117, 135,
  137, 138, 141, 145, 171, 202, 210,
  233, 241, 296
Taylor, Joan Kennedy, 65–67

Technology, 45, 46, 102, 104, 238, 250, 259
Temporary workers, 189–190
Third World countries, 126, 251–253
Thoreau, Henry David, 62
Thrift, 100
Trade, international, 245–248, 257–259, 260–262
Tragedy of the commons, 56, 289
Trespass, law of, 268
"Trickle-Down Theory," 112–114
Tuskegee Institute, 180

Ukraine, 19
Underwriters' Laboratories, 206
Unemployment, 63, 189, 195
U.S. Constitution, 9, 16, 24, 32, 45, 61, 62, 107, 121, 258
U.S. Department of Agriculture, 217–218, 222
U.S. Food and Drug Administration, 207, 208
U.S. Forest Service, 265–266, 271
United Nations Declaration of Human Rights, 18
Utilitarianism, 53

Van Gogh, Vincent, 238
Veblen, Thorstein, 46
Vernon, John, 208
Voluntary exchange, 141, 153, 187, 192, 279, 280

Wabash College, 283–286
Wages, determination of, 177–179, 194, 273
Walton, Sam, 63
War, 75–76, 78, 88
Wardell, William, 208
Washington, George, 122
"Washington Monument Ploy," 108
Wasley, Terree P., 203–205, 210–214
Wealth of Nations (Smith), 163
Wealth, 105–106, 112, 114, 115
Webb, Sydney, 19
Welfare state, 20, 71, 290
Wetlands, 265
Wickard v. Filburn, 58
Wilderness Act (1964), 273
Windsor (Ont.) Cardiac Emergency Care Center, 212
Women and the marketplace, 180–185
Women's Bank (Denver, Colo.), 180
Worker "exploitation," 186–188
Workers, temporary, 189–190
World Bank, 251
World economy, 42
World War I, 75–76, 88, 261
World War II, 134, 190
WPA, 289
Wright, Jim, 80

About the Publisher

The Foundation for Economic Education, Inc., was established in 1946 by Leonard E. Read to study and advance the moral and intellectual rationale for a free society.

The Foundation publishes *The Freeman*, an award-winning monthly journal of ideas in the fields of economics, history, and moral philosophy. FEE also publishes books, conducts seminars, and sponsors a network of discussion clubs to improve understanding of the principles of a free and prosperous society.

FEE is a non-political, non-profit 501 (c)(3) tax-exempt organization, supported solely by private contributions and the sales of its literature.

For further information, please contact The Foundation for Economic Education, 30 South Broadway, Irvington-on-Hudson, New York 10533; telephone (914) 591-7230; fax (914) 591-8910; e-mail freeman@westnet.com.

SUGGESTIONS FOR FURTHER STUDY

The following books from FEE are recommended to readers who wish to explore in greater depth the positive case for limited government, individual liberty, and the free market.

Frederic Bastiat
THE LAW   76 pages $ 2.95

The *Freeman Classics* Series
Each anthology in this series brings together essays on a single issue of lasting importance.

THE MORALITY OF CAPITALISM	150 pages	$14.95
PRICES AND PRICE CONTROLS	169 pages	$14.95
PRIVATE PROPERTY AND POLITICAL CONTROL	173 pages	$14.95
PUBLIC EDUCATION AND INDOCTRINATION	203 pages	$14.95
POLITICIZED MEDICINE	157 pages	$14.95
MAN AND NATURE	221 pages	$14.95
TAXATION AND CONFISCATION	206 pages	$14.95
BANKERS AND REGULATORS	176 pages	$14.95
AMERICAN UNIONISM: FALLACIES AND FOLLIES	230 pages	$14.95

The *Freeman Library* Series

THE FARM PROBLEM	144 pages	$ 9.95
FREE TRADE: THE NECESSARY FOUNDATION FOR WORLD PEACE	140 pages	$ 9.95
THE FREEDOM PHILOSOPHY	146 pages	$ 9.95

Henry Hazlitt
ECONOMICS IN ONE LESSON   218 pages $10.95

Ludwig von Mises

THE ANTI-CAPITALISTIC MENTALITY	114 pages	$ 8.95
HUMAN ACTION	907 pages	$49.95
PLANNING FOR FREEDOM	280 pages	$14.95

Leonard E. Read
ANYTHING THAT'S PEACEFUL   243 pages $12.95

Hans F. Sennholz
DEBTS AND DEFICITS   179 pages $14.95
THE GREAT DEPRESSION: 57 pages $ 4.95
  WILL WE REPEAT IT?
MONEY AND FREEDOM   102 pages $ 9.95
THE POLITICS OF UNEMPLOYMENT   356 pages $24.95
THE SAVINGS AND LOAN BAILOUT   57 pages $ 5.95

Henry Grady Weaver
THE MAINSPRING OF   270 pages $ 5.95
  HUMAN PROGRESS

Prices subject to change. Please add $3.00 per order of $25 or less; $4.00 per order of $26-$50; $5.00 per order of more than $50. To order, or to request FEE's latest catalogue of more than 400 books on economics and social thought, write or phone:

The Foundation for Economic Education
30 South Broadway
Irvington-on-Hudson, New York 10533
(914) 591-7230; fax (914) 591-8910